D0405906

Critical Praise for *Merton Miller on Derivatives*:

"Merton Miller does an excellent job in making a complex subject easily accessible to the non-professional. He achieves this with common sense, economics, and wit. This book provides a superb and comprehensive overview of derivatives in the context of free markets."
—Richard L. Sandor, Chairman and CEO
Centre Financial Products Ltd.

"Incisive, witty essays of and for the 90's, conveying an avowed academic's accumulated insight from a practical free-market perspective. For novices and sophisticates alike."
—Edward H. Fleischman, U.S. Consultant
Linklaters & Paines

"*Merton Miller on Derivatives* offers an insightful overview of the complex and diverse world of derivatives. The explanations and reflections by the 1990 Nobel Laureate in Economics are invaluable in understanding these sophisticated instruments of finance."
—Leo Melamed, Chairman Emeritus, Chicago Mercantile Exchange
Chairman and CEO, Sakura Dellsher, Inc.

"Merton Miller, the pre-eminent academic in the field, cuts through the static on the subject to present an intelligent perspective and insightful analysis of derivative markets—their value and their impact. Presenting a realistic, comprehensible look at the role derivatives play and their future, this book is a fascinating read for veteran market participants or anyone with an interest in the markets."
—William J. Brodsky, Chairman and CEO
Chicago Board Options Exchange

"Merton Miller makes the case that competition and innovation are the key issues when it comes to derivatives, and this book is a solid response to the hue and cry for tighter regulation that follows every market twist. This is a must read for everyone concerned with the health of our financial markets."
—Thomas R. Donovan, President and CEO
Chicago Board of Trade

"This book contains a wonderful collection of speeches delivered to diverse audiences of students, lay people, regulators, and financial practitioners over the last several years. Each chapter offers keen insights and clear analysis of topical financial concerns, using derivatives to illustrate many ideas. Even if you have no such concerns, Miller's humor alone provides reason to purchase the book."
—Myron S. Scholes, Principal, Long-Term Capital Management, L.P.
and Frank E. Buck Professor of Finance Emeritus, Stanford University

Merton Miller on Derivatives

Merton H. Miller

John Wiley & Sons, Inc.

New York • Chichester • Weinheim • Brisbane • Singapore • Toronto

Copyright © 1997 by Merton H. Miller.
Published by John Wiley & Sons, Inc.

ISBN: 0-471-18340-7

10 9 8 7 6 5 4 3 2 1

Contents

Part IV   Corporate Finance and Corporate Governance

Part V   Questions I'm Often Asked

Foreword

Merton Miller is that rare academic, a first-rate scholar and a skilled street fighter. If this seems too flattering a portrait, let me add that perhaps he'd be even better if he had some experience as a trader.

His seminal work in laying the foundation of the modern theory of corporate finance radically changed the way private firms approach their investment and financing decisions. For this he was awarded the 1990 Nobel prize in economics. Modern corporate finance theory not only describes the world of business and finance; it also shapes it. Few branches of economic theory are so close to actual decision making.

Those of us in the derivatives industry know Merton best for providing numerous insights on critical topical and conceptual issues relating to financial futures. When derivatives are assailed, as they routinely are, especially by regulators and the media, he can always be counted on to point out their value in managing financial risk, in tailoring a risk-return profile, and in price discovery. In all this, he is guided by his appreciation of the marketplace as the final decision maker. This is a key reason his work has so much value for the financial community.

He encourages the market to experiment with new products and ways of doing things—and is quick to oppose wrongheaded and reactive moves by regulators that might gum up the works. A more skilled or more enthusiastic supporter of the derivatives industry, particularly exchange-traded futures, would be hard to imagine. Merton has actively participated in public discussions on diverse issues ranging from the stock market collapse of 1987 to the Metallgesellschaft case of 1993. Currently, for example, he is the executive director of the Joint Strategic Initiative

Committee which is exploring potential collaborative efforts between the Chicago Mercantile Exchange and the Chicago Board of Trade. These efforts represent an ongoing theme in Merton's work which stresses the importance of increasing economic efficiency as a prime role of financial markets.

In these, as in all matters, Merton has strong views. These views, which are the result of years of carefully honed academic discourse, can, however, differ considerably from those of market participants. These differences can be seen on issues as general as the balance of trading power between the floor traders or locals on the exchange floors and the off-floor trades of financial institutions, hedge funds, and commodity pools or as specific as the importance of basis risk for the return to a portfolio.

In this volume Merton provides thoughtful and valuable insights into financial markets in general and the derivatives industry in particular. Practitioners as well as other interested observers will find them both thought provoking and enjoyable.

Tom Dittmer
Refco Inc.

Preface

The neighbor who rents and farms my Illinois corn-and-soybean second home asked me recently what I was doing now that I have retired. I have become a professional keynote speaker, I explained. Well, he said, at least it's indoor work; and it does seem to keep you busy.

It does indeed, because the number of conferences held each year keeps growing without bounds. And every conference must have at least one and sometimes several keynote speakers to set the tone and state the theme. The twenty-two essays in this volume are mostly just such keynote speeches that I have delivered at a variety of conferences around the world over the past half-dozen years.

Although the specific topics vary, two themes are constant. First, the so-called "derivatives revolution" of the last twenty years, in which I am proud to say the academic community has played such a major role, is not to be deplored, but applauded. Contrary to the widely held perception, derivatives have made the world a *safer* place, not a more dangerous one. They have made it possible for firms and institutions to deal efficiently and cost effectively with risks and hazards that have plagued them for decades, if not for centuries. True, some firms and some financial institutions have managed to lose substantial sums on derivatives, but some firms and institutions will always find ways to lose money. Good judgment and good luck cannot be taken for granted. For all the horror stories about derivatives, it's still worth emphasizing that the world's banks have blown away vastly more in bad real estate deals than they'll ever lose on their derivatives portfolios.

Which brings up the second major theme running through these essays.

That some firms and institutions will surely make mistakes in their handling of derivatives does not mean that the government has an obligation to keep them from hurting themselves. And, even though many regulators, notably our Commodity Futures Trading Commission, are only too anxious to assume that obligation, they can't possibly succeed. The notion that wise government rules actually *can* somehow prevent any and every derivatives calamity is incurably romantic because government regulation, at best, can deal only with the *last* reported disaster. New and totally unanticipated potential forms of disaster are evolving all the time! In fact, as I have argued in the past (and again in chapter 1) many of the innovations we see are introduced precisely to get around regulatory restrictions. The regulators are *always* behind the curve. And just as well. Can you imagine the size of the *Federal Register* if the regulators really believed they could *anticipate* problems and not just react to them?

People and businesses in the private sector, of course, *do* make forward-looking judgments and investments all the time. But that's because the genius of the free-market, private-enterprise system ties together the costs *and* the rewards of those decision makers. No such self-equilibrating mechanism applies, however, to the ordinary process of regulation as we have come to know it. Nobody really knows what the regulators are trying to maximize (in economics, what their "criterion function" is), nor how well they are succeeding or even think they are succeeding. The view of some academics of the "public choice" school that political competition can ensure the "efficiency" of the regulatory process, in the way that commercial competition supports the efficiency of the private sector, strikes me as no more than surface analogy with virtually no substantive content.

All this is not to suggest, of course, that the regulatory environment never changes, that the deadweight burdens of useless or, more often, special-interest protectionist regulations are never lifted. Sometimes they are, though for reasons not fully explained by public choice economics. We have good descriptive theories of why we get the regulation we do (see chapter 5), but no good theories of why we sometimes get deregulation. Pure chance probably has much to do with it, as does, though perhaps only to a minor extent, the steady stream of critical academic research (and keynote speeches!) seeking to remove the halo that the regulatory state has enjoyed in this country since the days of the Roosevelt New Deal (and that it still seems to enjoy in Japan and in much of Western Europe other than Britain).

Let me insist, however, that the very negative approach I take throughout to the current U.S. (and Japanese) financial regulation not be dismissed as simply University of Chicago antigovernment prejudice. Contrary to the widespread perception, University of Chicago economists have never argued that the government has no useful role to play in economic life. We are not anarchists! We obey traffic signs! We believe, in fact, that the coercive powers of the state—for that is what regulation ultimately comes down to—are a precious national resource. And, like all such other natural resources, that coercive power must be husbanded, and used sparingly only when the evidence shows overwhelmingly that the available noncoercive alternatives, essentially private contracting and competitive discipline, will lead to vastly inferior social outcomes. That has not in fact been shown, I argue in these essays, by the defenders of the current financial regulatory structure. And I refuse to be fobbed off by their standard nonsequitur that because the United States is the richest country in the world, its regulatory climate must be economically efficient in the technical sense, if not actually responsible for the country's success, as the most fanatic apologists for the Securities and Exchange Commission and the Commodity Futures Trading Commission seem to be suggesting. Our country is indeed doing well these days, but it could do even better if the rigorous standards of the cost/benefit calculus were applied to its regulatory superstructure.

My pounding away in these essays at so much of the useless and costly regulation afflicting the capital markets here and throughout the world is also intended deliberately as a call to arms to my colleagues in the academic field of finance. As I say in concluding my Nobel lecture (reprinted here as chapter 15):

> Unlike some of the older fields of economics, the focus in finance has not been on issues of public policy. We have emphasized positive economics rather than normative economics, striving for solid empirical research built on foundations of simple but powerful organizing theories. Now that our field has officially come of age, as it were, perhaps my colleagues in finance can be persuaded to take their noses out of their databases from time to time and to bring the insights of our field, and especially the public policy insights, to the attention of a wider audience.

No rush to mount the barricades and fight for more sensible regulation is yet detectable, however, on the part of my colleagues in finance, except perhaps more sensible regulation in the special area of banks and savings and loan associations.

The twin themes of derivatives and their regulation are the focus of the first three parts of the book. Parts I and II presume some, though not an awful lot, of knowledge about what derivatives are and how they work (especially stock index derivatives). Those coming to these subjects for the first time may find it easier to start with the introductory material of Part III before turning to the more contentious and polemical issues of Parts I and II.

Part IV breaks off into what at first may seem a totally different direction, corporate finance. That is the field of economics within which I had specialized for many years before concentrating on derivatives; it was for work in that field that I was awarded the Nobel Memorial Prize in Economic Sciences in 1990. My Nobel lecture "Leverage" is included in this part, along with three other talks on corporate finance and corporate governance issues in the United States, Japan, Germany, and China.

The last section, Part V, presents a variety of essays on more general economic topics of current interest. Derivatives play no particular role in these, but regulation in the broad sense still does, alas.

In presenting speeches delivered as many as six or seven years ago, the temptation is always present to touch up the record by removing examples of conspicuous failures of prediction. I have tried to resist that temptation by presenting the various speeches essentially as delivered. In a few cases, I have added brief references to subsequent major developments. In one instance, that of Orange County, California, I have altered the original texts of chapters 2 and 5 to reflect my own recent research on that episode. Although the texts are basically unchanged, the inevitable overlaps and duplications have been carefully pruned by my capable editor, Ida Walters, to avoid repetition. She has been invaluable throughout in helping me select and edit the materials (yes, there is more, much more!) into a coherent whole. The book literally could not have been done without her. A special word of thanks is also due Bob Kamphuis of Caledonia Group Inc. for his continuing interest and encouragement in getting this book to press.

Academic scribblers are aware, or should be aware, of the inevitable intellectual debts they incur just from interacting with their colleagues, and these debts are particularly large in my case. Many of the public policy issues raised here were discussed, often with some acrimony, at the University of Chicago's Quadrangle Club where I have had the pleasure over the years of sharing a lunch table with such luminaries from the university's economics department as Milton Friedman, the late George Stigler, Gary Becker and Robert Lucas, among many others. The tradition of lively informal discussions over lunch has also been maintained, I am happy to say, by my fellow board members of the Chicago Mercantile Exchange who have taught me on those occasions much about how futures exchanges really work. As I explain in chapter 6 in a related context, the inside game is often very different from what the outsiders see.

A third group of colleagues to whom I owe great debts are the students at the University of Chicago in my seminar on financial regulation. Papers presented over the last ten years by those students and subject to searching class discussion have dealt with many of the regulatory issues covered in these essays and more as well. Doctoral thesis candidates are still another group to whom I am indebted for intellectual stimulation, especially to Christopher Culp with whom I have coauthored both academic research publications and op-ed pieces on a variety of regulatory issues. I can only hope that the great benefits I have derived from working with him have not too long delayed the completion of his thesis.

A special word of thanks finally to Tom Dittmer of Refco Inc. who contributed a flattering foreword to this volume. I can reveal now that he is the long-time trader whose observations about the declining liquidity of the exchange floor are noted in endnote 8 of chapter 11. Nobody knows more about the derivatives business than he does. He would have made a great professor of finance. But I'm glad he chose another line of work. Who needs that kind of competition?

Merton Miller
Chicago, March, 1997

Part I

The Derivatives Revolution

1

The Derivatives Revolution: Accomplishments and Prospects

The wonderment of Rip Van Winkle, awakening after his sleep of twenty years and viewing the changes in his world, would pale in comparison to one of his descendants in the banking or financial services industry who fell asleep (presumably at his desk) in February 1970 and awoke two decades later. So rapid has been the pace of innovation in financial instruments and institutions over the last 20 years that nothing could have prepared him to understand such now commonplace notions as swaps and swaptions, index futures, program trading, butterfly spreads, puttable bonds, Eurobonds, collateralized-mortgage bonds, zero-coupon bonds, portfolio insurance, or synthetic cash—to name just a few of the more exotic ones. No twenty-year period has witnessed such a burst of innovative activity. What could have produced this explosive growth? Has all this innovation really been worthwhile from society's point of view? Have we seen the end of the wave of innovations; or must we brace for more to come? Those are the issues addressed here.

THE GREAT BURST OF FINANCIAL INNOVATIONS

Several explanations have been offered for the sudden burst of financial innovations starting some twenty years ago. (See, for example, Miller 1986 and Van Horne 1985.)

The Move to Floating Exchange Rates

A popular explanation locates the initiating impulse for the burst of financial innovations in the collapse of the Bretton Woods regime of fixed exchange rates. In the early 1970s, the U.S. government, with strong prodding from academic economists, notably Milton Friedman, finally abandoned the tie of gold to the dollar. The wide fluctuations in exchange rates following soon after added major new uncertainty to all international transactions. One response to that uncertainty was the development of exchange-traded foreign-exchange futures contracts by the Chicago Mercantile Exchange, or CME—an innovation that spawned in turn a host of subsequent products as the turbulence spread from exchange rates to interest rates.

But cutting the tie to gold cannot be the whole story because financial futures, influential as they proved to be, were not the only major breakthrough of the early 1970s. Another product introduced only a few months later, and almost equally important to subsequent developments, was not so directly traceable to the monetary events of the early 1970s. The reference, of course, is to the exchange-traded options on common stock of the CME's crosstown rival, the Chicago Board of Trade, or CBOT. That the CBOT's options did not precede the CME's financial futures was mainly luck of the bureaucratic draw. Both exchanges started the process of development at about the same time, impelled to diversify by the same stagnation in their traditional agricultural markets. Both needed the cooperation, or at least the nonhostility, of the appropriate regulators to break out in such novel directions.

The CME was the more fortunate in having to contend only with the U.S. Treasury and the Federal Reserve System, at a time, moreover, when both those agencies were strongly committed to the Nixon Administration's push for floating exchange rates.[1] The CBOT, alas, faced the U.S. Securities and Exchange Commission, a New Deal reform agency always hypersensitive to anything smacking of speculative activity.[2] By the time the SEC had finished its detailed review of option trading, the CME had already won the race.

Computers and Information Technology

Another explanation for the sudden burst of financial innovation after 1970 finds the key in the information revolution and especially in the electronic computer. Computers in one form or another had been available since the 1950s, but only in the late 1960s, with the perfection of transistorized circuitry did computers become cheap enough and reliable enough for designing new products and strategies such as stock index arbitrage or collateralized mortgage obligations. Certainly the immense volume of transactions we now see regularly could not have been handled without the data processing capacities of the computer. But the basic and most influential innovations, financial futures and exchange-traded options, did not require computers to make them commercially feasible.

Options on commodities in fact had been traded regularly on the CBOT until the U.S. Congress, in one of its periodic bouts of antispeculative zeal following the Crash of 1929, ended the practice in 1934. That this long prior history of option trading is not better known may trace to the arcane CBOT terminology under which options were known as "privileges." But traded instruments designated with the modern terms "puts" and "calls" go back much further than that, to the Amsterdam Stock Exchange of the late seventeenth century (de la Vega 1688). Routine exchange trading of futures contracts has a history almost as long.

Innovation and World Economic Growth

Still another possibility, and the one I find most persuasive (see Miller 1986), is that the seeming burst of innovation in the 1970s was merely a delayed return to the long-run growth path of financial improvement. The burst seems striking only in contrast to the dearth of major innovations during the long period of economic stagnation that began in the early 1930s and that for most of the world continued well into the 1950s.

The shrinkage in the world economy after 1929 was on a scale that few not actually experiencing it can readily imagine. The prolonged depression undermined any demand pull for developing new financial instruments and markets; and the increased regulatory role of the state throttled any impulses to innovate from the supply side. Much of this new regulation, particularly in the United States, was in fact a reaction to the supposed evils, notably the Crash of 1929, flowing from the development of exchange-traded, and hence relatively liquid, common stock as a major investment and financing vehicle in the 1920s.

Even in the depressed 1930s, of course, financial innovation, though muted relative to the 1920s, did not come to a halt. But the major novelties tended to be government sponsored, rather than market induced. Examples are the special housing-related instruments such as the amortizing mortgage, the Federal Home Administration loan guarantees and the support, direct and indirect, of what later came to be called (we now know somewhat ironically) as "thrift institutions." New U.S. Treasury instruments were developed, or at least used on a vastly expanded scale, notably Series E savings bonds for small savers and, at the other extreme, U.S. Treasury bills which quickly became the leading short-term liquid asset for banks and corporate treasurers, displacing the commercial paper and call money instruments that had previously served that function.

Financial innovation by the private sector might perhaps have revived by the 1940s had not World War II intervened. The war not only drained manpower and energy from normal market-oriented activity, but led to new regulatory restrictions on financial transactions, particularly international transactions.

Regulation and Deregulation as Stimuli to Financial Innovation

By a curious irony, the vast structure of financial regulation erected throughout the world during the 1930s and 1940s, though intended to throttle some kinds of financial innovation (and usually successfully), actually served to stimulate the process along other dimensions. Substantial rewards were offered, in effect, to those who successfully invented ways around the government-erected obstacles. Many of these dodges (or "fiddles" as the British call them) turned out to have market potential far beyond anything dreamed of by their inventors, and the innovations thrived even after the regulation that gave rise to them was modified or abandoned.

The most striking example of such a regulation-propelled innovation may well be the swap in which one corporation exchanges its fixed-rate borrowing obligation for another's floating-rate obligation, or exchanges its yen-denominated obligations for another's mark-denominated obligations, and so on in an almost unimaginable number of permutations and combinations. Some swaps are arranged by brokers who bring the two counterparties directly together, others by banks who take the counterparty side to a customer order and then either hedge the position with forwards and futures or with an offsetting position with another customer. The notional amount of such swaps, interest and currency, currently outstanding is now in the trillions of dollars and rising rapidly. Yet, according to legend at least, the arrangement arose, modestly enough, as vacation- home swapping by British overseas travelers who were long severely limited in the amount of currency they could take abroad. Two weeks free occupancy of a London flat could compensate a French tourist for a corresponding stay in a Paris apartment or compensate an American for the use of a condominium at Aspen. If the ingenious British innovator happened to work for one of the merchant banks in the city, as is likely, the extension of the notion to corporate currency swaps was a natural one.[3] The rest, as they say, is history.

The list of similar, regulation-induced or tax-induced innovations is long, and includes the Eurodollar market, the Eurobond market, and zero-coupon bonds, to name just some of the more far-reaching loopholes opened in the restrictive regulatory structure of the 1930s and 1940s. (For a fuller account of tax and regulation-induced innovations see Miller 1986.) Whether the private sector processes that produced the seemingly great wave of innovations after 1970 will continue to produce innovations if left unchecked is a topic to be taken up after first considering some of the arguments currently being advanced for not leaving them unchecked.

HAS THE WAVE OF FINANCIAL INNOVATIONS MADE US BETTER OFF OR WORSE OFF?

Free market economists have a simple standard for judging whether a new product has increased social welfare: are people willing to pay their hard-earned money for it? By this standard, of course, the new products of the 1970s and 1980s have proved their worth many times over. But why have they been so successful? Whence comes their real "value added?" The answer, in large part, is that they have substantially lowered the cost of carrying out many kinds of financial transactions.

Consider, for example, a pension fund or an insurance company with, say, $200 million currently in a well-diversified portfolio of common stocks. Suppose that for some good reason, the sponsors of the fund believe that the interests of their beneficiaries would be better served at the moment by shifting funds from common stocks to Treasury bills. The direct way would be first to sell the stock portfolio company by company, incurring commissions, fees, and market impact on each transaction. The cash proceeds, when collected, could then be put in Treasury bills, again incurring transaction costs. A second, and much cheaper alternative, however, is simply to sell about 1,000 (at present price levels) S&P 500 index futures contracts. Thanks to the way the futures contracts must be priced to maintain intermarket equilibrium, that one transaction has the same consequences as the *two* transactions along the direct route. And at a fifth or even less of the cost in fees, commissions, and market impact. (For more on this see chapter 9.)

Or, to take other kinds of financial costs, consider a bank maintaining an inventory of government bonds for resale. The availability of that inventory, like the goods on the shelf in a supermarket, means better and faster service for the bank's customers when they come to shop. But it also means considerable risk for the bank. Bond prices can fall, sometimes very substantially, even in the course of a single day.

To protect against such losses the bank can hedge its inventory by selling Treasury bond futures. Should the price of the bonds fall during the life of the futures contract, the gain on that contract will offset the loss on the underlying inventory. Without this opportunity to shift the risk via futures, the bank must seek other and more costly ways of controlling its inventory exposure, or it might well abandon the activity altogether.

Insurance and Risk Management

A bank's use of futures to hedge its own inventory does not, of course, eliminate the price risk of the underlying bonds; it merely transfers that risk to someone else who *does* want to bear the risk, either because he or she has stronger nerves, or more likely, because another firm or investor somewhere wants to hedge against a *rise* in bond prices. The futures and options exchanges have greatly reduced the time (and hence cost) that each risk-shifter might otherwise have spent searching for a counterparty with the opposite risk exposure.

The combined set of futures and options contracts and the markets, formal and informal, in which they are transferred has thus been likened to a gigantic insurance company, and rightly so. Efficient risk-sharing is what much of the futures and options revolution has been all about. And that is why the term "risk management" has come increasingly to be applied to the whole panoply of instruments and institutions that have followed in the wake of the introduction of foreign exchange futures in CME's International Money Market in 1972. Honesty requires one to acknowledge, however, that this essentially benign view of the recent great innovative wave is not universally shared by the general public or even by academic economists.

THE CASE AGAINST THE INNOVATIONS

Some of the complaints about the harmful social consequences of the financial innovations appear to be little more than updated versions of a once-popular eighteenth-century economic doctrine known as Physiocracy, which located the ultimate source of national wealth in the production of *physical* commodities, especially agricultural commodities. Occupations other than commodity production were nonproductive. Modern-day Physiocrats, disdaining any appeals to consumer sovereignty, automatically and enthusiastically consign to that nonproductive class all the many thousands on Wall Street and LaSalle Street now using the new instruments.

A related complaint is that the new instruments, by lowering transactions costs, have led to too much short-term trading—trading that not only wastes resources, but which has unduly shortened the planning horizons of both firms and investors. That the volume of trading has in fact skyrocketed in recent years there can be no doubt, though the key stimulus to the surge in trading in the underlying stocks appears to have been less the introduction of index futures and options than the ending of the regime of high, fixed commissions in 1974. For Treasury bonds, the spur was the huge expansion of Federal government debt beginning in 1981. But the critics are surely right in believing that lower trading costs will induce more trading. More trading, however, need not mean more waste from society's point of view. Trading is part of the process by which economic information, scattered (as it necessarily is) in isolated bits and pieces throughout the whole economy is brought together, aggregated, and ultimately revealed to all. The prospect of trading profits is the "bribe," so to speak, that society uses to motivate the collection, and ultimately the revelation, of the dispersed information about supply and demand.

Index Futures and Stock Market Volatility

Although many of the complaints against the new financial investments are merely standard visceral reactions against middlemen and speculators, some are specific enough to be testable against the available data. Notable here is the widespread view expressed almost daily in the financial press that stock market volatility has been rising in recent years and that stock-index futures and options are responsible. The evidence, however, fails to support this widespread public perception of surging volatility.

Volatility, measured as the standard deviation of rates of return (whether computed over monthly, weekly, or even daily intervals), is only modestly higher now than during the more placid 1950s and 1960s, and is substantially below levels reached in the 1930s and 1940s (Schwert 1989). Even the 1950s and 1960s had brief, transitory bursts of unusually high volatility with a somewhat longer-lasting major burst occurring in the mid-1970s. The number of large, one-day moves (that is, moves of 3% or more in either direction) has indeed been higher in the 1980s than in any decade since the 1930s, but almost entirely thanks to the several days of violent movements in the market during and immediately following the crash of October 19, 1987. Such increased volatility seems to accompany every major crash (as the Japanese stock market showed through much of 1990). In fact, the tendency of volatility to rise after crashes and fall during booms is one of the few, well-documented facts researchers have been able to establish about the time-series properties of the volatility series. These bursts of post-crash volatility typically die out within a few months, and that has been basically the case as well for the Crash of 1987. The 1930s were so different because the high levels of volatility following the Crash of 1929 persisted long into the next decade.

Index Products and the Crash of 1987

The failure to find a rising trend in volatility in the statistical record suggests that the public may be using the word volatility in a different and less technical sense. They may simply be taking the fact of the Crash of 1987 itself (and the later so-called mini-crash of October 13, 1989) as their definition of market volatility. Without doubt, the Crash of 1987 *was* the largest one-day shock ever recorded. (What we now know and have learned about the Crash of 1987 is the subject of chapter 18.) The mini-crash of October 13, 1989, at about 6%, was high, but far from record breaking. If the Crash of 1987 is the source of the public perception of increased volatility, the task of checking for connections between the innovative instruments and volatility becomes the relatively straightforward one of establishing whether index futures and options really were responsible either for the occurrence or the size of the crash. On this score, signs of a consensus are emerging, at least within academia, with respect to the role of two of the most frequently criticized strategies involving futures and options: portfolio insurance and index arbitrage.

For portfolio insurance, the academic verdict is essentially "not guilty of causing the crash," but possibly guilty of the lesser charge of "contributing to the delinquency of the market." Portfolio insurance, after all, was strictly a U.S. phenomenon in 1987 while the crash on October 19 seems to have gotten under way in the Far East, well before trading opened in New York or Chicago. The extent of the fall in the various markets around the world, moreover, bore no relation to whether a country had index futures and options exchanges (Roll 1988). Even in the United States, non-portfolio insurance sales on October 19, including sales by mutual funds induced by the cash redemptions of retail investors, were four to five times those of the portfolio insurers.

Still, portfolio insurance using futures, like some older, positive-feedback strategies such as stop-loss orders or margin pyramiding, can be shown, as a matter of theory, to be potentially destabilizing.[4] The qualification "using futures" is important here, however, because the potentially destabilizing impact of portfolio insurance is much reduced when carried out with index options (that is, essentially by buying traded puts rather than attempting to replicate the puts synthetically with futures via craftily timed hedges). With exchange-traded puts, the bearishness in portfolio insurance would make its presence known immediately in the market prices and implicit volatility of the puts. With futures, by contrast, or with unhedged, over-the-counter puts, the bearishness may be lurking in the weeds, only to spring out suddenly on a less-than-perfectly forewarned public (Grossman 1988).

Index Arbitrage: The New Villain

Whatever may or may not have been its role in the Crash of 1987, portfolio insurance using futures rather than options has almost entirely vanished. Certainly it played no role in the mini-crash of October 13, 1989. Its place in the rogues' gallery of the financial press has been taken over by computerized "program trading" in general and by index arbitrage program trading in particular.

Why index arbitrage should have acquired such an unsavory public reputation is far from clear, however. Unlike portfolio insurance, which can be destabilizing when its presence as an informationless trade in the market is not fully understood, intermarket index arbitrage is essentially neutral in its market impact. The downward pressure of the selling leg in one market is always balanced by the equal and opposite buying pressure in the other. Only in rather special circumstances could these offsetting transactions affect either the level or the volatility of the combined market as a whole.

Index arbitrage might, possibly, increase market volatility if an initial breakout of the arbitrage bounds somehow triggered sales in the less-liquid cash market so massive that the computed index fell by more than needed to bring the two markets back into line. A new wave of arbitrage selling might then be set off in the other direction. Despite the concerns about such "whipsawing" often expressed by the SEC, however, no documented cases of it have yet been found. (See, for instance, the very thorough searches by Duffie *et al.*, 1990.) They find the market's behavior after program trades entirely consistent with the view that prices are being driven by "news," not mere speculative "noise" coming from the futures markets as the critics of index futures have so often charged.

Nor should these findings be considered in any way remarkable. The low cost of trading index futures makes the futures market the natural entry port for new information about the macroeconomy. The news, if important enough to push prices through the arbitrage bounds, is then carried from the futures market to the cash market by the program trades of the arbitragers. Thanks to the electronic order routing systems of the NYSE, the delivery is fast. But arbitrage is still merely the medium, not the message.

That so much recent criticism has been directed against the messenger rather than the message may reflect only the inevitably slow reaction by the public to the vast changes that have transformed our capital markets and financial services institutions over the last twenty years. Index futures, after all, came of age less than ten years ago. The shift from a predominantly retail stock market to one dominated by institutional investors began, in a big way, less than fifteen years ago. In time, with more experience, the public's understanding of the new environment will catch up. Unless, of course, new waves of innovation are about to sweep in and leave the public's perceptions even further behind.

FINANCIAL INNOVATIONS: ANOTHER WAVE ON THE WAY?

Will the next twenty years see a continuation or perhaps even an acceleration in the flow of innovations that have so vastly altered the financial landscape over the last twenty years? I think not. Changes will still take place, of course. The new instruments and institutions will spread to every country in the developed world (and possibly even to the newly liberalized economies of Eastern Europe). Futures and options contracts will be written on an ever-widening set of underlying commodities and securities. But the process will be normal, slow, evolutionary change, rather than the "punctuated equilibrium" of the recent past.[5]

Long-range predictions of this kind are rightly greeted with derision. Who can forget the U.S. Patent Office Commissioner who recommended in the early 1900s that his agency be closed down because all patentable discoveries had by then been made? We know also that regulation and taxes, those two long-standing spurs to innovation, are still very much with us despite the substantial progress, at least until recently, in deregulation and in tax rate reduction. But something important *has* changed. In the avant-garde academic literature of economics and finance today, few signs can be seen of new ideas and concepts like those that bubbled up in the 1960s and 1970s and that came to fruition later in specific innovations.

The extent to which academic thinking and criticism prefigured the great wave of financial innovations of the 1970s and 1980s is still too little appreciated. Calls for the creation of a foreign exchange futures market and analysis of the economic benefits that would flow from such an institution were common in the 1950s and 1960s, as noted earlier, in the writings of the academic supporters of floating exchange rates, especially Milton Friedman. As for common stocks, major academic breakthroughs in the 1950s and 1960s were the Mean-Variance Portfolio selection model of Markowitz and, building on it, the so-called Capital Asset Pricing Model of Sharpe and Lintner in which the concept of the "market portfolio" played a central role. The notion of the market portfolio ultimately became a reality by the early 1970s when the first passively managed index funds were brought on line. That the world would move from there to the trading of broad market portfolios, either as baskets or as index futures and options was widely anticipated. The fundamental Black-Scholes and Robert Merton papers on rational option pricing were published in the early 1970s, though manuscript versions of them had been circulating informally among academics well before then. These and other exciting prospects abounded in the academic literature twenty years ago. At the moment, however, that cupboard seems bare of new concepts and ideas waiting for the day of practical implementation.

Such hints of future developments as the current literature does have, relate more to the structure of the exchanges themselves than to the products they trade. For academics, accustomed to spending their workdays staring at the screens of their PCs, the near-term transition of the markets from floor trading to electronic trading is taken for granted. Frequent references can be found in the many articles on the Crash of 1987 to the presumed failings of the current exchange trading systems during that hectic period. Those systems are typically characterized pejoratively as "archaic" and "obsolete" in contrast to the screen-based trading systems in such non-exchange markets as government bonds or interbank foreign exchange.

That screen-based trading will someday supplant floor trading seems more than likely, but whether that transition will occur even by the end of this century is far from clear. The case of the steamship is instructive. The new steam technology was clearly superior to sail-power in its ability to go up river and against winds and tides. Steam quickly took over inland river traffic, but not, at first, ocean traffic. There steam was better, but vastly more expensive. Steam thus found its niche in military applications and in the high-unit value fast passenger trade. Only as fuel costs dropped did steam take over more and more of the low-unit value bulk trade in ocean freight. For some bulk commodities such as lumber, in fact, sail was often the lower cost alternative up until the start of the First World War, more than a hundred years after the first practical steamboat.

The same laws of comparative advantage apply to electronic trading systems. The open-outcry trading pits of the major futures exchanges may seem hopelessly chaotic and old-fashioned, but they are, for all that, a remarkably cheap way of handling transactions in large volume at great speed and frequency in a setting of high price volatility. Until recently, at least, electronic trading could not have come close to being cost-competitive in this arena. Screen trading found its niche elsewhere. And electronic computer systems found their niche in futures in tasks such as order routing, data processing, and some kinds of surveillance rather than on the trading floor. (For more on the comparative advantages of trading floors versus electronic exchanges see chapter 11.)

Even successful electronic trading, however, need not doom the exchanges to disappear as functioning business entities. The transactions facilities the exchanges provide through their trading floors are currently the major and certainly the most glamorous, but by no means the only, services they offer. The exchanges also provide such humdrum, but critical functions as clearing and settlement, guarantees of contract performance, record- keeping and audit trails, and the collection and dissemination of price information. The market for these services in supporting financial transactions not currently carried out via exchanges is potentially huge. The futures exchanges, by virtue of their expertise and their substantial existing capital investments, are well positioned to enter and to capture a significant share of these new markets, just as they were twenty years ago when the shrinkage in their agricultural business propelled them into financial futures and options.

Based on "Financial Innovation: Achievements and Prospects," Journal of Applied Corporate Finance, Vol. 4, No. 4, Winter 1992.

REFERENCES

Brennan, Michael J. and Eduardo S. Schwartz, "Portfolio Insurance and Financial Market Equilibrium," *Journal of Business* 62 (October 1989), 455–472.

de la Vega, Joseph, *Confusion de Confusiones*, Amsterdam, 1688, translated by Hermann Kellenbenz, 1957, reprinted by Baker Library, Harvard Business School, 1988.

Duffie, Gregory, Paul Kupiec, and Patricia White, "A Primer on Program Trading and Stock Price Volatility: A Survey of the Issues and Evidence," Working Paper, Board of Governors, Federal Reserve System, Washington, D.C., 1990.

Grossman, Sanford J., "An Analysis of the Implications for Stock and Futures Price Volatility of Program Trading and Dynamic Hedging Strategies," *Journal of Business* 61 (July 1988), 275–298.

Hu, Henry T. C., "Swaps, the Modern Process of Financial Innovation and the Vulnerability of a Regulatory Paradigm," *University of Pennsylvania Law Review* 128 (December 1989), 333–435.

Melamed, Leo, "The International Monetary Market," in *The Merits of Flexible Exchange Rates*, Editor Leo Melamed, George Mason University Press, Fairfax, Virginia, 1988, 417–429.

Miller, Merton H., "Financial Innovation: The Last Twenty Years and the Next," *Journal of Financial and Quantitative Analysis* 21 (December 1986), 459–471.

Roll, Richard, "The International Crash of October 1987," *Financial Analysts Journal* 22 (September 1988), 19–35.

Schwert, William G., "Why Does Stock Market Volatility Change over Time?" *Journal of Finance* 44 (December 1989), 1115–1153.

Van Horne, James C., "Of Financial Innovations and Excesses," *Journal of Finance* 40 (July 1985), 621–636.

2

The Recent Derivatives "Disasters": Assessing the Damage

How much wealth has been destroyed over the last few years by derivatives deals gone bad? A lot, many may conclude if they read the newspapers. Procter and Gamble is reported to have lost $150 million in an interest-rate swap. Metallgesellschaft, the big German conglomerate, supposedly lost nearly ten times that amount on oil futures. Orange County lost even more, $1.7 billion by some accounts, on interest-rate derivatives. Barings Bank, in perhaps the biggest disaster of all, lost more than $2 billion in Nikkei index futures and options.

Don't those disasters signify that we need more regulation of derivatives? I considered that question in 1994 (Miller, 1995; reproduced here as chapter 7), and concluded that of the three most notorious disasters then in the news (the Barings debacle having not occurred until February 1995) none could reasonably be attributed to holes in the regulator net. We already had enough—some would argue more than enough—regulatory machinery in place. What we really needed was better understanding of derivatives and how to manage them.

I turn here once again to the issue of more regulation for derivatives, but in a somewhat different way. This time I'll be stressing the kind of cost/benefit considerations that should, in a free society, always be central when invoking the coercive powers of the state for any public purpose, however worthy. On the principle that minus a minus makes a plus, this paper seeks to measure the potential benefits of more regulation for derivatives by estimating the real damage in the sense of the social costs that *might have been avoided* had regulation by any or all of the Securities and Exchange Commission (SEC), the Commodity Futures Trading

Commission, and the multitude of bank examiners somehow kept those disastrous deals from ever happening.

The social costs of disasters avoided, it bears emphasizing, can give at best only an upper bound on the net benefits from regulation. Regulation of derivatives is not a free good, particularly when you factor in the indirect costs imposed on end users forced to find less efficient risk-management substitutes for any derivatives made too expensive by regulation. Regulation, moreover, unless strict vigilance is maintained, will often deteriorate. Some people, such as my late colleague George Stigler, would say regulation will *usually* deteriorate into simple special-interest protectionism of the Japanese variety. (These issues of Japanese protectionist regulation of financial services are considered at length in chapter 5.) Let me put aside for now those concerns about the social costs of regulation and home in on the narrower issue of estimating the real social costs of the disasters that have for so long been dominating public discussions of derivatives.

THE DIRECT SOCIAL COSTS OF THE DERIVATIVES DISASTERS

The easiest place to start my tabulation of the social losses in the recent derivatives disasters is with Procter and Gamble, or P&G, whose treasurer negotiated with Bankers Trust an exotic swap in the notional amount of $200 million. The deal, known as a "five/thirty-year linked swap," amounted to P&G selling Bankers Trust a put option on long-term bond prices. When bond prices fell in March 1994, the put option came into the money and P&G had to pay Bankers Trust $150 million to buy it back.[1]

But even if $150 million was P&G's *private* loss on that deal, can that $150 million be taken as a measure of the *social* cost? Keep in mind that for every dollar P&G lost, Bankers Trust *made* $1. Did anyone else in society suffer any harm? I know I certainly didn't, if only because the College Retirement Equities Fund (CREF), which manages my pension, holds stock in both P&G *and* Bankers Trust. What my pension fund lost on its P&G stock it gained right back on its Bankers Trust stock. It was just a wash. (Or should have been. More on that later.)[2]

That offset of gains and losses is in no way peculiar to the P&G incident, of course. Derivatives *always* have two sides, a long and a short. And, at all times, the positions cancel. The gains and losses thus simply represent what economists call pure transfers of wealth between the parties, not changes in aggregate social wealth. Note the difference from something like the Kobe earthquake. That event did represent a true net destruction of aggregate social wealth—homes, factories, roads and, of course, lives.

Aggregate net wealth can be destroyed, of course, not just by natural disasters, but by man-made events like a stock market crash, though one must be very careful there. Economists distinguish between company-specific risks (gains and losses on individual stocks that can be diversified away, as in the example of my college retirement fund) and marketwide risks affecting every stock at the same time. When the whole stock market crashes across the board, no offset like in the P&G case exists because society as a whole is net long in stocks, almost by definition.[3]

But while every derivatives deal has two equal and opposite sides, the offset may not always be as easy to see as in the P&G example. Consider the case of Orange County. Orange County's treasurer bought structured notes known as "inverse floaters" whose payoff was of the form, say, 15.5% minus twice the London Interbank Offer Rate, or LIBOR. Hence, their stream of interest receipts goes up when LIBOR and other short-term interest rates fall. The treasurer of Orange County also made heavy use of so-called "reverse repos," which may sound like exotic derivatives, but really aren't. They are functionally equivalent to buying securities, in this case long-term Treasury bonds, on margin. Buying long bonds on margin can make sense if you believe interest rates will remain unchanged over the life of the bond (in which case you pocket the difference between the long-bond rate and the normally lower short-term rate).

For a time the Orange County treasurer's bet on stable or falling interest rates paid off handsomely. From 1991 to early 1994, the Orange County fund made over $750 million in profits, representing a cash payoff more than 400 basis points over that on the State of California's investment pool. That's why so many municipalities in the county kept depositing more and more money into the fund! But when short-term interest rates rose, as they did in mid 1994, the value of the county's inverse floaters and leveraged long-term bonds fell, by a whopping $1.7 billion or so below the value of the county's liabilities. On December 6, 1994, the county filed for bankruptcy (a subject to which I'll return later). (Author's note: In the original version of this speech, I had assumed, based on the press accounts, that Orange County had no choice but to file for bankruptcy. Subsequent research I have undertaken jointly with David Ross of Lexicon establishes, however, that the Orange County investment pool was, in fact, neither insolvent nor illiquid at the time the county filed for bankruptcy. The fund had a net worth of over $6 billion in December 6, 1994, and cash was flowing into (not out of!) the fund at a rate of $30 million a month. The bankruptcy decision may simply have been a tactical ploy to justify the filing of damage suits against Merrill Lynch and other brokerage firms who sold the securities to the Orange County investment pool.)

The people who sold Orange County those inverse floaters gained, of course, from the rise in interest rates. And who may they be? The counterparties on the structured notes were the Home Loan Bank Board and other government housing finance agencies like the Federal National Mortgage Administration, or Fannie Mae. The wealth transfer in that case would thus be from the citizens and taxpayers of Orange County to the general body of U.S. taxpayers.[4]

The transfers of wealth involved are harder yet to see in the case of Metallgesellschaft, or MG, because the oil-products marketing program of MG Refining and Marketing (MGRM), its U.S. subsidiary, had so many different components. On the one hand, MGRM was long short-term oil and oil-products futures (and swaps) so that when oil prices fell in the last quarter of 1993, MGRM had to lay out $1.3 billion or so in maintenance margin calls. In the first instance, of course, that margin money was simply transferred to those fortunate enough to have been on the short side of the futures and swaps during the same interval. But that's only the beginning. MGRM was also a short, *viz.*, a short in long-term fixed-price forward delivery contracts to its customers. MGRM held its long position in futures and swaps, in fact, precisely to hedge its short position in the forward delivery commitments. As with any other hedge, the fall in value of one leg is offset by the rise in value on the other, so that in principle at least, in a world with no transactions costs, MGRM should have washed out of the picture entirely. The wealth acquired by the lucky futures and swaps shorts when oil prices fell would thus have come ultimately from MGRM's customers who were long the fixed-price, forward-delivery contracts.

In principle the deal should have been a wash for a hedged MGRM but in practice no hedge is ever perfect. Thanks in part to the "rollover" costs under its strategy, the company did sustain a net loss for 1993 when short-term futures prices fell by more than longer-term futures (i.e. when the market's typical "backwardation" turned into "contango"), though the loss was far less than the numbers usually cited in the press. Despite a cash drain of as much as $1.3 billion on the futures and futures-equivalent leg of its hedge, Culp and Miller (1995b) estimate the net loss to the company from its combined marketing/hedging program during 1993 at no more than $170 million.[5]

Whatever the occasion for the wounds suffered by P&G, Orange County, Barings, and Metallgesellschaft, my point here is that the loss figures cited so frequently by the press do not measure the true social costs involved. Unlike the Kobe earthquake or Hurricane Andrew, very little of the world's hard-won accumulated patrimony was actually dissipated in those derivatives episodes. Properly understood, the derivatives horrors turn out to be mostly—not entirely, as I'm about to explain, but mostly—just wealth transfers.

SHOULD WE BE CONCERNED ABOUT WEALTH TRANSFERS?

Some may regard as too casual (or too callous) my dismissal of these highly publicized derivatives losses as mere wealth transfers of little social significance. They might argue that when someone sticks a gun in your ribs and takes your wallet, that's just a wealth transfer too. And surely, they suspect, even I would see adverse social consequences in that kind of transfer. I must insist, however, on a critical and fundamental difference in the two cases. Robbery is what we economists in our quaint way call an uncompensated wealth transfer. That very definitely does not describe the wealth transfers I have been talking about.

Again take the P&G case, and suppose that interest rates had gone down in 1994 instead of up. Then P&G would have done just fine. Under the terms of its deal with Bankers Trust, P&G would have received five years of financing not just at low interest rates, but at rates seventy-five full basis points below the commercial paper rate, no matter how low that rate fell. The company treasurer would then have been hailed as a genius by the whole financial press. Bankers Trust, or somebody to whom it had peddled the contract, would have taken the loss and all the hee-haws.

Bankers Trust knew, of course, that they would take a big hit if interest rates fell. What led Bankers Trust to expose itself that way? Not the commissions earned, which were tiny relative to the embedded cash flows. Instead, it was mainly the prospect that P&G would assume the corresponding exposure and cover for Bankers Trust if interest rates rose. A swap is not robbery. It is a voluntary and mutually beneficial exchange of interest-rate risk exposures between two companies.

The phrase mutually beneficial must be emphasized because derivatives are so often described as zero-sum games. And indeed, *ex post*, they are zero-sum in terms of dollar values—or even slightly negative sum on balance when you factor in commissions and other transaction costs. But *ex ante*, before the event, they're very definitely positive sum transactions. Each party to a derivatives deal is free to choose which of the two equal and opposite risks it feels better able to bear. Hence, no matter what the final outcome in dollars, every derivatives deal at the time it is entered leaves both parties better off. The proof is simple: if both parties didn't feel better off, they wouldn't have done the deal.[6]

THE INDIRECT SOCIAL COSTS IN THE DERIVATIVES DISASTERS

To insist that the direct social costs of recent derivatives disasters are essentially zero is not to suggest, of course, that no social costs whatever have been incurred. The "externalities" (any fallout or adverse side effects of the deals) must also be considered.

One externality might be the litigation costs some of these cases have generated. MG, for example, has been involved in at least six high profile lawsuits that I am aware of. P&G, rather than admit that its top management either did not understand or did not properly supervise the deals its treasurer was getting into, cried fraud and sued.[7] Lawyers fighting suits, of course, cannot be doing something productive for the GNP (Gross National Product), like producing automobiles or even flipping hamburgers. Keep in mind, however, that the volume of derivatives-related litigation has actually been quite small in the aggregate. That is remarkable really, given that, by definition, a loser and hence a potential plaintiff is present in every one of the thousands and thousands of derivatives deals.[8]

Another and possibly more serious type of social cost of the recent derivatives disasters might be listed under the general heading of bankruptcy costs. Bankruptcies have occurred in two of the cases, Barings and Orange County, and a possible bankruptcy was narrowly averted in the case of Metallgesellschaft, or so the current management would have us believe.[9]

The word bankruptcy is surrounded by such negative connotations, however, that we must be careful not to overreact to the term. My concern here, after all, is with the collateral damage likely to be inflicted on the bystanders in a derivatives-induced bankruptcy, not on the pain and suffering of the stockholders of the unfortunate firm. Apart from the deadweight legal and negotiation costs, the loss of underlying real social capital in a bankruptcy is often surprisingly small. Walk down Michigan Avenue in Chicago and you'll see many hotels and office buildings that have been in bankruptcy, some of them several times. The buildings are still standing where they always were and are still renting out space exactly as before. The stockholders and the original managers are gone, but the properties remain.[10]

Even when a business is liquidated rather than reorganized, its physical assets do not disappear from the face of the earth. They usually get transferred to other businesses; another form of recycling, as it were. No true social loss is occasioned by liquidating a firm unless society's wealth is actually destroyed in the process, or put to such less valuable alternative uses that it might just as well have been. That can happen in a bankruptcy, but it need not happen, as the recent Barings bankruptcy shows. The Dutch bank ING, by agreeing to assume a billion dollars of Barings' past acknowledged futures and options losses, took over the rest of Barings pretty much intact. ING managed to preserve as much of Barings' going-concern value as possible, given the inevitable blow to Barings' reputation.

True, ING subsequently did fire most of the upper echelon of Barings's former managers and destroyed much of their accumulated human capital which, in principle at least, is just as much social capital as any other kind. ING destroyed it, however, on the ground that it really wasn't valuable capital. While the fired top managers may well not have known of or been told about the problems developing in their Singapore branch, they should have been alerted by the sudden calls for more cash from their Singapore branch. Surely, they *should* have seen the dangers in allowing a trader to run his own back office (that is, allowed both to make the deals and to record the settlements). Anticipating just such problems, after all, is presumably why competent top managers get such high pay.[11]

The contrast of managerial fates at Barings and at MG is quite striking on this score. The head of MG's bank-dominated supervisory board, appointed in April 1993, is still very much in charge and still insisting that he did not know or was not told that the oil marketing program would face significant cash drains on its futures hedge if oil prices fell.

In the case of the Barings bankruptcy, it's natural to wonder also what might have happened if ING had not felt that Barings, or what was left of it, was worth $2 billion plus one pound Sterling. Then the losses would have been borne not just by the Barings stockholders, who were wiped out, but by the banks and other creditors that had, sometimes unknowingly, been financing Barings's futures positions. Those creditors could not have been paid after Barings's $400 million or so of initial stockholder capital had been exhausted, which brings us to the much-mooted subject of "systemic risk"—the fear that a failure by one big bank will bring down another big bank which will bring down another until the world's whole financial system melts down in some cataclysmic Chernobyl. That can happen, of course, but it's most unlikely. The major derivatives dealers are all big banks. The big banks of this world—and remember that Barings was not a big bank—are all very heavily capitalized, highly diversified in their portfolios, thanks in part to derivatives, incidentally, and constantly monitoring their aggregate risk exposure.[12]

The central banks of the world, moreover, have the power, though, alas, not always the will or the wisdom, to stop in its tracks any downward cascading financial spiral. Our own Federal Reserve System failed miserably on that score in the early 1930s, but at least learned some important lessons in the process that have made the prospect of a recurrence of the 1930s virtually unthinkable. The Bank of Japan, however, apparently still hasn't mastered the art of avoiding self-reinforcing spirals, upward or downward, in its asset markets. A strong case can be made, in fact, for the proposition that the governors of the central bank of Japan have destroyed far more of their country's wealth over the last five years by their monetary policies than have been or will ever be destroyed in derivatives transactions in the next hundred years.

THE ORANGE COUNTY BANKRUPTCY

The issue of possible bankruptcy-related externalities has now taken on still another dimension, thanks to recent developments in the Orange County case. In November 1996 the bankruptcy court discharged the county from bankruptcy and authorized the flotation of additional new securities to help pay off outstanding creditors. Additional funds needed to pay off the debts were to be raised by cutting the municipal payroll, or selling off county assets, obviating any default that would leave outside creditors holding the bag.[13]

In one sense, of course, a decision of Orange County taxpayers to stiff their creditors would have been a perfectly rational one for them. People pay their debts, after all, not just because they think it is the right thing to do, but because they have to. In an ordinary corporate or personal bankruptcy, the court-appointed bankruptcy judge can *force* the debtor to hand over assets to satisfy legally binding claims. That may not hold true for municipal bankruptcies, however, so that the taxpayers of Orange County might have been able to walk away and conclude, like the fabled financial buccaneer Jim Fiske after Commodore Vanderbilt had forced him to flee from New York to avoid arrest, that: "Nothing was lost, save honor."

A decision by Orange County to default on its debts would surely have led to some rise in interest rates on future borrowings not just for Orange County, but for all other county and local government units particularly, though by no means only, in California. Does such a rise in interest rates for Orange County and for other states and localities represent a true social cost properly chargeable to the Orange County derivatives disaster? If the event signifies merely that the probability of municipal defaults, when things go bad and taxes would have to be raised, is now actually higher than the market had been expecting, then any losses on the already outstanding bonds are clearly private, not social costs; just transfers, on a mark-to-market basis, from the old creditors to the debtors. Any higher risk premiums on new borrowings, moreover, can even be regarded as socially beneficial. By correcting the previously over-rosy view of default prospects, higher risk premiums help reduce an otherwise too large flow of resources to the municipal sector

An Orange County default could have a darker interpretation, however. The market could interpret the event to mean that municipal bodies will now feel free to repudiate past commitments under one pretext or another, not just in bad times when they can't raise more taxes, but even in good times when they can. That would be close to pure robbery, of course, and if it were considered likely to occur on any significant scale, further borrowing by municipalities and local governments would be cut off. Nothing can kill a financial market faster than uncertainty about whether you will be paid.[14]

How serious are the social consequences of killing a market depends, of course, on the size of the market killed and the available alternatives. In the particular case of the municipal bond market, some cynics (and conservatives) might even see the demise of the municipal bond market as a social blessing in disguise. Think of it, they would say, as just a "balanced budget" requirement for our profligate cities and counties. But erosion of faith in the rule of law in society must never be taken lightly.

CONCLUSION: PRESERVING THE INTEGRITY OF THE MARKET

These broader implications of the Orange County disaster can serve finally to highlight what most real-world regulators will surely regard as the fatal flaw in my assessment of the derivatives disasters as mere wealth transfers of little social significance. While conceding, perhaps, that the *measurable* costs of those disasters have indeed been negligible when the offsetting gains—and there are always offsetting gains—are taken into account, they would insist that the case for more regulation of derivatives cannot be reduced to simple numerical calculation of measurable costs and benefits. The real case for regulation, they argue, rests on preserving public confidence in the honesty and integrity of the marketplace. The widespread belief that our derivatives disasters really are disasters—and preventable ones, at that—is, by itself, the essential case for more regulation.

This public confidence argument is invoked by regulators in their own defense not just on derivatives, of course, but universally across the board. And why not, since it's virtually irrefutable by direct evidence? It's an automatic argument-stopper, and a perfect cover for frequent attempts by segments of an industry to capture the regulatory apparatus for their own benefit. (For some examples see Miller 1995, represented as chapter 7 in this volume.)

Fortunately, however, economics gives us another way to measure any perceived loss in the integrity of a market. If the public really was losing confidence in the derivatives market, then the volume of business would be drying up, which is not the case.[15] And the calls for more regulation would be coming not just from the public and the press, and from regulators seeking to expand their turf, but from firms in the industry feeling the pinch of lost business most directly. That's certainly the way it was in the early 1930s when major parts of the securities industry accepted the SEC and its Good Housekeeping Seal of Approval as a way of reviving the industry after the crash of 1929 and the subsequent dry-up in volume.

That the derivatives industry is in no such comparable state is clear not only because the volume of business remains high, but because the industry still seems to believe that nothing beyond normal public relations campaigns are needed to overcome the bad publicity on derivatives. (The recent Voluntary Trading Guidelines introduced to much fanfare by the New York Federal Reserve Bank and the International Swaps and Derivatives Association in August 1995 are a case in point.) The only businesses calling for more regulation of derivatives these days are some corporate end users seeking tougher "suitability" rules, hoping thereby to strengthen their hands against the dealers in any subsequent lawsuits over losses. (Why the end users think the dealers won't charge them for the extra risks of being sued is far from clear, however.) In times past, those seeking suitability regulations could have counted on many in Congress to support their efforts to substitute *caveat vendor* for the once accepted principle of caveat emptor. But prospects for such legislation on derivatives—analogous to the "dram shop" laws permitting victims of drunk drivers to sue the bartender—have been dramatically reduced by the power shift to the Republicans after the November 1994 election.[16]

While the derivatives industry as a whole continues to thrive, some parts of the market (notably collateralized mortgage obligations, or CMOs, and inverse floaters and other exotic structured notes) clearly are suffering severe declines in volume. Those products have been hit with a combination of hostile rulings by the regulators which have raised dealers' costs. Much more important, in my view, is the belated recognition by many corporate treasurers that, as occasional dabblers in the market, they're not likely to come out ahead selling exotic options to specialized professional swap dealers, especially given their lack of (or only very primitive) valuation technology.[17]

Structured notes and CMOs thus may have died (though it's still too early to tell for sure), but so what? If the services they represent really do fill a valid social need, then, despite all the bad publicity, they will revive again when the conditions are appropriate, just as did junk bonds, which many in the press wrongly assumed were just worthless paper kept in play by Michael Milken's daisy-chain strategy as a market maker. If, on the other hand, structured notes, CMOs and exotic options do not fill a void—do not help to "complete the market" as economists would say—then they will be gone for good. And their demise should be regarded not as a social cost, but as one of the social benefits of recent derivatives disasters. In short, a vivid demonstration (if one more were needed) that our financial markets and institutions are fully capable of recognizing and rejecting "toxic waste" without intervention by government regulators.

Keynote address given at the Seventh Annual Pacific Basin Capital Market Research Conference, July 7, 1995, Manila, the Philippines, and published in Pacific-Basin Finance Journal 2 *(1996), ©1996 Elsevier Science B.V. All rights reserved. Thanks for helpful comments on earlier drafts is owed to Christopher Culp and Jesús Saá-Requejo.*

REFERENCES

Culp, Christopher L. and Merton H. Miller, "Metallgesellschaft and the Economics of Synthetic Storage," *Journal of Applied Corporate Finance* 7 (1995), 4.

———, "Auditing the Auditors," *Risk* (1995), 8, 4.

———, "Hedging in the Theory of Corporate Finance: A Reply to Our Critics," *Journal of Applied Corporate Finance* 8 (1995), 1.

Gamze, Michael S. and Karen McCann, "A Simplified Approach to Valuing an Option on a Leveraged Spread: The Bankers Trust, Proctor and Gamble Example," *Derivatives Quarterly* 1 (1995), 4.

Jorion, Phillipe, *Big Bets Gone Bad: Derivatives and Bankruptcy in Orange County*, Academic Press, San Diego, California, 1995.

Magee, Stephen P., *A Plague of Lawyers*, Warner Books, 1995.

Meguire, Philip G., "Aggregate Consumption, Fiscal Policy, Wealth, and the Rate of Interest: Extending the Consolidated Approach," a dissertation submitted to the Graduate School of Business, University of Chicago, Chicago, Illinois, 1995.

Miller, Merton H., "Do We Really Need More Regulation of Financial Derivatives?" *Pacific Basin Finance Journal* 3 (1995), 2.

Miller, Merton H. and David Ross, "The Orange County Bankruptcy and its Aftermath: Some New Evidence," December 10, 1996, Working Paper.

3

The Economics and Politics of Index Arbitrage

The stock exchanges, the brokerage industry, and the security regulators have for many years been waging economic and political war against the competing futures exchanges. The battle has evolved very differently in the United States and Japan, however. The U.S. brokerage industry, after a long and largely inconclusive struggle, has opted for the strategy once proposed for ending the entanglement in Vietnam: declare victory and then pull out. In Japan, the fight against index futures rages on. Only a massive (and long overdue) deregulation of Japanese financial markets will let the two sectors coexist in peace.

Before explaining why, a brief word first about index arbitrage, the presumed villain of the piece. Economic logic and mountains of empirical research have long since found index arbitrage not guilty of increasing market volatility or of causing markets to crash. The two equal and offsetting legs of an intermarket arbitrage move the cash index and the futures price closer together (and perhaps do so a bit faster than if left solely to the actions of the "good shoppers" who can and do trade on both exchanges). They do not, and indeed cannot, effect the *net* level of share prices. In the political war between the exchanges, which is chronicled here, the term "index arbitrage" should be seen as just a convenient tactical weapon—a smokescreen masking the real point of the attack by the brokerage industry and its allies.

THE POLITICS OF INDEX ARBITRAGE IN THE UNITED STATES

The S&P 500 index futures contract, introduced by the Chicago Mercantile Exchange, or CME, in May 1982, was a success from the very start—something quite rare as new futures contracts go. After only three years, in fact, the share-equivalent daily volume of trading on the CME surpassed by a substantial margin that on the New York Stock Exchange (NYSE) itself. Some part of this futures volume was surely net new business—a movement down the demand curve as it were, in response to the lower level of transactions costs for rebalancing institutional portfolios. But some was also, or at least appeared to be, a diversion of business that might otherwise have gone directly to the NYSE via the normal stock brokerage routes.

The response of the NYSE and the brokerage industry to this new, lower-cost competition was perfectly natural and understandable: they went to Washington and demanded protection. The conventions of U.S. politics are such, however, that appeals must be couched not in terms of crass private advantage, but of supposedly overwhelming social benefits. The specific social benefits from eliminating futures exchanges were never quite spelled out, of course, but "index arbitrage" and its sometimes surrogate "computer-driven program trading" were phrases with a ring sufficiently ominous to make the public-interest case sound plausible, at least to the financial press.

The brokerage industry directed its appeal for protection initially to the powerful chairman of the Committee on Energy and Commerce of the U.S. House of Representatives, Congressman John Dingell of Michigan. Dingell's committee was overseer for the Securities and Exchange Commission, or SEC, which regulates the stock and options exchanges, but *not* the futures exchanges. Dingell himself was then, as now, a leading "populist" defender of the little man against the moneyed interests. Arbitrage, he thundered, was not something for you or me. Only Morgan Stanley and other Wall Street fat cats could make money at it; and, their profits from arbitrage were obtained, as any dictionary definition of arbitrage will attest, with no risk and no net investment of capital. That was a heavy load of negatives for the futures industry to overcome with standard, colorless academic arguments about maintaining the law of one price. In fact, when one academic witness before his committee opined timidly that arbitragers, too, had their place in the capital markets, Chairman Dingell replied scornfully: "Yes. About the same place as cockroaches in a kitchen."

Despite support from Congressman Dingell, the brokerage industry made little headway in Washington against the futures industry until October 19, 1987—Black Monday. The NYSE, the press, and almost everyone other than a few academic finance specialists blamed the futures markets for the Crash of 1987. A presidential commission, chaired by Nicholas Brady, an old-line Wall Street banker, put the futures industry further on the defensive. Retail volume on the NYSE also dried up in 1988, as it always does after a crash, lending further credence to the charge that futures trading and index arbitrage were driving retail stock customers away by increasing the market's volatility and undermining investor confidence. By early 1989, moreover, Nicholas Brady had become the Secretary of the Treasury in the Bush Administration and its point man on matters of financial regulatory policy. When the so-called mini-crash of October 13, 1989, provided him the necessary border incident, he joined the war against the futures industry in earnest. Legislative hostilities commenced when Congress returned from its Christmas recess in early 1990.

Secretary Brady's proposed "reforms" had two main features: one, the transfer of regulatory jurisdiction over stock index futures from the Commodity Futures Trading Commission, or CFTC, to the far less friendly SEC; and two, the transfer of authority to set margins (or performance bonds, as the futures industry prefers to call them) on stock index futures from the exchanges to the Federal Reserve System, which sets the margins on stock exchange transactions—and which has set them very high indeed. So high, in fact, that margin buying now plays only a minor role in stock market transactions. For futures, however, *every* transaction is margined. Raising futures margins above "prudential levels" (that is, above levels needed to protect the exchange's clearinghouse) thus makes futures trades more costly to customers and makes the exchanges that much less competitive.

The futures exchanges, nevertheless, perhaps taking a leaf from the Japanese automotive industry, "voluntarily" raised stock index futures margins far above prudential levels. On the more critical jurisdictional issue, however, the industry fought back hard and refused to give ground. Ways could be found to live with higher margins, but not with a hostile regulator. In their struggle to fend off the SEC, the futures exchanges found powerful natural allies in the Agriculture Committees of both the House and the Senate, which strongly resisted any dilution in their authority over the CFTC. The result, as so often happens in our Congress, was a legislative stalemate on the jurisdiction front, still unresolved.

Meanwhile, the NYSE, pressured by some of its retail-oriented member firms to "do something" about index arbitrage, had by mid-1990 instituted its own Rule 80A, making index arbitrage transactions much slower and more costly after the market has moved fifty points on the Dow in either direction. The futures exchanges, and many academics, myself included, had feared initially that Rule 80A would weaken the linkage between the exchanges. Fortunately, however, substitutes for formal arbitrage transactions are plentiful enough to keep the markets from separating noticeably even on big-move days. Better yet, the absence of crashes since Rule 80A was instituted has apparently convinced the NYSE and the financial press that the problem of index arbitrage has now been "solved" and that further "reforms" are no longer needed. Even a sudden cut in margin requirements by the futures exchanges on June 18, 1992, went largely unnoticed. The NYSE, having declared victory, is less concerned currently with the futures exchanges than with off-exchange trading—a common foe against whom both can unite.

THE POLITICS OF INDEX ARBITRAGE IN JAPAN

Although the intersectoral conflict has diminished in the United States, outright and open hostility still persists in Japan, with the conflict now even spilling over the borders of the country itself.

The point of the struggle in Japan, of course, was never really whether the Tokyo Stock Exchange and the brokerage industry could enlist the machinery of government in their battle with the futures exchanges. The Japanese government, in the form of Ministry of Finance, or MOF, bureaucrats, had not only long since enlisted on the side of the stock brokers but had actually become their shock troops. The late George Stigler may have developed his capture-theory of regulation by observing our own SEC, but MOF would have made an even more compelling case study.

MOF is, unashamedly, the managing director of the domestic stock brokerage industry cartel in Japan. And I use the term cartel deliberately, in its standard economic sense of a scheme to enhance the profits of its member firms by fixing prices—in this case, by fixing brokerage commissions and underwriting fees. MOF not only fixed them, but at levels that placed them among the highest in the world.

As every cartel manager knows, however, industry profits can not be maintained at monopoly levels for long unless entry to the industry can be restricted. And until the late 1980s, MOF was able to do just that. But ultimately, and only after intense pressure from U.S. trade negotiators, MOF finally gave way, and allowed some large U.S. brokerage firms and investment banks to operate in Japan and even to become full-fledged members of the Tokyo Stock Exchange. At roughly the same time, and again under some considerable pressure from abroad, MOF also agreed to allow trading in stock index futures and options.

Rereading today the discussions and controversies surrounding MOF's 1988 decision to allow cash-settled stock index futures suggests that MOF's instincts were sound in suspecting that these new instruments might well knock down the house of cards that the Japanese equity sector had become. But MOF was looking for the trouble over the wrong shoulder. Like so many others in Japan then and now, MOF was fixated on the *level* of stock prices. The high, and rising, stock market of 1988–1989 was a cornucopia that benefitted everyone—the brokerage firms got profits, their customers got capital gains, the corporations got low capital costs, the banks got hidden reserves, and the politicians got cash payoffs. MOF feared that futures trading threatened this universal wealth machine by undermining the strong cultural taboos in Japan against *selling* stocks—not just short-selling, but *any* selling. Short-selling was already hard enough to do thanks to MOF rules and the practice of many companies of encouraging stockholders to show their loyalty by reregistering their shares at frequent intervals. (That way, the companies would also know who had lent the shares to the shorts.) The much re-marked Japanese custom of cross-holdings of shares between firms, and between firms and banks further reinforced loyalty by what amounts to a mutual exchange of hostages.

Futures trading undermined these taboos against selling because futures were effectively impersonal instruments. Equity exposure could be reduced at any time merely by taking a short position in futures. The underlying shares need never actually leave the vault. The shares could be presented for registration whenever called upon. Yet those shares, for all practical purposes, had been converted into riskless, money market instruments. MOF's nightmare was thus that the Japanese insurance companies and other major financial institutions, taking advantage of the anonymity of futures trading, would hedge their portfolios and unleash a torrent of concerted selling like that supposedly associated with portfolio insurance in the United States.

As it turned out, of course, MOF need not have worried about the migration of portfolio insurance selling to Japan. The accounting and tax rules in Japan made hedging uneconomic for insurance companies, the biggest institutional holders of equities. And, in fact, the Japanese insurance companies, rather than *selling* futures as the Nikkei index was falling in 1990 and 1991, actually became heavy net *buyers* of futures. They were increasing their equity exposure with futures as the market dropped, not decreasing it.

Though MOF's initial fears over institutional hedging proved groundless, the prolonged decline in share prices after 1989 left MOF both concerned and puzzled. Their instincts told them that the index arbitragers had to be the real culprits, if not for causing the crash, at least for making it worse and dampening every tentative recovery. After all, the more the market went down, the more money the foreign arbitragers seemed to be making. There *had* to be a connection between the market's fall and their profits. But what was it?

The explanation couldn't be that the arbitragers were dumping shares? The foreign arbitragers were selling *futures*, but were actually *buying* shares, and in fairly substantial amounts at that. MOF saw, or thought it saw, how the huge volume of shares purchased and held by the arbitragers might some day put great downward pressure on the market when those positions were eventually unwound. But that was a nightmare for the future. And, anyway, MOF had an informal understanding with the foreign arbitragers to keep rolling over those positions—a policy that the foreign firms were delighted to follow for reasons to become clear shortly. So MOF still faced the mystery of how the arbitragers could be taking so much money out of a falling market.

When MOF turned to consult their own academic experts, they must surely have heard the same tale academic experts in every country always tell: that the arbitragers make their money by exploiting small differences in prices between the two markets. MOF must have scoffed. Millions of dollars in profits being taken out of Japan's capital markets month after month just from differences between Tokyo prices and Osaka prices? Ivory tower academics might fall for that, but not the hard-bitten pros from MOF.

MOF's thrashing around to explain the huge arbitrage profits being sucked out of their markets by the foreigners reminds me of the story told in Belgium about the farmer who rode up to the customs toll booth at the Dutch border carrying a bag of sand in the basket on his bicycle. The Dutch customs officers suspected he was smuggling something into Holland so they thoroughly sifted the bag of sand. Nothing there. A week later he came again, again with a bag of sand. They sifted once more and still found nothing. After several trips and fruitless searches, the Dutch customs officers could stand it no longer. "We know you're smuggling something," they told him. "Just tell us what it is, and we'll grant you immunity."

"It's obvious," the farmer said. "I'm smuggling bicycles."

MOF too must surely have decided to take some foreign arbitrager firms aside, and offer immunity to learn what they were arbitraging. "It's obvious," was the answer. "We're arbitraging commissions."

Brokerage commissions on common stocks can be expected to be higher than those on index futures if only because the broker's costs of handling and processing stock orders are greater. But thanks to MOF's brokerage cartel policies of high, fixed retail stock commissions, the cost to the customer for establishing or adjusting diversified portfolios of equities, was not just three or four times higher with stock than with futures, as is the case currently in the United States, but anywhere from thirty to fifty times higher! Higher to *outside* customers, that is. But not, of course, to any foreign arbitrage firms with membership on the Tokyo Stock Exchange. Members could buy stocks directly, without paying commissions, and then hedge by selling futures to ordinary Japanese investors.

The futures contracts, though quoted at a substantial premium to theoretical cash value, were still a bargain for *Japanese* investors relative to direct stock purchases at full retail commissions.

Even nonmembers of the Tokyo Stock Exchange could profit from arbitraging commissions if their trades were big enough to qualify for such volume discounts as MOF's commission schedule allowed. Many foreign firms did qualify and many more presumably would have if they had been allowed to enter the market. Japanese firms might equally well have captured these arbitrage profits, of course, but chose to leave the field to the foreigners, not because the foreign firms had any overwhelming technological edge in arbitrage—the biggest index arbitrager in New York, after all, is Nomura—but because the Japanese firms preferred to allocate their capital to their own retail networks, a highly profitable area effectively closed to foreign competitors. And even if they had wanted to enter the arbitrage business, a frown from MOF would have been enough to dissuade them.

That MOF has finally figured out commission arbitrage is suggested by its many and frantic moves in the spring of 1992 to counter this back door undercutting of its retail commission structure. MOF has been struggling to protect its domestic cartel constituents in all the old familiar ways such as by imposing strict quotas on the index arbitrage activities of foreign firms, and by new ways such as requiring foreign firms to disclose their arbitrage positions to MOF (and hence, in all likelihood, to competing Japanese firms).

Actions targeting foreign firms so directly have their downside these days, however, by further straining the already tense relations between Japan and the United States on trade matters. In fact, an irony of the whole arbitrage affair in Japan is the indignant letter fired off recently to MOF by Congressman Dingell, complaining of the "onerous and unfair" restrictions placed by MOF on U.S. arbitrage firms in Japan. Arbitragers may be cockroaches to Congressman Dingell; but, by God, they are *his* cockroaches.

MOF fired back an equally indignant reply to Congressman Dingell, promising no concessions and filled with the standard stock market boilerplate about raising capital and tails wagging dogs, plus some additional homilies on the presumed evils of brokerage firms' trading for their own accounts rather than solely as agents for their customers. To further support that agency business of its stock-brokerage cartel constituents, MOF has increased the costs of trading index futures for *everyone*, domestic users and foreign arbitragers alike. Commissions on futures have been raised substantially. Performance bonds or margins on index futures have been raised to levels that are clearly punitive even in light of the high volatility levels that typically accompany prolonged bear markets of the kind Tokyo has been enduring recently. Hours of trading on the Osaka

Stock Exchange have been reduced and elaborate price limits and circuit breakers have been installed that further restrict the effective time for trading in Osaka.

All this and more, but to no avail. The Nikkei index keeps dropping; the share volume on the Tokyo Stock Exchange remains depressed, and more and more of the volume in Nikkei futures gets transferred to the Singapore International Monetary Exchange, or Simex. The recent attempts by MOF and the Tokyo Stock Exchange to staunch that flow by cajoling or browbeating Simex to bring its fees and margins in line with those in Japan have been embarrassing failures.

Watching MOF struggle so valiantly and so futilely to shore up its retail brokerage cartel brings to mind that somber film masterpiece *Suna no onna* by Hiroshi Teshigahara, titled in English, *The Woman in the Dunes*. The film tells of a man and a woman trapped in a cave at the bottom of a sand dune. They must spend their daylight hours shoveling out the sand that drifts through their cave during the night and that threatens to overwhelm the whole village. Eventually, of course, the man realizes that his task is hopeless, but feels that it's his duty and destiny to keep struggling on.

MOF by now must surely also be coming to a similar realization over its struggles to sustain brokerage industry profits. The sand just keeps pouring in through too many cracks. MOF's constituents, however, along with much of the financial press, still don't seem to understand that the struggle really *is* hopeless. MOF's seeming past successes have built up expectations that MOF cannot fulfill. That can have ominous political consequences for MOF and the entire Japanese financial establishment.

MOF's immediate problem is thus to end these unreasonable expectations about its power to control profits and prices. And what better way than for MOF to join the rest of the world in deregulating its financial markets?

To gain credibility, MOF could declare an immediate end to fixed commissions. Removing the long-standing, MOF-enforced floor under commission rates would not only signal convincingly that a new policy era was beginning, but would solve two of MOF's currently most vexing concerns. First, freeing up stock commissions would take much of the profit out of index arbitrage and shrink that activity back to the more modest role it plays in other world markets. Intermarket arbitrage won't disappear completely, of course, because the Japanese markets contain so many other obstacles (many of them induced by regulation) to efficient price discovery. But at least the newspapers will soon lose interest in the subject, as they already have in the United States. If not, something like the Rule 80A placebo might help.

Second, and in the long run even more important, removal of the floor under commissions would eliminate the root cause of the scandals undermining the confidence of ordinary Japanese citizens (and voters) in the honesty of their financial markets and in MOF's stewardship thereof. Brokerage firms, unable to compete for business by cutting prices openly will do so under the table by guaranteeing favored customers against losses or by undertaking transactions for them at fictitious prices, to mention just two of the endlessly ingenious kickback schemes that have made headlines in Japan in recent years.

Ending fixed commissions will surely force many brokerage firms out of business. One of the main consequences, after all, of artificially high cartel prices is the waste of resources it encourages in service competition—too many firms, too many branches, too many salesmen, too many newsletters. Squeezing this useless fat out of the bloated Japanese retail brokerage industry will not be painless (though compensation schemes can surely be devised to cushion the blow). But if the U.S. experience is any guide, the long-run benefits of having financial institutions disciplined by competition rather than by administrative guidance will also be substantial both for investors managing wealth and for firms raising capital. And for Japan, it will mean, at long last, financial markets that may someday hope to match that country's already substantial achievements in culture and technology.

Keynote address given at the Fourth Annual Pacific-Basin Capital Market Research Conference, Hong Kong, July 6-8, 1992; published in Pacific-Basin Finance Journal, *Vol. 1, No. 1, March 1993, with the title "The Economics and Politics of Index Arbitrage in the U.S. and Japan."* © 1993 Elsevier Science B.V. All rights reserved.

4

Swaps, Derivatives, and Systemic Risk

I remember years ago taking one of my kids to the doctor. The kid kept fussing until the doctor finally said, in exasperation: "If you don't stop crying and tell me exactly what's bothering you, how can I help you?" I feel much the same way about all the crying I've been hearing recently from regulators about the systemic risk to the banking system posed by swaps. I wish they would stop crying and tell us what *exactly* is bothering them?

Some are pointing at the huge nominal dollar size of the swap book. With $4 trillion (or is it $6 trillion) of notional swaps out there, there *has* to be a problem, they seem to be saying. These notional values for swaps, however, are just bookkeeping conventions, not serious money. They remind one of the fabled stock market traders keeping their skills honed on a slow day by trading two $25,000 cats for one $50,000 dog. The whole point about swaps, after all, is that you *don't* swap the notional capital values, but only the income flows, which is a number at least one order of magnitude smaller (that is, smaller by a factor of ten). And not even the full flows change hands, but only the *difference* between the two flows, which cuts the exposure at least in half again.

There is, of course, a credit-risk element in swaps as there is with any system of forward contracts. But if one party defaults, the counterparty only loses to the extent it had been "in the money" on the deal. And even then, only if the counterparty could not net the deficiency against other deals in which it is out-of-the-money to the defaulter or against any collateral previously posted by the defaulter. It's hard not to be impressed with how effectively the swaps dealers have dealt with credit risk by creatively and ingeniously combining credit management practices from the interbank forward markets and from the clearinghouses of the futures exchanges. Unwinding the swaps books of Drexel Burnham and of the Bank of New England proved far simpler and less costly than liquidating most large failed S&Ls or the loan portfolios of failed commercial banks. In fact, I believe that a persuasive case can be made for the proposition that the banking industry proper, which is where all of the currency swaps and most of the interest rate swaps are located, actually becomes safer, not riskier, when insured deposit banks switch from commercial and real estate loans to swaps.

So where's all the systemic risk coming from that's producing so much crying by the regulators? From *outside* the banking system perhaps? That may well have been on the mind of Richard Farrant, deputy head of banking supervision of the Bank of England, and chairman of the Basle Supervisors Committee on Off-balance Sheet Risk. He got the whole flap about systemic risk started with his famous keynote address at the 1992 conference of the International Swap Dealers Association in Paris. His ominous remarks there have triggered more private and government reports than even the great stock market Crash of 1987.

Let me regale you once again with regulator Farrant's oft-quoted warning on swaps:

> Different markets are being tied more closely together, greatly increasing the potential for shocks in one market to be transferred to others *in ways that are not fully understood.* (Italics supplied.)

Those are pretty hard charges for mere economists to deal with. Like my kid's doctor warned, regulators can't expect help if they don't fully understand what's bothering them.

When you probe the regulators a little further and ask questions like a good doctor should, what you get, all too often, are metaphors such as, "We're worried that the whole wall might collapse if one major brick falls out" or "We're worried that the whole suit might fall off if you pull out a thread." These metaphors are obviously conveying some serious concerns on the part of the regulators, but still nothing specific enough to suggest any particular course of action either by the players or by the regulators.

When you push the regulators further still they usually go from vague analogies to individual horror stories, notably the Great Crash of October 19, 1987. Thanks to the Brady Commission report and the Securities and Exchange Commission report the conventional wisdom among securities and banking regulators, among congressmen, and among financial journalists is that: (1) the U.S. payment system came close to gridlock or total systemic collapse on the day of the Crash of 1987 and, to echo Richard Farrant, (2) that the shocks that almost brought the house down originated in the insufficiently regulated derivatives markets—not the swaps markets, of course, which were then very tiny—but the futures and options exchanges.

If you really believe that and I'm sure many of you do—it's become as much a part of American folklore as the story of George Washington and the cherry tree—there's no way I can disabuse you in a few minutes. All I can do is urge you, if you ever get some free time, to look into the post-mortem crash reports by the CME blue ribbon committee which show clearly that the tidal wave of selling on the October 19, 1987, did not originate in the futures market. It struck both the New York and the Chicago markets simultaneously. It just *looked* like it started in Chicago because so many stocks in New York had delayed openings. As for portfolio insurance, you may be surprised to learn that sales by other investors, including mutual fund redemptions by retail customers, were five times as large as portfolio insurance sales on October 19.

I am not suggesting, of course, that October 19 was just a pleasant picnic lunch in the park—although let's face it, the crash, for all the ballyhoo surrounding it, appears to have left no permanent trace on the economy. Nor am I saying that financial gridlock and possible collapse was not being *rumored* on October 19 and 20. But *rumors* are what they were: rumors of a big brokerage house default that was threatening to bring down the CME's clearinghouse.

We know now (and the CME's clearinghouse people knew even then) that the brokerage firm in question *was* slow in putting up its margin money because there were misunderstandings about the CME's settlement rules and because there was confusion about the precise amounts required, not because the firm couldn't come up with the money; that is to say, not because it was in real danger of default. In fact, despite the unprecedentedly large flows involved during the Crash of 1987, the CME's clearing and settlement procedures (the margins, the intraday margin calls, the marking to market and the elimination of big credit buildups, the prearranged transfer connections and letter-of-credit arrangements with the banks—all of them) functioned so well, on the whole, in preventing any snowballing of financial defaults that some are urging that the same clearinghouse apparatus should be instituted for swaps and over-the-counter derivatives products generally.

And let me just add that no avalanche or gridlock—choose your own metaphor—occurred during the Crash of 1987 even though the CME clearinghouse rules back then allowed for much less in-house netting of margin flows than they do now, and hence involved much more cash flow to and from the banking system than would currently be the case.

In principle, a clearinghouse for derivative products might thus provide some additional comfort for the regulators' concerns about systemic risk to the banks. But if a clearinghouse *does* come, let it evolve naturally, and not as a result of some congressional mandate to the Federal Reserve, the Securities and Exchange Commission or the Commodity Futures Trading Commission, or any combination thereof, to come up with a national derivatives clearinghouse. That was the kind of recommendation, you may recall, that the Brady Commission made for unified clearing and cross-margining of stocks, options, and futures. Their recommendation for a forced merger of the clearinghouses, mercifully, died aborning. I say mercifully because the Brady commissioners, who were all Wall Street types, never realized just how difficult it is to merge different clearinghouses. Even for two futures exchanges, as similar in most essentials as the CME and the Chicago Board of Trade, no unification of clearing is in sight even after three years of negotiation and discussion. Negotiations for merging the leasing units of the CME and the CBT were restarted in 1996 under the auspices of the Joint Strategic Initiatives Committee. (See Chapter 11 for more on this committee.) It's true that the CME and the CBOE *did* manage to come up with (but only after several years of difficult negotiations, especially with the regulators) some cross-margining of index options and futures, but at the moment only for CBOE market makers in index options and for the proprietary trading accounts of member firms, not the general public. It's always a trickier matter to perfect the title, as the lawyers put it, in intangible derivatives like futures and options than for hard assets like stocks or bonds.

Not only is it difficult to unify exchange clearinghouses, but the Brady people never realized—or maybe they did—that for futures exchanges, their clearinghouses are important competitive tools. The CME's clearinghouse takes great pride in its famous slogan: "We're good to the last drop" (of our members' wealth). It would be a serious loss to the exchange's competitive posture if that pledge were watered down by a forced merger with clearinghouses following less rigorous regimes. There are more than hints, incidentally, in the swaps community of this same reluctance by the strong credits to be forced into multilateral arrangements with those less strong. The big banks *know* that their credit ratings are their major marketing tool, and so do the newly formed AAA-rated subsidiaries of the big Wall Street investment banks.

In the normal course of events, then, we would expect the extension of futures-style clearing and settlement to the swaps sector to proceed by bottom-up expansion by the existing strong clearinghouse of the futures exchanges, rather than from some top-down mandates like the Brady Commission recommendations. The trouble is that market evolution in this area is *not* allowed to proceed normally under our obsolete and hopelessly inefficient regulatory structure. Thanks to something known as the exclusivity clause of the Commodity Exchange Act, futures exchanges and anything connected with them come under the jurisdiction of the CFTC and via the commission under the agriculture barons who have congressional oversight over the CFTC.

Turf protection by those agriculture barons proved most valuable indeed to the futures exchanges in the past when the SEC was seeking to take over (and presumably to throttle) stock index futures. But it has turned out to be a Faustian bargain because it has disadvantaged the futures exchanges in their current competition with swaps. Yes, I know swaps are *complementary* with futures, as the growth in CME's Eurodollar contract clearly shows. But futures and swaps are also *competitive*.

So let them compete. Who can be against that? But here, alas, is where the exclusivity clause comes in. The CFTC, to preserve its independence, had to buy political support from the swap dealers and their regulators by agreeing to waive its jurisdiction over swaps. But the CFTC still keeps its jurisdiction—and hence its costly, agricultural, Ma and Pa Kettle, retail-trader rules—for any swap-type products (competitive swap fighters, as it were) developed by the futures exchanges and their clearinghouses. The CME has petitioned the CFTC to exempt these contracts too from their regulatory oversight, but so far to no avail. (Author's note: At the time of this writing, February 1997, congressional legislation to rein in the CFTC was under active discussion. But past experience suggests that killing that agency will not be easy.) After all, what's in it for the CFTC?

To sum up and conclude, then, let me say that I do believe that systemic risk in interbank markets can be reduced by forward integration of the futures industry's clearinghouses into the spot market for currencies and hence into the foreign exchange swap market. And since that process will also increase the competitiveness and the transparency of the swap market, the sooner we can eliminate current regulatory obstacles to that forward integration, the better.

A talk given at the Banking Structure Conference of the Federal Reserve Bank of Chicago, May 6, 1993, as part of the Panel on Systemic Risk in Interbank Markets and published in Proceedings of the 29th Annual Conference on Bank Structure and Competition, *May 1993.*

Part II

Financial Market Regulation in Theory and Practice

5

The Modern Theory of Regulation

Thirty years ago my late, and much missed friend and colleague, George Stigler, fired the opening shot in what has become a revolution in the economic theory of regulation. The shot was aimed at the U.S. Securities and Exchange Commission—that jewel in the crown of reform agencies created by the Roosevelt Administration in the 1930s in response to the supposed financial excesses of the 1920s. After noting the substantial volume of new regulations the SEC had introduced in its first three decades, Stigler asked the following, somewhat startling question. What empirical evidence has the SEC ever provided to show that its regulations accomplished their announced public policy objectives?

No evidence at all, said Stigler. He thereupon undertook some empirical research studies that the SEC, with its vastly greater resources, *should* have done either before the regulations and their attendant costs were imposed on the public or, if that was not practical, after the regulations had been in force long enough to measure the benefits produced.

That Stigler could find no evidence of social benefits for the specific regulations he studied posed even more puzzling and disturbing questions. Why does a regulatory agency keep imposing regulations that don't seem to produce as promised. The people running the regulatory agencies are not stupid, after all. Can it be that their regulations really *are* working, but are actually accomplishing objectives very different from those advertised?

Stigler followed up that thought with a number of subsequent papers culminating in his justly famous 1971 paper entitled "The Theory of Economic Regulation." That classic paper is the foundation on which the modern theory of regulation has been erected, not only in economics but in law and in their lively joint offspring, the spectacularly growing field of law and economics.

The many examples Stigler introduced to illustrate propositions and predictions of the economic theory of regulation were drawn, understandably, from American regulatory experience. But on rereading his paper recently I was struck by how aptly the reasoning applied to *Japanese* regulatory experience, especially the financial regulation maintained by the Japanese Ministry of Finance or MOF. The fit was tailor-made, amazingly so, since to my knowledge, Stigler had no firsthand knowledge of what MOF was up to.

What I propose to do today is an out-of-sample prediction of Stigler's model, as it were (the only kind of empirical work one can really trust), by showing in some specific detail how Stigler's economic theory of regulation can explain MOF's policies; and can explain also why those policies are likely to persist in the face of their complete, abject, and in some respects humiliating failures to meet their announced objectives.

THE THEORY OF REGULATION

Let me begin with what in some ways was Stigler's most fundamental contribution, namely transferring the economic theory of regulation from normative, to positive economics. Specifically, he assigns the theory of economic regulation the task—not of listing the many possible sources of market failure (like monopoly or asymmetric information or externalities) along with neat schemes of taxes and subsidies to achieve first-best, or second-best solutions—but instead the task of explaining "who will receive the benefits or burdens of regulation, what form regulation will take, and the effects of regulation upon the allocation of resources." In his 1971 paper, Stigler takes the central insight of that new positive theory to be, again to quote him, that "as a rule, regulation is acquired by the industry and is designed and operated primarily for its benefit" even though the regulation might initially have been thrust on the industry against its opposition.

Stigler acknowledges the possibility that some regulations may exist whose net effects are onerous. But he regards these as rare, and as explainable by the same theory, just pushed one or two layers deeper. I'll present later, in due course, some examples, both Japanese and American, of these seeming exceptions to the industry-benefit presumption.

Let me also hasten to say that I will be talking about Stigler's 1971 paper which got the field started and which stimulated so much further academic research on the positive theory of regulation. The 1971 paper, with its oft-called "capture theory of regulation," has aged surprisingly well in my view, but it has been substantially expanded and broadened since then. James Buchanan and the public choice school, for example, have added the regulator's own preferences and instincts for self-preservation back into the regulatory objective function. Others, notably Edward Kane, have emphasized the essentially competitive nature of what he would call the "regulatory service industry" especially in this age of the global market place, to invoke the current cliché.

Still others have stressed the important role in practice of what has been dubbed "regulatory slack" and regulatory inertia. Human beings grow old and die and pass from the scene, but not regulations and regulatory agencies. They have to be *killed* when the conditions that gave rise to them have changed. That's not easy. The classic example, of course, is the U.S. Rural Electrification Agency, instituted in the 1930s when less than 10% of U.S. farms had electricity; and continued on into the 1990s when less than 10% *don't* have electricity.

Anomalies due to regulatory inertia have multiplied in recent years in' the United States thanks to the master budget agreements negotiated between our congress and our executive branch. Under these agreements, it has become all but impossible to retire by legislation any regulatory rule that brings in money to the government even if *everyone* agrees that the social costs inflicted by the rule are many times the size of the revenue earned. To kill it, you have to replace with other taxes any revenue lost. Or, more accurately, you have to replace the revenue *estimated* to be lost, taking all relevant elasticities as zero.

A particularly outrageous example in financial regulation in the United States at the moment involves a ruling by the Supreme Court that the Internal Revenue Service has interpreted as levying profits taxes on ordinary, zero-profit, pure hedging transactions by business firms. Everybody knows the IRS ruling makes no economic sense, but if the IRS's ruling is upheld on appeal, it will cost $2 billion or more in alternative tax revenues to overturn the rules by legislation.

Regulatory inertia is an important extension indeed to Stigler's 1971 version, and I don't mean to downplay it. But for explaining the regulations we observe, the best strategy is still to begin, with Stigler, by assuming that someone in the regulated industry must be benefiting.

MOF, the SEC, and the Brokerage Industry

For both MOF and the SEC I will refer to the industry receiving the benefits of regulation as the "brokerage industry," construed broadly as the entire set of firms earning commission income from buying and selling (including underwriting) securities (mostly corporate securities) to outside investors.

I recognize, of course, that MOF's jurisdiction extends well beyond the brokerage industry even as I have broadly defined it, but I want to focus here on the brokerage side to highlight the differences and similarities between the MOF and the SEC. Our SEC's jurisdiction is still limited largely to those dealing in corporate securities, even though former SEC Chairman Richard Breeden fought valiantly, though unsuccessfully, during much of his tenure to expand the SEC's turf up to MOF-like dimensions— at the expense, it hardly needs pointing out, of other regulatory agencies, notably the Commodities Futures Trading Commission for jurisdiction over stock index futures, the Treasury for the right to supervise dealers in Treasury securities, and the Federal Reserve System for the right to set rules for reporting the values of securities held by banks.

I should add also that though the SEC's nominal jurisdiction is smaller than MOF's, the brokerage industry itself is much larger in the United States than in Japan, and I don't just mean in terms of nominal dollar value. It was common to hear in recent years that the value of Japanese equities had actually surpassed that of the United States, but that was never true even at the peak in 1989, when due allowance was made for the substantial amount of cross-holding among Japanese corporations and banks. And, of course, it's even less true today after the Tokyo market has lost 50 to 60% of its peak value.

But regardless of how size is measured, the U.S. industry is clearly vastly more complex in terms of the variety of products and services it offers and of its constant innovation of new ones. In terms of complexity, the second largest industry is not really in Japan, but in Great Britain.

The Alternative View of Regulation

The Stiglerian view that both MOF and the SEC and their counterparts elsewhere operate primarily for the benefit of the brokerage industry is very different, of course, from the public positions advanced by those agencies themselves. It is also different from how their roles are perceived by the general public.

The commonly held "alternative view," as Stigler dubs it, is that: "Regulation is instituted primarily for the protection and benefit of the public at large or some large subclass of the public." Thus our SEC would surely see its mission as protecting investors, particularly small and presumably less sophisticated investors, against fraudulent and unfair practices by brokers, dealers, and other industry professionals. And that vision conforms well with the public perception in the United States, which sees the SEC not essentially as an agency dealing with "economics" as that term is usually understood, but as part of our criminal justice system— the scourge of the inside trader and the purveyor of worthless securities.

That the SEC sees itself and is seen as policing fraud in the industry actually confirms rather than contradicts Stigler's industry-benefit theory of regulation. When the SEC was set up originally in the early 1930s, the brokerage industry's volume of business was in near total collapse—a collapse widely, if erroneously, attributed to fraudulent and illegal activities by Wall Street professionals.

The industry hoped that a tough-cop stance by the SEC would enhance the industry's tarnished image and restore investor confidence, even if a few victims, like the chairman of the NYSE, had to be ritually sacrificed in the process. Unlike the SEC in the United States, however, MOF in Japan does not see itself, and is not seen by the public, as an agency concerned mainly with rooting out fraud in the marketplace. In fact, many newspaper accounts I have seen (in translation, of course) have accused MOF of displaying too little zeal in stamping out fraud and corruption—a charge no one has ever leveled at our SEC.[1] In fact, our SEC has recently brought its regulatory thunder down on the heads of some of MOF's constituents by bringing civil charges against Daiwa, Yamaichi, Nikko, and Nomura for a long list of securities law violations in the United States, including submitting false bids in the auction of U.S. Treasury securities.

Unlike the SEC, MOF is concerned less with law enforcement in the small than with managing the economy in the large. MOF sees its main task as maintaining high and rising levels of stock prices. High and rising prices not only benefit the investing public, MOF would argue, but make it easier and cheaper for Japanese firms to raise equity capital. And they create hidden reserves on the books of Japanese banks, making it easier for them to meet international capital requirement standards and thus to compete more effectively for loan business both at home and abroad.

So rosy, in fact, is MOF's view of its own regulatory role that one wonders why no other regulatory agency, and certainly not our own SEC, has ever sought to follow MOF's example, that is, make supporting stock prices its main responsibility. Stigler's theory of economic regulation does indeed suggest why MOF alone has sailed on that tack, but that must wait until after documenting the specific ways in which MOF's regulation of the Japanese financial sector actually serves mainly the interests of the brokerage industry, to say nothing of MOF itself.

HOW REGULATIONS BENEFIT THE BROKERAGE INDUSTRY

Stigler identifies four main channels by which the regulatory authorities can exert the power of the state to benefit particular industries: subsidies, price fixing, entry controls, and restrictions of substitute products. I want to focus mainly on the issue of substitute products, but first, a few words about each of the others, beginning with subsidies, the most obvious form of regulatory benefit.

Subsidies

Direct subsidies to the brokerage industry have not so far been a conspicuous feature in the United States. But *indirect* subsidies do exist. A particularly controversial one at the moment concerns who pays for the salaries and other expenses of the regulators. The bills for our CFTC, for example, currently $50 million per year, are picked up by the general body of taxpayers. But in Washington during the Bush years, some economists, many of whom had read the Stigler paper, wondered why the public should be paying for regulation when it was the industry that was benefiting. Accordingly, they proposed that a so-called user fee or transactions tax be imposed to defray the budget of the CFTC. The Clinton Administration, even more desperate to find budgetary savings, has recently revived the proposal.

The segment of the financial industry most directly affected by the proposed new charge have been resisting it desperately for several reasons. Nobody *likes* to pay taxes, after all. And the tax is economically inefficient. It's not a tax on the ultimate retail customers, but bears on market makers as well. But perhaps above all in feeding the industry's resentment is the belief that the benefits being obtained from CFTC regulation are not worth the price. The CFTC has much less credibility than the SEC as a market watchdog, and its attempts to increase its reputation capital have only driven up the industry's costs and further weakened the industry's competitive position vis-à-vis foreign futures exchanges.

When it comes to MOF in Japan, however, direct subsidies to the industry are far more important than merely shifting MOF's salary burden to the taxpayers. MOF buys and warehouses stocks like our agriculture department buys and warehouses farm commodities. MOF has de jure control over investing the portfolio of the huge Japanese postal saving system and has de facto control over insurance company portfolios. It has not hesitated to use both portfolios in its price-support activities.

Entry Controls

Getting direct subsidies can be a neat way of adapting the coercive powers of the state to the benefit of your industry, if, of course, you have the political muscle to swing it, and if you don't have to pay too big a price for it in other dimensions.

The classical example of paying too high a price is the U.S. airline industry which, in its early years, was more than willing to accept heavy-handed micro regulation by the Civil Aeronautics Board in return for the government's huge airmail subsidies. (I mean heavy-handed; the CAB virtually told airlines how much lettuce they could put in a salad in first class.) But when the growth of regular air travel eventually dwarfed the mail subsidies, the industry suddenly became converted to free markets and led the charge for airline deregulation.

Short of direct subsidies, Stigler observes that "the second major public resource commonly sought by an industry is control over entry by new rivals." Here, of course, MOF has been masterful in defense of the incumbents in its brokerage industry, far more so than our SEC which has no power to issue, and hence restrict, brokerage licenses. The best our SEC has been able to do is to slow down entry somewhat by imposing high capital requirements on brokerage firms, which inevitably bear disproportionately on small and struggling new entrants.

Even MOF's protective walls, however, have buckled in spots, though its task initially was much easier than that facing the U.S. regulators. The main potential new entrants feared by the incumbent Japanese firms were foreign brokerage firms and investment banks like Merrill Lynch or Morgan Stanley. And, of course, keeping foreign competitors out of its market had become almost an art form in Japan. But eventually even MOF had to cave in to relentless pressure, mainly from the United States. The big Wall Street firms finally did enter and the consequences were about what you would expect from major new entrants, though, as I'll explain, in somewhat unexpected ways, at least unexpected by MOF.

I do not mean to suggest that MOF is in any way unique in its attempts to protect its domestic clients by blocking the entry of foreigners. The U.S. financial regulators do much the same thing whenever they think they can get away with it. It surely wasn't easy or automatic for Japanese firms to qualify as primary dealers in U.S. Treasury securities, even when Japanese citizens were major buyers of those bonds; similarly for Japanese investors seeking to acquire a major stake in a U.S. futures trading firm. In fact, one of the few examples I know where the local regulators did not try to block out a foreign entrant was in London, where the Swedish option market firm, OM, tried to enter and did so easily and quickly, first for options on Swedish stocks and then more generally. But then, option markets were never a big thing in London or it might have been different.

Price Controls

The third class of public policies sought by an industry is price-fixing. Stigler notes: "Where there are no diseconomies of large scale for the individual firm, price control is essential to achieve more than competitive rates of return" even when the industry has achieved entry control. MOF certainly has carried out its side of the bargain on this score. Profits and volume in the industry may be low at the moment, but the minimum fixed retail commissions set by MOF are still among the highest in the world, as are their mandated minimum underwriting fees.

MOF's price-fixing policies are sometimes contrasted unfavorably with the supposedly free-market approach of the SEC. But that comparison is not entirely fair to MOF. Before 1975, the fixed commissions mandated by our SEC were even higher than those of MOF. Nor was it some sudden excess of free-market zeal that led our SEC to abandon its price-fixing policies. Market evolution had simply made those policies untenable.

The SEC's mandated single fixed-commission rate of seventy cents a share on round lots of 100 shares discriminated enormously against the pension funds and other institutional investors trading in lots of 10,000 or 100,000 shares. These institutional investors knew that they were being exploited—that $7,000 on a 10,000-share trade was at least one and possibly two orders of magnitude above the marginal cost of processing that order. To better control their trading costs, the big pension funds tried to enter the brokerage business themselves by buying existing firms or by buying seats on a regional stock exchange. All to no avail. The SEC was able to thwart them at every turn. About all institutional investors could do was to extract kickbacks and other concessions from the brokerage firms to whom they directed their order flow.

The SEC tried to slow this under-the-table erosion of its rate structure by grudgingly permitting some modest quantity discounts. But they were too little and too late. Under pressure of the great bear market and volume dry-up after 1973, the fixed-rate structure was close to collapse. In the face of the inevitable, the SEC, with some not-too-gentle prodding by the Justice Department's Antitrust Division, finally abandoned its price-fixing policies on May 1, 1975.[2]

MOF in Japan is clearly going through much the same evolution. Kickbacks, under-the-table payments, and associated scandals have become far too notorious in Japan to require further comment here—beyond wondering why each new scandal seems to come as a surprise. Government-mandated price restrictions, after all, are always and everywhere an open invitation to corruption.

MOF in the 1980s and 1990s has had, in some ways, an even more difficult task than our SEC in the 1970s in defending its fixed-rate structure, thanks to certain important technological developments in the securities industry. And that brings me to the last of Stigler's four classes of public policies sought by an industry from its regulators, namely the encouragement of complementary products and especially the suppression of substitute products.

The Suppression of Substitutes

As a specific illustration, Stigler cites the case of the butter producers who were able for many years to suppress the production and sale of margarine altogether. When the ban eventually had to be relaxed under the pressure of butter shortages during World War II, the butter producers were able to prevent the margarine producers from coloring their product yellow. It had to look as unappetizing as so much lard.

Stigler's reference specifically to margarine was also a Chicago in-joke whose point is probably lost on most younger economists whose memories don't go back that far. In the 1940s, Stigler's long-time friend and mentor, Theodore (Ted) Schultz, then just a promising young agricultural economist, came to prominence by criticizing the ban on margarine and thereby getting himself fired from the University of Iowa. Iowa's loss was Chicago's gain, needless to say.

Compelling as the margarine-suppression example was for Stigler, an almost limitless supply of such examples can be found in financial regulation, especially with respect to what have come to be called derivative securities—options, futures, and swaps. These derivative products, after all, are designed precisely to be cheaper substitutes not for *owning* the underlying securities, but for *trading* them. Trading, with its attendant commissions and related fees, is precisely what the traditional brokerage industry lives on. Calls for the regulators to suppress these cheaper substitutes are thus all but inevitable.

Stigler couldn't have mentioned equity derivatives in his 1971 article because they didn't then exist. Strictly speaking, equity options *did* exist, but only as a small and highly specialized sector of the over-the-counter market. Volume was minuscule, secondary trading was cumbersome, and commissions were high.

Exchange-traded equity options *might* have existed as early as 1971, however, save for regulatory inertia of the SEC. The Chicago Board of Trade, confident that it could trade options on its floor far more cheaply than the OTC put-and-call brokers in New York, had applied to the SEC for permission to list options as early as 1969.

The SEC reacted slowly, however. The reason was not so much to protect its main constituents in the stock brokerage industry (it didn't really believe option trading would amount to much) and not to protect the regular put-and-call brokers (who were too small and too few to command much influence), but to protect the SEC itself. The commission had to avoid being blamed for setting off a speculative explosion like the one that supposedly occurred in the 1920s, which in turn led to the Crash of 1929 and eventually to the SEC in 1933.

We can smile today at these and related concerns (such as that giving risk takers the opportunity to trade options might dry up the flow of equity capital to the corporate sector), but options were very poorly understood in those days. The Black-Scholes option-pricing model, for example, was still two or three years away. And not everyone at the SEC realized the world of difference between a substantial reduction in option *premiums* (the price paid for the option) and a substantial reduction in option *trading costs*. The latter, of course, was all that the CBOT was actually promising.

But the SEC had more than just these macro concerns. A major worry was that opening a second market in options might outflank some of the key regulations in its main market, the NYSE, notably the insider trading restrictions and the so-called "uptick rule." The uptick rule is a uniquely American way of regulating short sales. In some other countries, short sales are either banned altogether by the regulators (as they were in Sweden before the recent capital market liberalization). Or they may be regarded as unenforceable in law (which ruling, and not the Tulip bubble, is what really killed the Amsterdam Stock Exchange in the seventeenth century). Many among the general public of stock owners undoubtedly *wish* the SEC would ban short sales. But there are too many legitimate technical reasons for short sales, particularly on the part of dealers and market makers, to prohibit them completely. So the SEC compromised. You *can* sell short, but you must actually borrow the shares physically, put the proceeds from the sale of the borrowed shares into escrow, and make the sale of those borrowed shares at a price no lower than that of the previous transaction.

That last restriction is the uptick rule. It's a very popular restriction indeed. Even though there is no evidence that it's effective, many in the brokerage industry and among its customers see it as a fundamental protection against "bear raids" (cascading waves of short sales hammering prices ever lower). And those views are shared by other SEC constituencies such as underwriters of new stock issues and the owners of corporations who would *like* to bring out primary or secondary offerings of their shares if only those awful speculators would just stop undermining the underwriter's efforts to keep the offering price high.

The SEC soon realized that it couldn't just extend the uptick rule to options, if only because CBOT-style, open outcry markets don't have sequential ticker tapes. That's strictly a stock exchange feature. So to keep the bears from exerting their downward pressure on prices via the option market, the SEC agreed to approve trading initially only in calls, not puts—surely one of the silliest rulings ever made by a regulatory agency. By the time the SEC learned about the Put-Call Parity Theorem a few years later, the CBOT's substitute market, now known as the Chicago Board Options Exchange (CBOE) was too firmly entrenched to be dislodged.

Ten years after options first appeared on the scene, another low-cost derivative substitute product suddenly appeared to compete vigorously with the traditional brokerage industry. The options approved for trading in 1972 had all been single company options. The new development was stock index futures, especially the CME's S&P 500 Index contract— a product with great appeal to the pension funds and other institutional investors who not only held (and traded) large diversified portfolios but who regularly used the S&P 500 Index as a benchmark for measuring performance.

So appealing was the new index futures product and so rapidly was it embraced by institutional investors that within three years the per share equivalent of futures trading exceeded that of the NYSE itself. Some part of this huge futures volume was surely net new business because it really *is* cheaper to rebalance big portfolios between equities and cash with a single futures transaction rather than hundreds of separate stock transactions. There's also more price impact to the separate trades in individual stocks because the market is less sure that the trades are not being driven by special information advantages. Some of the futures volume, of course, fed back to the NYSE via index arbitrage, but that hardly mollified the old-line retail firms who believed that those computer-driven arbitrage programs were using up too much of the market's normal liquidity and were frightening away too many of their small, but still lucrative, retail customers.

The SEC had to listen with some embarrassment to these complaints from its constituents because, in a way, it really *had* let them down. When index futures were first being proposed in the early 1980s, the CME actually had approached the SEC as the presumed regulator of equity products, much as the CBOT had approached the SEC ten years earlier for permission to trade options. The SEC, however, spurned the offer, misled perhaps by the very modest volumes of trading for individual stock options up to that point.

But basing the contract on an index made all the difference in the world, not just for the CME, but also for the CBOE which introduced that same year its own S&P 100 option contract, a contract whose volume of business quickly surpassed that of all the individual options combined even though the SEC initially set position limits so low as to make the product unattractive to large institutional investors. By the time the SEC realized its mistake in signing off on the CME's S&P 500 futures contract, it was too late to get the jurisdiction back. The contract was now regulated by the CFTC, a smaller and less prestigious agency, surely, but like any other agency, not willing, voluntarily, to relinquish any turf. The best the SEC could get out of its prolonged negotiations with the CFTC was the so-called Shad-Johnson accord of 1984 under which the CFTC agreed not to authorize any index so narrowly based or so heavily weighted by a single stock as to be an effective substitute for a single stock (that is to say, for purposes of insider trading)

The SEC, its brokerage industry constituents, and its congressional overseers (notably Congressman John Dingell of Michigan) continued to complain about the competition from index futures with absolutely no success until the fateful day of October 19, 1987. They all thereupon immediately blamed the CFTC-regulated futures industry for the Crash of

1987 and demanded that jurisdiction over index futures be transferred back to the SEC. Their "one-market, one-regulator" cry was soon taken up by the Presidential Commission on Market Mechanisms chaired by Nicholas Brady. Brady himself was a leading member of the old-line investment banking community, and his other commissioners were drawn entirely from the ranks of the Wall Street and corporate establishments. No one who actually knew anything about index futures or options was asked to serve and no economist, not even George Stigler who had volunteered to serve.

The Brady Commission report would have had its justly-earned fifteen minutes of fame and then been forgotten save for one special circumstance. Nicholas Brady soon thereafter became Secretary of the Treasury and a most influential person indeed in the councils of the Bush Administration.

I shall not review here in any detail the subsequent history of the bitter jurisdictional dispute between the SEC and the CFTC (which some have dubbed the Brady-Breeden attempted hostile takeover of the CFTC) beyond noting that the proposed regulatory takeover was a failure. (The subject is taken up in more detail in chapter 3.) The futures industry and the CFTC were able to fend off their seemingly much more powerful political and economic rivals for reasons long stressed by the public choice theorists. The cost of our sugar import quotas, for example, when spread over the whole consuming public amounts to only a few dollars each per year. But for the smaller number of sugar producers, the gains are a tidy sum, providing both the motivation and wherewithal to fight and win the political battles to retain the quotas; similarly for the CFTC and its futures industry constituents. The retail stock brokerage industry is larger than the futures industry but it is also more diffuse.

The futures industry was not only more heavily concentrated regionally but, thanks to the historical origin of futures trading in hedging corn, wheat, and other farm commodities, supervision over the futures industry was lodged with the agriculture committees in Congress, even though by 1989 trading was mostly in interest rate, stock index, and foreign currency futures. No one needs to be reminded how politically potent the agricultural bloc in any country can be. There was never any real prospect that the powerful agriculture barons in the U.S. Congress would not resist the takeover threat to their jurisdiction.

The agriculture bloc was not powerful enough to actually checkmate the securities bloc, but it could and did force a stalemate. During the more than two years of delay and maneuvering after the Brady-Breeden attack was launched, the brokerage industry lost its enthusiasm for continuing the fight. More and more stock brokerage firms have added a futures trading capability to their regular lines. The two segments of the industry have intermarried, as it were. Retail stock volume has recovered substantially from its 1988 lows. The NYSE has also taken a number of steps on its own that have managed to quiet the clamor over index arbitrage and program trading without actually affecting either. The NYSE has shifted its attention from the futures exchange to the far more serious competitive threat it faces from off-exchange trading of its listed stocks.

Let me add a brief postscript for the benefit of those who have read recent accounts of the futures industry's call—yes, the *futures* industry's call—for a single financial regulator.

What's *that* all about and how do we reconcile it with their past all-out resistance even to the mention of the idea? How do we reconcile it with the Stigler model?

The answer is, basically, that the industry is trying to get better (that is, lower-cost) regulatory service. The futures industry came to realize that in seeking the protection of the agriculture bloc against the securities industry, it had made a Faustian bargain. The agriculture bloc *did* protect them, but exacted a heavy price by imposing its own farmer-oriented agenda on an industry that was now part of the financial sector.

The futures exchanges would dearly like to get out from under their agriculture overseers, but don't want to turn to the SEC. The SEC commissioners can't be trusted because their hearts lie elsewhere. So the futures industry has recommended that a new, cabinet-level department of financial regulation be set up, organized along functional lines into eight separate (but equal) operating divisions: (1) prudential and systemic risk (mainly capital requirements); (2) fiduciaries and pooled vehicles (mutual funds); (3) disclosure and reporting; (4) investment securities markets (mainly debt and equity instruments); (5) risk-shifting markets (futures and options); (6) banking and insurance; (7) customer insurance (FDIC, SIPC, and PBGC); and (8) consumer protection.

That an organization so structured would indeed reduce much of the wasteful duplication in current arrangements is clear enough. But that a unified structure along MOF-like lines offers a safe haven for the futures industry is certainly *not* clear.

For while the U.S. brokerage industry and its regulator have adapted, albeit grudgingly, to the competition from futures and options, the fight to suppress these substitutes continues unabated in Japan, and is even spilling over the borders of the country itself.

The difference in evolution reflects undoubtedly MOF's previously noted self-view of its main function as that of propping up the level of stock prices. Left to its own devices, MOF would probably never have permitted the trading of index futures. MOF authorized futures trading only reluctantly and only after intense pressure from the United States in support of firms in its financial services industry who saw trading in derivatives as the one area in which they had the expertise to compete effectively for business in Japan.

MOF saw index futures as a threat to its policies for discouraging sell-ing—not just short-selling, but any selling. Futures trading could un-dermine these policies because futures were effectively impersonal in-struments. Equity exposure could be reduced at any time merely by taking a short position in futures. The underlying shares need never even leave the vault. They could be presented for reregistration when-ever called upon. Yet, for all practical purposes, they had effectively been converted to cash.

MOF's nightmare was that the Japanese insurance companies, tak-ing advantage of the anonymity of futures trading, would hedge their portfolios and unleash a torrent of selling, like that associated with port-folio insurance in the United States. But MOF needn't have worried. Their accounting and tax regulations had already made hedging un-economic for insurance companies. And, despite the steady erosion in equity values after 1989, Japanese insurance companies were actually *buying* futures not selling futures. Who, then, was selling futures? The answer, of course, was the foreign investment banks, especially those that had been allowed to buy seats on the Tokyo Stock Exchange. These firms were making literally hundreds of millions of dollars a year, de-spite the steady fall of Japanese stock prices, merely by a simple and straightforward arbitrage. The arbitrage, however, was not the same as that between the New York and Chicago markets. In Japan, what was being arbitraged was not small price differences but large *commission* differences.

That MOF did not at first understand this process of arbitraging com-missions is clear from MOF's frantic attempts to dissuade the foreign ar-bitrage firms from unwinding their arbitrage positions. MOF knew enough to realize that unwinding the positions meant selling the stocks. But not enough, apparently, to realize that it also meant buying futures, which would exert an equal and opposite effect on the price level. The foreign firms, of course, were more than eager to accommodate MOF. Every time they rolled over their positions at MOF's behest, they made more money.

That MOF has finally figured it out, however, is clear from a num-ber of MOF's more recent actions which have greatly increased the cost of trading index futures for everyone, domestic users and foreign arbi-tragers alike. Commissions on futures have been raised, as have mar-gin requirements. Hours of trading on the Osaka Stock Exchange have been cut and elaborate price limits and circuit breakers have been in-stalled that further restrict the effective time for trading futures in Osaka. All that did was move huge chunks of the business offshore to Singapore.

MOF's attempts to staunch that flow to Singapore by browbeating the Singapore International Monetary Exchange, or Simex, to bring its fees and margins back into line with Osaka have been an embarrassing failure. The Simex people simple laughed at the visiting delegation from MOF and the Tokyo Stock Exchange. Nor have MOF and the Tokyo Stock Exchange been any more successful in their efforts to get IOSCO (the International Organization of Securities Commissions) to support their position against Simex or to enunciate a policy of giving each country exclusive rights to regulate futures on indexes whenever traded.

The Simex case is not the first time, of course, that MOF's policies have driven Japanese markets overseas. MOF restrictions, plus MOF-mandated high fixed underwriting fees "hollowed out" the Japanese bond and warrant market, creating a Eurobond market in which both Japanese firms and Japanese investors trade in London.

CONCLUSION

The natural inclination of most academic economists confronting so much evidence of the damage MOF has inflicted on the Japanese capital markets is to recommend a thoroughgoing deregulation. Tear MOF down and start over. Why should a twentieth century economy be saddled with a seventeen century regulatory structure?

And, in that spirit I and many others have suggested recently that a useful first step to establish some credibility for a major deregulation would be to end the fixed brokerage commissions like we in the United States did in 1975. That would also help solve two other problems vexing MOF. It would reduce the pressure for kickbacks and also reduce index arbitrage.

Stigler would deride proposals like mine as hopelessly naive. He writes:

> The idealistic view of public regulation is deeply imbedded in professional economic thought. So many economists, for example, have denounced the ICC for its pro-railroad policies that this has become a cliché of the literature . . . The fundamental vice of such criticism is that it misdirects attention. . . . The only way to get a different commission would be to change the political support for the Commission and reward commissioners on a basis unrelated to their services to the carriers.

Read hastily, that passage too may misdirect attention to the overly narrow matter of the pecuniary rewards (in the form of future jobs) flowing to the regulators from the industries they regulate. That's important surely, particularly in Japan, though it's not much different here.

But there are also real differences between the SEC and MOF. The SEC did, after all, however reluctantly, abandon fixed commissions. And, except to the limited extent of its uptick rule, the SEC has never held itself out as supporting the level of stock prices.

Our SEC has carefully avoided taking on any such responsibilities, even by implication, and for two reasons. First, unlike MOF, the SEC knows that the policy won't work. It may *seem* to work for short periods if great sums of money are pumped in, but stock prices can't be kept indefinitely from reflecting their true economic fundamentals. If those fundamentals are bad then sooner or later the level of stock prices will be adjusted downward, possibly abruptly.

And that's the second and decisive reason for the SEC's unwillingness to accept responsibility for prices: When the inevitable adjustment comes, they will take the blame for the failure of a policy that attempts to support prices. They and their political sponsors will be swept out of office. Now we're getting to the heart of the matter. MOF and its sponsors don't have to pay the costs of failure of its policies, even abject failure, because there is no effective political competition in Japan.

Stigler, referring to the political environment in the United States, notes that:

> If one party becomes extortionate (or badly mistaken in its reading of effective desires), it is possible to elect another party which will provide the governmental services at a price more closely proportioned to the costs of the party.

Until that kind of political competition comes to Japan, I am sorry, as an academic, to have to conclude that all talk of financial deregulation and reform in Japan is likely to be just that—academic.

Keynote address given at the Hitotsubashi International Symposium, Financial Markets in the Changing World, Tokyo, March 23-4, 1993; published in Hitotsubashi Journal of Commerce & Management 28, 1, December 1993.

REFERENCES

Stigler, George J., "Public Regulation of the Securities Markets," *Journal of Business*, Vol. 37, April 1964, pp. 117–142.

———,"The Theory of Economic Regulation," *Bell Journal of Economics and Management Science*, Vol. 2, Spring 1971, pp. 2–19.

6

Financial Regulation: The Inside Game

I have decided to try a new approach to the deadly dull subject of derivatives and regulation—a sort of Miller Lite version, as it were.

I've called this version Financial Regulation: The Inside Game, and I've patterned it on TV sports shows like *Inside Baseball* or *Inside Basketball,* whose point is the vast difference between the simple game as it appears to ordinary fans at the park or in front of their television screens and the complicated and often quite subtle game as it appears to the athletes and coaches, the insiders. The same difference exists in the game of financial regulation: one game as seen by financial journalists and their readers, and the other (and much more intricate game) as seen by the professionals, the insiders. So different are these games in fact, that the outsiders in the press and the general public often don't even know who's playing, let alone who's winning.

The outsiders, in their naivete, worry about a derivatives-induced financial meltdown and hope the threat can be headed off by new government regulations. But the insiders know better. They know that derivatives have actually made the world *safer,* not riskier, and that no serious likelihood of a derivatives-induced financial meltdown actually exists. Note, however, how I have carefully phrased that: no derivatives-induced financial collapse. Firms will continue to lose money on bad judgment and bad derivatives deals, just as they always have in straight deals on the underlyings. And a major crack in one of the world's many bond and stock markets is always possible, of course. But when that crunch comes, it will trace not to derivatives or other transactions between consenting, *private-sector* parties, but to the actions of one or more of the central banks of the world—slamming on the monetary brakes and producing a credit crunch, usually overreacting to their own past excesses in the other direction.

The insiders know also that none of the proposals calling for more government regulation of derivatives would, in fact, make the world a safer place, or even that that's what the constant cries for more regulation of derivatives are really all about. To understand why, however, you first have to know the inside game. Explaining that real inside game, and especially the poorly understood role the regulators play in it, is what I propose to do here, much in the same spirit as I might try, say, to explain American football to a British audience.

Let me begin by introducing the players, their teams, and the league in which they play, focusing mainly on the U.S. Financial Derivatives League, since we originated the game—but we have no monopoly. The big European banks, having seen how much fun we're having with the game— that is, how much money we're making—have overcome their squeamishness and have been entering in a big way, typically by the free-agent route of buying teams like O'Connor & Associates.

At the moment, our U.S. Financial Derivatives League has three full-fledged teams. Each team has three sets of players. One set comprises the stars out front, the running backs carrying the ball and scoring the touchdowns as we would say. The other two sets of players comprise the defensive side of the ball, acting mainly as linebackers.

The three teams currently active in the U.S. Financial Derivatives League—and I'll refer to them by the names of their star running backs— are the Exchange Team, the Bank Team, and the Securities Broker/Dealer Team. The largely Chicago-based Exchange Team is to derivatives what the Chicago Bears were to modern T-formation football. The Exchange Team popularized the modern game of financial derivatives in the early 1970s when it introduced exchange-traded currency futures, followed soon thereafter by exchange-traded puts and calls, interest rate futures, and cash-settled stock index futures and options. The Exchange Team dominated for a considerable time, much as the Ivy League teams once dominated college football. But just as the Ivy League teams were overtaken by the semipro state schools, and later by the acknowledged professionals in the NFL, the Bank Team has now become dominant, with the Securities Broker/Dealer Team a distant, but gamely struggling second.

After the ballcarriers come the two remaining sets of players on each team, known as the Primary Regulator and the Congressional Overseer, funny sounding names and not terribly descriptive of their real roles, perhaps, but no more so really than the tight end in football, or the shortstop in baseball, or the silly mid-on in cricket. The outsiders, of course, don't think of the Primary Regulator and the Congressional Overseer as players but as referees, handing out red cards to the players for flagrant fouls and sending them to appropriate penalty boxes. And, indeed, that is precisely what the insiders want the spectators to believe. A poll taken some years ago showed the public thought the SEC was part of the Department of Justice, like the FBI, and that the SEC's main job was to catch insider traders. But enforcement is actually only a small part of what the Primary Regulator and the Congressional Overseers do. Their main concern, apart from their own personal power and perks, of course, is to help their team win.

On the subject of government regulation, let me digress a bit to note that the anti-regulatory tradition of the University of Chicago actually has two quite distinct streams. One stream, best personified by Milton Friedman, emphasizes errors in reasoning by the public and Congress. Some people sincerely believe that the country would be better off, say, by imposing tariffs on Japanese autos, and it is the task of the economist to expose the fallacies in that line of thought. The other Chicago stream, typified by my late colleague George Stigler, and tracing back ultimately to Adam Smith himself, is much more cynical. The regulations we see, Stigler insisted, are not there by error or by accident. They're there by design. Whatever the rhetorical arguments invoked in their favor, their real purpose is normally to benefit their sponsors at the expense of their competition.

If that oft-called capture theory of regulation strikes you as too cynical, you should spend some time in Japan, where the techniques of regulatory support for the home team have been raised to an art form. (For a wider and deeper introduction to the modern theory of economic regulation, see chapter 5 in this volume.) My all-time favorite Japanese trick for building a sense of solidarity among teammates is a play they call *amakudari*, which translates literally as "the descent from heaven." Every hardworking Japanese bureaucrat in the ministry of finance who can maintain a reputation as a team player can look forward on his retirement to a well-paying sinecure on the board or on the top management of some Japanese bank or insurance company or brokerage firm. It's not really all that different here, of course. Rick Ketchum, for example, the former head of the SEC's key Division of Market Regulation, is now executive vice president of NASDAQ. Perhaps we have more of a two-way flow than the Japanese do. Arthur Levitt, for example, former chairman of the American Stock Exchange, is now chairman of the SEC. But the real difference is that our regulators, unlike those in Japan, at least have to pretend that everything they do is really only for the benefit of the fans.

For the Exchange Team, or at least the futures part of it, the Primary Regulatory is the Commodities Futures Trading Commission, or CFTC, and the Congressional Overseers (even though the game is *financial* derivatives) are the Agriculture Committees in the U.S. House of Representatives and the U.S. Senate. Why such unlikely players have assumed their roles as overseers of financial futures is an accident of history, but one that, nevertheless, has seriously weakened the playing strength of their team, because they're not really committed to winning. Their heart isn't in the game. To the Agriculture Congressional Overseers, the financial derivatives game is just a sideshow to their main interests. To the CFTC, the Primary Regulator, the main concern seems to be to look busy and hope that the Futures Exchange Team doesn't lose so much ground to other teams that their own jobs are jeopardized. (In that connection, incidentally, I sometimes wonder whether the CME and the CBOT find their relations with the CFTC so adversarial because their industry is too small to offer much in the way of post-regulatory employment. Lacking the prospects of *amakudari*, the CFTC bureaucrats have come to think they're in business for themselves.)

For the Securities Broker/Dealer Team, the Primary Regulator is the Securities and Exchange Commission, the celebrated SEC, once hailed by the crowd as a veritable Maradona of regulation, but now, like the once great Argentine soccer player himself, aging visibly, putting on weight and no longer a threat to break any match open. The team's Congressional Overseers are powerful, but at least in the Senate, not flashy, unlike their counterparts in the House.

For the third or Bank Team, the regulatory and oversight part of the team is still more complicated, as would be expected given the size and age of the banking industry proper, with every bank in the derivatives business subject to at least one of three separate regulators (The Federal Reserve System, the Comptroller of the Currency, and the Federal Deposit Insurance Corporation), and most subject to more than one. At the congressional oversight level, the Senate Banking Committee is far and away the dominant influence. The House Banking Committee, chaired until recently by Congressman Gonzalez of Texas, is strictly "bush league."

Such are the teams and their main players. But what is the object of the game? The same as in any other game, of course—winning, which in this game means capturing market share from the other teams in the league and, above all, keeping them from taking market share from you. Hence, the Primary Regulators and Congressional Overseers—the linebackers, as I have called them.

Linebackers, of course, are never entirely happy with their secondary, defensive status and will, from time to time, try to pick up a fumble and score for their team. The classic case, of course, was the attempt by the SEC, egged on by its teammates, the NYSE and the retail brokers, to wrest control over stock index futures from the Exchange Team and its regulator, the CFTC, by blaming exchange-traded futures for the 1987 crash. The New York Team and their regulatory linebackers were claiming that the Chicago futures were raising market volatility, which was false. The real complaint, of course, was that they were losing commission income to Chicago, which was true.

Despite the SEC's writhing on the ground, clutching its knee, and crying foul in standard soccer fashion, its histrionics didn't succeed. The SEC failed to gain jurisdiction over stock index futures. The agriculture barons in Congress may have no stomach to fight to acquire more turf for their exchanges, but they don't like to give up turf they already have and certainly not turf populated by deep-pocketed political action committees. The agriculture barons, however, to keep from being double-teamed by the other two strong Congressional linebackers, had to strike a deal forcing the CFTC to abandon its claims to regulatory jurisdiction over the swaps products of the other two teams. (What happened is that, long ago, before swaps were invented, Congress gave the CFTC exclusive regulatory jurisdiction over futures and anything resembling futures. Swaps, of course, are equivalent to futures in everything but name, and a really aggressive, team-playing CFTC could have hammered the swap dealers with litigation if it had really wanted to fight. But with its reauthorization in jeopardy, and with no permanent chairman until very recently, the CFTC wasn't looking to pick fights. The newly appointed chairman, however, has been doing some trash-talking on the subject of swaps recently, but we'll have to wait and see whether it is anything more than talk.)

Meanwhile, the swap dealers on the Broker/Dealer Team, with the threat of the CFTC removed, have been looking to gain ground in the other direction against their competitors on the Bank Team. The Bank Team, as noted earlier, has become far and away the dominant force in the swaps game, particularly the so-called plain vanilla interest-rate and currency swaps; not because the Bankers are necessarily more talented than the other teams, but because the league officials won't let them lose. For making swap deals, the key is always counterparty credit risk and, as a customer dealing with a bank, you can take comfort in knowing that our government will not allow the bank to stiff you, at least if the bank is big enough.

Unable to match the Bank Team's high-quality counterparty status directly, the Broker/Dealer Team has sought to boost its own credit ratings up to and even beyond the Bank Team levels by splitting their derivatives business off into separate subsidiaries with dedicated capital of their own. This triple-A subsidiary move by the Securities Broker/Dealers was clever but, like blitzing on the third down, strategically dangerous. It might easily have backfired against the Broker/Dealer Team by provoking hostile retaliation from the regulatory players on the other teams, especially the Bank Team, which had just stopped some of its own smaller and weaker players from introducing separately capitalized triple-A subs of their own.

Indeed, the retaliation is exactly what many of us thought was happening when we read the prepublication copies of the General Accounting Office (GAO) report in May 1994 and saw that it called for substantial new regulatory restrictions on the derivative subs of the Broker/Dealers, but gave a clean bill of health to the Bank and Exchange Teams. (Note the delicious irony here that seems to have escaped our GAO. The credit ratings of the so-called unregulated triple-A subs are actually higher than those of their regulated bank competitors.) Our feeling that the other teams might be ganging up on the Broker/Dealers seemed confirmed when Congressman Edward Markey announced his committee's hearings on the GAO report and convened what he must have considered a hanging jury of long-time critics of derivatives like Gerald Corrigan, the former chairman of the New York Fed who had started the whole flap over derivatives with some ominous words of warning about financial meltdowns some two or three years ago, and Richard Breeden, the former chairman of the SEC and, at that post, a ferocious foe of stock-index futures. But this time, Markey's calls for more regulation received absolutely no support from what he assumed were his natural allies.

A cynic might suspect their change of heart came from changing roles, for Corrigan and Breeden have since become players, Corrigan for Goldman and Breeden for Coopers & Lybrand. But more humiliation was still to come for Congressman Markey. Arthur Levitt, the current chairman of the SEC, declined Markey's offer to expand the SEC's regulatory role over the triple A subs—an act of renunciation about as rare as a basketball player's turning down the coach's offer to increase his playing minutes. And Alan Greenspan, representing the Bank Team—a team that might normally have been expected to support the further hobbling of its Broker/Dealer rivals—backed away from the GAO report completely. Greenspan, concerned that Congressional meddling with regulation might drive business abroad—the only antiregulation argument they ever take seriously in Washington these days, incidentally—declared that the existing regulatory structure was more than adequate, thank you. Poor Congressman Markey was left like the man in the old song: he brought his harp to the party, but nobody asked him to play.

What Markey failed to realize was that the derivatives industry, for all its fierce rivalries, had reached a state of competitive balance that no one really wanted to risk upsetting. The Broker/Dealer Team members are still far behind the Banks on simple swaps but are more than holding their own on the more exotic options and structured deals—deals in the spirit of some recent TV commercials: off the Nikkei, behind the Deutschemark, nothing but net!

Even the much-put-upon exchanges are participating indirectly in the success of the others. The CME's Eurodollar contract, for example, has become the vehicle of choice for banks and other swap dealers seeking to balance their exposure books without having to put up more regulatory capital.

Mutually satisfactory accommodations of this kind within an existing league can be expected to last, however, only as long as attendance is booming. A rising tide does lift all boats, as President Kennedy many times noted. But what happens when business falls off? Then you *will* begin to hear serious calls for a new regulatory deal, calls initiated, as George Stigler has suggested, by the teams themselves, not by bystanders or outsiders like the GAO.

That, alas, may be where we are now. The torrent of bad publicity has made corporate CEOs and CFOs gun shy. The prevailing mood at the moment is well conveyed by the cartoon showing a panhandler and his tin cup, on which is written "No derivatives please." Corporate officers are afraid to use derivatives even for hedging, unlike the Procter & Gamble case, where a know-it-all corporate CFO took a leveraged bet on interest rates and then doubled up to recoup his losses.

This is taking its toll on the derivatives dealers, many of whom, particularly the Wall Street broker/dealers, are in downsizing or layoff mode at the moment. They're beginning to look for some kind of dramatic action to restore confidence in the market, like in the early 1930s after the Great Stock Market Crash of 1929. So low had public confidence in the industry fallen by 1933, and trading volume along with it, that the leading teams actually welcomed the SEC and the tough-cop image it brought to the table. For nervous investors, it was like a Good Housekeeping Seal of Approval and, by and large, the strategy seems to have worked. Even today, the NYSE proudly bills itself in some of its ads as "The World's Most Regulated Stock Exchange."

What might some of these new, confidence-building measures be?

First, of course, the Broker/Dealers will try to repeat what seems to have worked in the past. And that means "disclosure." As for who will be asked to disclose what, one group will surely be the mutual funds, and especially the money market funds already under the SEC's jurisdiction. Some of these supposedly no-risk funds have tried to steal a march on their competitors by using exotic securities of one kind or another like inverse floaters (which, strictly speaking, aren't really "derivatives"), and they will be reined in, either by the disclosure route or perhaps even by outright prohibitions. And the money funds won't be getting much sympathy from the rest of the league because they've clearly let the side down.

I don't see detailed disclosures on derivatives usage being applied to other end users, such as regular business corporations, even though that was a major part of the GAO's recommendations and even though it's much in the news at the moment. (Author's note: I was clearly wrong in this prediction. Both the SEC and the Financial Accounting Standards Board have since promulgated elaborate derivatives disclosure rules despite the objections of dealers and many end users.) That would be costly and cumbersome—just one more source of lawsuits—for the corporate users, who are in a separate league of their own with even more powerful linebackers, as the Securities League has found out to its sorrow on many occasions in the past. It's still true that the national pastime is business, not finance. So powerful, in fact, is the Corporate Business League that we are more likely to see them imposing stricter suitability requirements on the Bank and the Broker/Dealer Teams that are peddling derivatives to corporate clients.

Will these admittedly almost trivial and largely cosmetic regulatory changes now under discussion be enough to overcome the recent scandals and bring the fans back to the stadiums? Baseball, after all, was able to do it after the Black Sox Scandal of 1920. Let us hope history can repeat itself once against because the stakes are so much higher this time. We have shown, as a country, that we can carry on without baseball, at least for a few months. But I'm not sure that American banks and businesses could last even that long without using the fundamental risk management tool of derivatives, given the harsh international competition they face today.

7

Regulating Derivatives: Enough Already!

Financial derivatives, for those who may have been too preoccupied with their own concerns to notice, come these days in basically three different flavors, like the quarks in nuclear physics.

Historically, the first derivatives to burst on the scene in their modern form were exchange-traded futures and options in the early 1970s, in Chicago, naturally (though their ancestry traces back to Holland in the seventeenth century and, surprisingly, to Japan at about the same time). Next in time came so-called swaps. Swaps are contracts in which, as the name suggests, two counterparties exchange payment streams, typically a floating interest-rate stream for a fixed-interest rate stream or a stream in dollars for a stream in marks or yen. Finally, and most recently, has come an explosive revival in so-called "structured notes" that might, to take one wild example, let a Brazilian firm, say, borrow at 5% in U.S. dollars plus the amount by which the returns on the Brazilian stock market exceed that on the Mexican market. These customized structured deals, admittedly, may sometimes strike outsiders as a bit bizarre, but the fact remains that the use of derivatives of all three flavors has grown rapidly over the last twenty years. And why is that?

Their use has grown, I insist, because they have satisfied an important business need. They have allowed firms and banks, at long last, to manage effectively and at low cost, business and financial risks that have plagued them for decades, if not for centuries.

But despite what I and most other economists, at least of the Chicago variety, see as the social benefits of these financial derivatives, they have, let us face it, also been getting a very bad press recently. Everyone by now surely has read about Procter and Gamble, that sweet little old Ivory soap company that dropped $150 million or so on derivatives, and about the big German conglomerate, Metallgesellschaft, that supposedly dropped ten times that amount on oil futures. Derivatives horror stories have created the impression that derivatives have brought us close to a financial Chernobyl that threatens to bring the whole economy down around our ears unless derivatives are brought under strict government control and supervision.[1]

THE REAL THREAT: DERIVATIVES OR CENTRAL BANKS?

So, before going any further, let me emphasize that no serious danger of a derivatives-induced financial collapse really exists. Note, however, how I have carefully phrased that: no *derivatives-induced* financial collapse. Firms will continue to lose money on bad judgment and bad derivatives deals, just as they always have in deals on ordinary assets like stocks and real estate. And a major crack in one of the world's financial markets is always possible. But crashes in financial markets are not exogenous calamities like earthquakes. They are *policy* disasters, tracing not to transactions between *private-sector* parties, but to the deliberately deflationary actions of a central bank somewhere, usually overreacting to its previous policy errors in the other direction.

A classic example, of course, has been the turmoil in the U.S. bond market since the spring of 1994 after our Federal Reserve System suddenly nudged up short-term interest rates. And why did the Fed feel it had to nudge them up? Because the Fed had previously driven short rates far too low, hoping that lower short rates would lead to lower long rates which in turn, the Fed hoped, would pull the U.S. economy more rapidly out of recession. That announced policy of driving interest rates down gave the banks, the hedge funds, and the big institutional investors generally what seemed a surefire, money-coining strategy: borrow short and lend long. The low short rates kept their cost of borrowing small and the Fed's fears of throttling the then still-weak economic expansion would keep them low. Prices of long-term bonds, then, could go only one way: up. For more than a year, those leveraged bets on falling long-term interest rates paid off handsomely.

But the Fed eventually discovered, or should I say rediscovered, that the short-term rate could be held below its warranted level only by rapidly expanding the money supply and risking a resurgence of price inflation. The Fed thereupon suddenly stepped on the monetary brakes by raising short-term interest rates, hoping that its anti-inflation rhetoric would keep the more inflation-sensitive long-term rates from rising. But the Fed guessed wrong. Long-term rates rose right along with short-term rates and blood began to flow on Wall Street (and in Orange County). So far, the fallout on the U.S. real economy from the Fed's monetary tightening has been small. But more tightening may be on the way and we must not become complacent. We need only look to the mismanagement by the Federal Reserve System in the early 1930s to see how much permanent damage a central bank can inflict on an economy.

THE CURRENT STATE OF DERIVATIVES REGULATION

For what further comfort it may offer to those worried about the dangers from unregulated derivatives, let me also assure them that derivatives already are very extensively regulated. The futures exchanges, for example, are regulated (and very heavy-handedly) by the Commodities Futures Trading Commission, or CFTC, one of the largest producers of bureaucratic red tape this side of Japan. The securities broker/dealer firms like Goldman Sachs or Salomon Brothers are regulated by the Securities and Exchange Commission, or SEC, an agency with a world-recognized reputation as a tough cop.

On that score, however, some critics, including our U.S. General Accounting Office, have complained recently that while the SEC may regulate the dealer firms and their capital requirements, the agency has no special or specific requirements for their derivatives operations. But if you know how the derivatives business is structured in Wall Street these days, that line of argument by our GAO makes no real sense. The name of the game in the derivatives business is *credit quality*. Nobody will deal swaps with you if you can't convince them that you have adequate capital, or unless you post substantial collateral if you don't. For further reassurance to the particularly credit-sensitive sector of the market, moreover, some of the big brokerage firms have even split parts of their derivatives business off into separate subsidiaries, with dedicated capital of their own. These "subs" have received triple-A credit ratings from the private credit-rating agencies like Moody's and Standard & Poors, agencies who do a more stringent capital and credit analysis, incidentally, than the SEC ever has or ever could. And far from suggesting any looming capital inadequacy, the ratings of the subs, in fact, are actually higher than that of the banks that do most of the derivatives business.

Those banks, moreover, which currently account for about 70% of the derivatives business, are themselves heavily regulated, to say the least. The derivatives activities of every bank dealer are regulated by at least one, and sometimes by as many as three separate regulators. The bank officers often find themselves saying good-bye to one group of examiners going out the back door just as another group is being ushered in at the front door.

THE S&L CRISIS AND THE SUPPOSED DANGERS OF INADEQUATE REGULATION

But if derivatives, as I insist, are already adequately (or more than adequately) regulated, how do I answer people who say we've heard that same talk about overregulation back in the early 1980s when the savings and loan industry was insisting that *its* regulation was adequate. And look what happened.

But are the two cases really parallel? Very definitely not. The so-called deregulation of S&Ls in the early 1980s was less a matter of allowing free market magic to do its work than an attempt by Congress to prolong the life of an industry that a truly free market would have ended years before. The industry was not allowed to die a natural death because residential housing and everything connected with it had become a sacred cow of U.S. politics. Congress in the 1930s and even more so in the years after World War II was encouraging U.S. citizens to buy homes and finance them with thirty-year fixed-rate mortgages from local savings and loan associations funded by insured deposits. By the mid 1960s however, as inflation and hence interest rates began to rise in the United States, the S&Ls found themselves having to pay 6% or more to keep from losing their deposits, while the thirty-year fixed-rate mortgages on their books had been made years before at 4 to 5%. By the late 1970s, in fact, as inflation accelerated, most of the industry had become technically insolvent on a mark-to-market basis.

At that point, rather than face up to closing down the politically potent local S&L industry and bailing out their federally insured depositors with tax money, Congress gave the S&Ls one last chance to stay alive, by allowing them to invest in more than just the mortgages on single-family homes, their traditional market niche. They could now invest in commercial real estate, luxury condos, and resort properties, a form of diversification which, by itself, might not have been so troublesome. But the S&Ls were allowed to support commercial property developments of that kind, without having to face the normal market tests for funding such risky ventures. Congress, in the dark of night (that is to say without holding hearings or any public debate), had raised the limit on government guaranteed deposit accounts of S&Ls from $10,000 to $100,000 per *account*. Not per individual or per family, but per account. In today's prices that would be equivalent to close to $200,000 per account, a non-trivial sum. S&Ls could thus raise virtually unlimited funds for speculative property development merely by offering to pay fifty or seventy-five basis points above the going deposit rate. Deposit brokers would then funnel them money from all over the country. The depositors didn't ask any questions about how the S&Ls hoped to earn those extra fifty or seventy-five basis points. Why should they care? The U.S. government was guaranteeing their deposits.

To cite the S&L bailouts as grounds for regulating derivatives is thus not only to miss the point of that government-spawned disaster, but is doubly ironic. Financial derivatives, if they had only been more readily available in the early 1980s, could have kept the S&L industry viable as a residential housing lender without massive life support from subsidized deposits. If maturity mismatch between floating-rate deposits and fixed-rate mortgages is your problem, then interest-rate swaps and futures and options can be your solution. Indeed, that is precisely the direction in which what's left of the S&L industry is going at the moment. The industry has also been helped, of course, by the development of variable-rate mortgages and even more by its ability to securitize its locally raised mortgages by bundling them into mortgage pools. Those pools in turn, serve as inputs to still another class of derivatives securities, the so-called CMOs or collateralized mortgage obligations. CMOs support many new strategies for controlling interest-rate risks, though, alas, also some new ways for the unskilled or the unlucky to lose big chunks of money.

DERIVATIVES AND THE SAFETY OF THE BANKING SYSTEM

Not only are the S&Ls much safer institutions today, thanks to derivatives, than they were in the past, but so too are the commercial banks. Despite all the hullabaloo in the press, and all the bad publicity surrounding derivatives, banks are safer today, not riskier. And for several reasons.

For one thing, the customers in a bank's derivatives book are now much better credit risks, on the whole, than those in their regular loan portfolio. Top-rated, blue-chip clients had been leaving the banks steadily for many years in favor of public-market funding, especially commercial paper. Swaps and options have brought them back. And even for some of the banks' so-so, intermediate credits, swaps strengthen a bank's hand on long-term fixed-rate credits. They let a bank pull the plug on a firm when its condition is just beginning to deteriorate, without having to wait for an actual default.

The swaps and options book, moreover, is typically highly diversified whereas banks' commercial portfolios are often heavily concentrated by region, or by industry (like Continental Bank and its oil credits) or by foreign country (like Citibank and its Latin American credits). And, of course, as noted earlier for the S&Ls, a bank's swaps and derivatives book can be managed to control interest-rate risk. If more of a bank's customers want to take the floating-rate side than want the fixed-rate side of interest-rate swaps, the bank simply lays off the excess directly with other dealers who happen to have the reverse position. Or, I am happy to say, the bank can make an offsetting transaction using exchange-traded financial futures, like the Eurodollar futures of the Chicago Mercantile Exchange, or CME.

But if swaps and derivatives have really made the financial system safer, not riskier, as I have claimed, why are we hearing so many calls these days for more regulation? Part of the answer, I suspect, comes from misunderstanding by the public and the financial press about how serious the risks really are. (For more on this, see chapter 4 in this volume.) A telltale sign of how deep those misunderstandings go is the almost universal practice of citing the nominal size of swaps outstanding and treating that number as if it were the amount at risk. Last year the conventional number was $8 trillion, this year it's $12 trillion. But whether eight or twelve, it's a huge amount. If it really did measure the risk exposure, it would be hard to blame people for being worried.

Those multitrillion dollar numbers, however, are just bookkeeping entries, or better, score-keeping entries, not transaction amounts. And similarly for interest-rate swaps. What gets swapped is *not* the trillions of principal amount, but only the *interest* on the principal, which is an order of magnitude smaller. And even that is an overstatement, because only the *difference* between the fixed and the floating rates is exchanged, which cuts it in half again. So we're talking not about $12 trillion at risk, but something like 1 to 2% of that amount, which is certainly not trivial, but it's not terribly frightening either, given the elaborate risk-control programs installed by all the major banks and dealers.

PROSPECTS FOR CONGRESSIONAL ACTION ON DERIVATIVES

While congressmen in the United States have deep and enduring ties to the industries they oversee, they also have other constituencies as well, and it is perhaps these constituencies that are fueling the calls for regulation. Congressmen know they will be blamed by those constituents if a disaster occurs on their watch. And often even if it's not really a disaster.

The reaction of Congress to news sometimes reminds me of my undergraduate college where the rules for governing our behavior were: There *are* no rules governing off-campus behavior, as long as you don't get the university's name in the papers. But if newspaper stories did appear, the university would have to do something. Our Congress too has been wondering whether to do something in response to what seem like horror stories about derivatives in the newspapers recently. Barring a catastrophe, however, and it's hard to imagine one, I don't see them doing anything of great consequence. We may well see more calls for disclosure, which has long been a magic word in Washington. It's not clear, of course, as a matter of purely scientific evidence, whether the SEC's disclosure rules really ever *have* saved anybody from a bad investment or even that an SEC prospectus is readable by anyone other than a plaintiff's lawyer looking to levy some extortion on a luckless corporation willing to settle rather than fight. But it's hard for anyone, except perhaps a cynical academic, to argue against the proposed therapeutic value of disclosure.

As for who will be asked to disclose the details of their derivatives holdings, one group will surely be the mutual funds and especially the money market funds. Some of those supposedly no-risk funds were trying to steal a march on their competitors by using exotic options of one kind or another to raise their advertised yields. The stakes in playing the yield-enhancement game can be enormous, not in terms of the investment returns themselves, but thanks to the presence of firms that specialize in ranking fund performance. An edge of even a few basis points can sometimes move a money market fund well up in the rankings, leading to a big surge to the fund in deposits (and fees to the managers). But when interest rates rose in early 1994, some of the more aggressive no-risk funds that had been enhancing their reported yields with derivatives took big hits and had to be bailed out by their parent brokerage firms; in one case, the fund had to be liquidated.

Although money market funds will almost surely be reined in by the disclosure route (or possibly by outright prohibitions on derivatives), I don't see detailed disclosures on the use of derivatives being applied either to the corporate customer end users of derivatives or to the dealers who peddle them. Nobody has yet figured out what it makes sense to disclose. A derivative is not like a piece of real estate you put on your books and appraise from time to time. The dealer's book and risk-exposure changes from minute to minute. And estimates of "value at risk" often can be quite sensitive to the particular risk model being used. Model errors are *always* a problem, of course, but for these errors of mandated disclosure you could wind up as a defendant in a class-action lawsuit. Despite these concerns, both the SEC and the Financial Accounting Standards Board have recently issued elaborate disclosure mandates for both dealers and corporate users of derivatives. Many years of confusion and litigation lie ahead.

Even if Congress or the regulatory agencies are tempted to win publicity points by imposing disclosure requirements on dealers, the threat of foreign competition will quickly cool the ardor. The European banks may have been somewhat slow at getting into the derivatives game, but they are in it now in a big way. These latecomer European banks are much larger than the American banks that pioneered the derivatives business. They also have much better credit ratings, which is always the key in this field. Tough disclosure requirements for U.S. dealers make it harder and riskier for them to do business. I don't see any U.S. Congress cheerfully conceding this industry to Europe.

If Congress feels it must do *something* to allay the public's concerns over derivatives, it may try imposing so-called suitability requirements; that is, giving dealers the affirmative obligation of assuring that the risks in the derivatives peddled to their customers are both carefully explained and appropriate to the customers' circumstances. If not, and the derivatives later go bad, the dealer can be sued. This is a uniquely American approach to regulation, replacing the doctrine of caveat emptor with *caveat vendor*. Pushed to an extreme (for example by applying securities law rather than common law to swaps) that approach could effectively kill the U.S. swaps industry (or, at least move it to subsidiaries abroad). Remember that one party loses on *every* derivatives deal.

A CLOSER LOOK AT SOME RECENT DERIVATIVES HORROR STORIES

The public's concerns over derivatives may also be allayed, we can hope, by further academic research into the reality behind some of the recent conspicuous horror stories about derivatives disasters. Just as a child's fears that something is lurking under the bed can be made to vanish by shining a light down there, so perhaps will the public's fears diminish when the true facts of the seeming horror stories become known. (And that, of course, is precisely the subject of chapter 2 in this volume.)

Although the horror stories were painful indeed for all concerned, they may serve at least to bring a better sense of perspective to the current agitation over derivatives. The real problems at MG, and at Orange County and P&G as well, trace not to the derivatives as such, but ultimately to top management's failure to ask their technicians the right questions *before* the programs were set under way. Top managers do that routinely with most other big-money commitments, but derivatives are just too new and unfamiliar to set managements' standard control reflexes into motion. And understandably so.

The derivatives revolution, after all, is barely twenty years old; and some parts of it are much more recent than that. The top managers of most U.S. or German corporations and banks are too old to have studied derivatives during their college or MBA days. Derivatives hadn't been invented yet. The tools themselves, though far less complicated, when properly taught, than the "rocket science" image they have acquired, do require some diligent study and homework—something for which busy CEOs cannot always and perhaps should not be expected to find the time. So we will just have to live with travails like the MG case or the P&G case for another decade or so until a new generation of corporate leaders who have grown up with derivatives and computers finally takes over.

Many present-day executives wrestling with the problems and the opportunities posed by the derivatives revolution may envy their younger, soon-to-be successors with all their glib talk of megabytes and modems and knock-out options. But the current group of business leaders shouldn't really be envious. Today's young Turks, they should remember, will eventually become old fogies themselves. The next generation of business leaders will have to face technical revolutions of their own—revolutions whose outlines today can still only dimly be perceived. That's the way it has always been in vibrant and progressive societies. And who really would want it any different?

Keynote address given at the Sixth Annual PACAP Finance Conference, Jakarta, Indonesia, July 6-8, 1994; published in the Pacific Basin Finance Journal, *Volume 3, No. 2 (1995). © 1995 Elsevier Science B.V. All rights reserved.*

REFERENCES

Culp, Christopher L., and Merton H. Miller. "Hedging a Flow of Commodity Deliveries with Futures: Lessons from Metallgesellschaft," *Derivatives Quarterly*, Vol. 1, No. 1 (Fall 1994).

———, "Metallgesellschaft and the Economics of Synthetic Storage," *Journal of Applied Corporate Finance*, Vol. 7, No. 4 (Winter 1995).

Miller, Merton H. "The Economics and Politics of Index Arbitrage in the U.S. and Japan," *Pacific Basin Finance Journal*, Vol. 1, No. 1 (March 1993).

———, "Functional Regulation," *Pacific Basin Finance Journal*, Vol. 2, No. 2 (May 1994).

———, "Inside Financial Derivatives," *Taxes*, Vol. 72, No. 12 (December 1994).

Part III

Derivatives Markets and Risk Management

8

Futures and Options Exchanges as Insurance Markets

The importance of the role of futures and options exchanges is not as well understood as it should be, perhaps because the explosive growth of the financial futures industry is not as widely appreciated as it should be. As recently as the mid 1980s, the futures industry was largely concentrated at the Chicago Board of Trade and the Chicago Mercantile Exchange. Now, financial futures exchanges can be found in virtually every major country in the world and even in some not so major countries.

Why do we see this great success of financial futures and the financial futures industry? The reasons are the same as the reasons for the successful growth of any other industry: the industry is offering a product that people want. To show that they want it, they are actually willing to pay for it.

What is the product that the world seems to want and that is so much in demand? The answer is: insurance. The world wants insurance against price risk.

Suppose you are a treasury bond dealer and suppose you have just bought at a Treasury Bond auction $500 million worth of U.S. Treasury securities. You plan to take that $500 million, break it up into smaller pieces and sell it to your customers in the normal course of your business; $25 million here, $50 million there, and so on.

You're basically in a wholesaling business and you can make a living at it when all goes well. But you could be wiped out by a relatively small drop in the value of those securities occasioned by rising interest rates. And remember, moreover, that you have probably borrowed against that inventory. That is, you hold it on the basis of short-term loans, so that when interest rates rise suddenly and unexpectedly, you can take a very sizeable hit in terms of your net equity position.

How can you insure against being wiped out by rising interest rates? Sell interest rate futures. If the interest rate goes up you lose on your inventory, as before, but you will have an offsetting gain on your futures contract. You are "hedged." Then, as you sell your inventory out in retail, you gradually lift the hedge by buying back the futures contracts.

The futures you sell and buy back are clearly doing their job of insuring against price risk. But many of you may be wondering—as some of my children wonder when they ask me, "Daddy, what did you do before there was television?"—what did people do in this business before there was a futures industry?

Well, of course, we listened to the radio, and we actually read books, although they find that hard to believe. There are always substitutes for everything. Even if there were no futures markets, the people who are in the government bond business would be able to get by. But, not as well or as efficiently. If there were no futures markets for hedging, there would be more dealers dealing in smaller amounts. Instead of one dealer buying in big $500 million lots, there would be ten dealers buying in smaller $50 million lots. Similarly, if dealers couldn't hedge their inventories, they wouldn't bid as high at the auctions. And, when they did sell the bonds to their retail customers, they would have to sell them at higher prices to compensate for the added risks they assumed while waiting to sell out.

That's why the U.S. Treasury Department has always been one of the strongest supporters of T-Bond futures. They know that giving dealers the chance to hedge their inventories lowers the cost of managing the public debt. In fact, there's a famous incident in which a Treasury bond auction was scheduled for a day on which the futures market was to be closed, which meant the dealers could not hedge their inventory. Under those conditions, the U.S. Treasury postponed its auction.

Ah, but, maybe you'll say, "The Treasury is so favorable to financial futures in the United States because the country has such huge deficits that it has to keep financing all the time." What about countries that don't have big deficits to worry about? Well, curiously enough, financial futures exist and thrive even in countries where there is a government surplus. Because, even though the government may not be running a deficit, many of the firms in the economy are. They have to float securities, and they have to have underwriters. The underwriters of those securities face exactly the same problem that underwriters of the government bonds do, and they use financial futures and T-bond futures in precisely the same way: to hedge their inventories against unexpected changes in interest rates.

Financial futures markets not only provide price risk insurance but they do so in a way that is cheaper, that is more liquid, and that is more reliable for the customers than the next best alternative. All three terms are important—cheaper, more liquid, and more reliable. And you must understand them if you want to understand why the growth of financial futures has been so rapid.

I could spend an hour talking about each one of these and how futures markets have structured themselves to deliver price insurance cheaply, with great liquidity, and greater reliability than the substitutes, but instead let me move away from the subject of insurance and on to something I know is of great concern to many of you, namely: Isn't all this talk of hedging and insurance a smokescreen to conceal what futures exchanges really are, namely, just glorified gambling casinos? Doesn't allowing futures trading expose a society to all the evils of speculation on a massive scale? Hasn't futures trading, in fact, destabilized the stock market?

Well let me dispose of the last charge first, and do it very briefly. Despite what you may have read in the U.S. financial press, stock index futures trading has not, in fact, increased the volatility of the U.S. stock market. Nor has the introduction of futures trading increased the volatility of any other market. We've had literally dozens of careful academic studies to that effect over the last fifty years. Yet, the myth and image persists: that the futures markets destabilize the economy and other markets. One reason may be that we economists simply haven't made a sufficient effort to get the facts before the public. That is part of the reason why I've written and spoken in this vein on so many occasions.

As for speculation and its relation to future markets, let me begin by asking what is "speculation"? Actually, there are many possible definitions. There are many senses in which one uses the term speculator and one of the most important is "the opposite of a hedger." A speculator is someone who isn't hedging.

I had the occasion recently to talk with the treasurer of a medium-size oil company in Chicago. He was moaning that, after the war in the Gulf ended, the price of oil dropped very sharply and the firm suffered substantial losses on its oil inventory.

I said, "Well, it serves you right for speculating and gambling."

But, the treasurer insisted: "Oh, no, we didn't speculate. We didn't use the futures market at all."

"That's exactly the point," I replied. "When you hold inventory, nonhedging is gambling. You gambled that the price of oil would not drop and you lost."

There's another narrower sense in which the term speculator is used. In the futures market, a speculator is technically any user who doesn't actually qualify as a hedger; that is, a speculator is anyone who doesn't hold the underlying commodity.

People are often surprised at how few speculators or nonhedgers there are in the market. No more than a quarter to a third of all people trading in the futures market would be classified as "speculators" in this technical sense. The rest are all hedgers.

You might wonder, "How can this be?" After all, for every short there has to be a long. For every hedger, there has to be someone on the other side of the transaction. The answer is that the person on the other side of one hedger's transaction is often another hedger.

Let me give you the example of another local Chicago firm, which is in the business of making photographic film. It sells this film to hospitals and others for X-ray purposes. Since it has undertaken long-term delivery commitments with fixed prices, it would get hurt quite substantially if silver prices should rise suddenly because silver is a major part of its raw material costs. The firm hedges that risk by *buying* silver futures.

Hedging against a price rise by buying futures is called a "long" hedge, in contrast to a "short" hedge that protects against price falls by selling futures. This offsetting or two-sided hedging is a particularly important feature of financial futures markets. Consider interest rates. For every borrower that's worried that interest rates may be going up, there's a lender that's worried that interest rates may be going down. And they make a natural market when they can find each other.

But though the markets involve both short hedgers and long hedgers, some markets may sometimes have a net predominance of short hedgers— people wanting to buy insurance against price *falls*. The speculators are, in effect, the people who sell them that insurance.

But, you may say, isn't calling speculators "insurance sellers" overdignifying them, perhaps like the street sweepers who insist that they be called "waste-management engineers"? You may say, we know these people; they're just gamblers and they're seeking a fast return.

But, in economics, what counts is results, not motives. *You* may think they're gambling. *They* may think they're gambling. But from a social point of view, they're selling insurance. Not only are they selling insurance, but, if they lose money at it, as many of them certainly do, then they're selling insurance at a loss. That's a great benefit to us insurance buyers. In other words, futures markets put the gambling instincts of the speculators to work for society. I don't know why some government people are so upset about that. They do the same thing with the national lottery after all; put people's gambling instincts to a social purpose.

But, of course, there's another way that gamblers and futures speculators can lose money that does not benefit society: they, and the hedgers as well, can be cheated and defrauded. This is particularly likely to happen, I'm sorry to say, in the countries that prohibit futures trading, because if there exists a demand for gambling that is strong enough, it will be supplied. People will set up what we call "bucket" shops and call them futures markets to fool the unsophisticated.

To set up these phony futures markets is easy enough; all you need is a storefront, a cash register and a trade-reporting screen. Some of them can go for a long time with no problems because the in-flows on one side roughly balance the out-flows, and because the profit margin of the owners is large enough to cover any ordinary discrepancies. But, the law of averages is such that, eventually, there will be an imbalance. Eventually, there are going to be too many people on the winning side of the contract and not enough losers on the other (or at least losers willing to pay up in full). The bucket shop is going to be unable to meet its obligations.

So, it collapses, and the presumed "winners" find that they haven't won at all. They can't collect. That's why perhaps the most reassuring message I can bring is that, if anyone decides to use the U.S. futures markets—either as a hedger or as a speculator—they can be absolutely sure that they will never become a victim of contract defaults.

The Chicago Mercantile Exchange and the Chicago Board of Trade, between them, have been in business for 150 years combined and *not once*, despite all the economic turmoil we've had over the years, *not once* has a single user suffered from a contract default. And let me assure you that it's not just a matter of luck. It's not just an accident waiting to happen. It hasn't happened because our markets are structured in such a way as to keep contract defaults from happening.

How can this be done? Send your technical experts over to Chicago and we'll show you how it can be done. It's our stock in trade.

But let me mention one small part of our customer protection strategy that is not as well known as perhaps it should be. When you buy stock on margin in the United States and most other countries, even from an honest broker, the broker is a creditor to you. But you are also a creditor to him to the extent of the equity in your account. That's part of his capital and, if he goes broke, you may lose your equity. But, in the case of futures, your account is not part of the broker's capital. It's segregated in a separate bank account and the broker's other creditors can't get at it.

That's just one of the many defenses that the futures markets have developed over the years to maintain financial integrity and reliability. Reliability, as I stressed earlier, is one of the three key elements that's been behind the huge financial growth of the futures markets.

An address to the joint Chicago Board of Trade-Chicago Mercantile Exchange Workshop on Futures Markets in Taipei, Taiwan, March 21, 1991.

9

Derivative Markets and Their Cash Market Counterparts

How do derivative products relate to the cash markets? My answer is that they relate like two doors into the same house. This is not what people in the retail stock brokerage business in the United States or Japan would tell me. Their response would quite probably be that the derivative markets relate to the stock market like a dog to a lamppost.

The retail brokerage industry based in New York (or in Tokyo) has never much liked the futures and options exchanges in Chicago (or in Osaka). The disdain shows up even in the words they use for futures or options exchanges: mere *derivative* markets. Not the *real* market, that is, the stock market, but derivative or parasite markets, living off the prices in the cash market like ivy on an oak tree, sucking out its vital juices and undermining its strength.

Actually, of course, when it comes to the pricing of Equity with a capital E, as opposed to the pricing of stocks of particular companies, you can make a case these days for saying that the stock market is really derivative of the index futures and options exchanges. The Chicago futures and options markets, and I include under that heading the warrant and options markets of the American Stock Exchange even though it happens to be in New York, have come to be the natural entrance doors for certain important kinds of news. I refer to news that affects the economy as a whole or the investment climate, in particular news about interest rate changes, exchange rate movements, shifts in tax policy, and the like. Those broad-reaching economywide events, of which there have been plenty in recent years, are likely to register first in the Chicago markets. The prices of the individual stocks in the cash market of the New York Stock Exchange then adapt to the new price level for Equity—the new price level "discovered," as they say in the trade, on the Chicago exchanges.

Why these so-called derivative markets have become the major arena for the pricing of Equity will be the leading theme of my remarks here. I will also address the advantages of derivative products for establishing and altering positions in Equity.

Derivative markets have won the role of pricing Equity away from the traditional stock exchanges. This has happened not only in the United States, but in the many other countries that have established index derivative markets in recent years. We hope to soon see the name of Mexico added to that long and growing list—not by luck and not by unfair tactics, but for the same reasons that *any* new product succeeds and wins a big market share: it provides a valuable service cheaper than its competition.

Some of the critics of equity derivatives claim, in fact, that they are *too* cheap. They make it too easy for ill-informed speculators to rush into the market, driving it up to absurd heights only to see it come crashing down later, ruining not only themselves, but threatening the whole economy with financial collapse. These charges, though often repeated, are completely unfounded. But before turning to confront them, let me first review the valuable services that equity derivatives can and do offer to investors.

The term equity derivative products means so many different things these days that I cannot hope to cover all or even a representative sample of them. Instead, I will focus on just one product, exchange-traded index futures, whose cost advantages relative to transactions in the cash market are, in some ways, easiest to explain.

To see why and how institutional investors use index futures, imagine you are the manager in the United States of an insurance company, or a large portfolio, a pension fund, perhaps, or a bank trust fund. You know that over longtime horizons, the returns on well-diversified portfolios of Equities tend to exceed those of alternative investments like corporate or government bonds. You know also, however, that your cash outflows for pensions or medical benefits or other guaranteed returns to the beneficiaries may sometimes exceed your cash inflows. Since stocks do well in the long run and in the average year but not necessarily in every year, when the shortfall is unexpectedly large you may have to liquidate a portion of your portfolio. If that forced liquidation comes at a time when the stock market is depressed, the damage to your clients' interests can be substantial. So you try to protect against this danger by holding government and corporate bonds in your portfolio as well as stock. The long-run return on those bonds will be less than on your stocks, but so will be their year-to-year variation in market value.

A portfolio that includes both stocks *and* bonds (a so-called balanced portfolio) has thus become the standard strategy for pension funds and trust funds. As to how much you should put into bonds, Modern Portfolio Theory, alas, can offer you no firm guidance. The fixed-income proportion is what portfolio managers get paid to choose, and it will depend on how they view the risk-return tradeoff, or, as the old saying has it, whether you and your clients prefer to eat well or sleep well.

A typical split might be, say, 60% stocks and 40% bonds. If you are like most portfolio managers, you would not fix those proportions once and for all time. For any number of good reasons, at some point you might feel that 60% was just too much Equity exposure. At that point you might feel that, say, 50% Equity and 50% Debt would be a safer mix for the fund and its beneficiaries. You reserve always, of course, the right to restore the old balance or even increase the Equity share in the future if conditions or market prospects change.

It's precisely at this point in the decision cycle, when you are reconsidering your Equity exposure, that you should think about index futures. Before I try to explain more specifically what you should be thinking about, let me say a word or two about terminology. In all the examples to follow, the particular derivative product I will use for illustration will be an exchange-traded futures contract. In every case, however, I could equally well have used exchange-traded options, or over-the-counter options or swaps negotiated with a bank. The results are the same, but futures contracts are somewhat easier to visualize.

THE USE OF DERIVATIVES
FOR ADJUSTING PORTFOLIO PROPORTIONS

Let's suppose, for concreteness, that you want to cut your Equity exposure by $20 million and transfer it to your fixed income portfolio. You can do so in two different ways. One way to cut your Equity exposure is to use the underlying cash markets: sell $20 million of the stocks in your equity portfolio, issue-by-issue, and collect the cash proceeds. Then take that cash to the bond markets or to the bond dealers and buy some appropriate short-term fixed-income instrument such as Treasury bills. That is certainly a way to reduce your Equity exposure that is familiar and easy to understand. But it can be slow, even in this day of the Superdot and program trading. And it can also be expensive.

There is another way of doing exactly the same thing. Suppose instead that you simply sell $20 million of S&P 500 index futures contracts (about 100 contracts at the present level of the S&P 500 index). That one transaction—which can be accomplished in a matter of minutes, or even seconds—is exactly equivalent to the two-step procedure of first selling the separate stocks and then buying bills.

How can one simple transaction do so much? It seems like magic (and black magic at that). But like most magical tricks, it has a straightforward explanation. When you sell the $20 million of futures contracts, you have eliminated any risk in $20 million of the stocks. Let me note that although I speak loosely of selling a futures contract, you don't actually *sell* anything. You simply take a *position* in a futures contract by agreeing to pay money to or to collect money from the exchange's clearinghouse, depending on how the index happens to move over the duration of your futures contract. If you take a short position in futures, which is the functional equivalent of short selling in the cash market, and if the index rises, you must pay the clearinghouse for the loss on your futures position. But that loss will be offset exactly by the gain you make on the underlying stocks which you continue to hold. And vice versa if the index falls; you will gain on your futures and lose on your stock. Because you are thus completely protected, or hedged, against price moves in either direction, your $20 million of stocks has effectively been converted into a riskless asset, like Treasury bills. And thanks to the way futures contracts must be priced relative to the underlying cash index to eliminate any arbitrage opportunities, your return on your newly risk-free $20 million will be the same as you would have earned on an equivalent, stand-alone, risk-free holding of Treasury bills.

So you really do get to the same destination by either strategy. But, and this is the key point, taking the index futures route can be cheaper by a factor of five in the United States and by a factor of ten or even more in Japan.

Why is it so much cheaper to change Equity exposure with futures? Brokerage commissions are part of the answer and a major part in a country like Japan whose Ministry of Finance deliberately supports its brokerage cartel by mandating very high fixed brokerage commissions on all stock transactions, including those of large, institutional investors. The bid/ask spreads are also typically much lower for index futures than those on the underlying stocks. And so too are the market impact costs for orders of large size, as would be expected when you are trading a standardized product, in heavy volume, in the presence of many competing market makers.

Taking the futures route can also help when, like so many pension plan sponsors these days, you have delegated the tasks of day-to-day portfolio management to a number of competing submanagers—one focusing, say, on growth stocks, another on cyclical stocks, another doing "bottom fishing," and so on. Should you seek to reduce your equity exposure by $20 million you won't have to allocate the cut among the managers or risk disrupting their strategic plans (or their performance-based bonuses). Just one transaction in index futures takes care of it.

For these and related reasons, then, you can cut costs by using equity index derivatives to reduce or increase your fund's exposure to Equity, with a capital E. That much is well known. What is only just beginning to be appreciated, however, is how great the advantages can be for both foreign and domestic investors in using index futures to *establish* an Equity position in a country's market.

The idea itself is actually an old one. It goes back, legend has it, to a South Sea island archipelago whose inhabitants settled their interisland balance-of-payments accounts not with gold but with huge, intricately-carved boulders which they hauled on rafts from one island to another.

One day, so the story goes, a sudden storm arose, sinking the raft that was carrying a boulder from a debtor to a creditor island. At first, all were in despair at having lost such a valued piece of national wealth. But the deficit island's high-priest, who also happened to be its central banker, paddled out into the lagoon with his surplus-island counterpart on board. He pointed down to the bottom of the lagoon, where the boulder could clearly be seen—the waters were much clearer in those ancient times—and he said: "That's *your* boulder, now."

And that's essentially what you can do these days with index derivative futures: leave the physical assets in place and just move their returns.

You do it by reversing the process I described earlier in which you reduced your Equity exposure by selling futures, that is by taking a short position in index futures contracts. You still retained physical possession of the underlying stocks, but your futures transaction had eliminated their risk, converting them effectively to Treasury bills. In fact, buying stock, and selling futures against them, is sometimes actually called, for that reason, creating *synthetic* Treasury bills.

In much the same way, you can also create synthetic *Equity*. A U.S. or other foreign portfolio manager, for example, seeking to give his clients the chance to participate in the growth of the Mexican economy, or simply seeking to give them the benefits of additional international diversification, could add Mexican Equity, with a capital E, to the portfolio by buying, say, two billion pesos worth of Mexican Treasury bills and taking a long position of the same nominal amount in Mexican index futures. That strategy will give results in terms of market price appreciation that are exactly the same as if two billion pesos of Mexican stocks had been purchased directly. But it will do so without the portfolio manager having to research dozens of separate companies; without having to incur the high commission costs, spread costs and market impact costs for lightly traded securities; without having to take physical custody of the stocks; and without all the tax and accounting paper work involved in actually collecting the dividends from a multitude of small companies. And it can be done with futures far cheaper than with closed-end funds or ADRs (American Depository Receipts), the two alternatives now available.

The advantages to foreign investors from taking the synthetic Equity route are thus quite substantial and they are obtained without any of the disadvantages, real or imagined, of foreign ownership or control of Mexican businesses. The boulders, as it were, stay at the bottom of the lagoon. Mexican investors can still continue to own the underlying stocks and to exercise all the voting and other relevant ownership rights. They transfer to foreigners just the market risks and returns of Mexican Equity, by taking the opposite or short side of the foreign long position in futures. That renders their portfolios of Mexican stocks riskless, as we saw, so they can sell the Treasury bills they own to the foreigners who need them to complete their synthetic Equity positions. Mexican investors can then use the proceeds to diversify cheaply into U.S. or other foreign synthetic Equity. Everyone winds up with more efficient portfolios.

STOCK MARKETS AND FUTURES MARKETS: THE PROBLEMS OF COEXISTENCE

Up to this point, my focus has been on how equity derivative instruments relate to an underlying cash equity index. I used index futures in my specific illustrations, but, as noted above, the stories could have been told equally well in terms of options, warrants, or any of a number of over-the-counter instruments including interbank swaps. Interbank swaps and futures, in fact, are basically the same thing, as the banking regulators are beginning to realize. Futures contracts just happen to be traded on exchanges, out in the open, where everyone can see the prices and the quantities of the deals being made.

But this very openness of the futures exchanges is also the source of their greatest competitive vulnerability. The threat by the politically powerful cash market sector and its regulators to close down the competing index futures exchanges, or, what amounts to the same thing, to impose regulations on those exchanges that will negate their cost advantages, is an ever-present one.

The history of the U.S. index futures industry, now being painfully replayed in Japan, may provide some lessons in this respect for Mexico. Index futures, when they first burst on the scene ten years ago were not taken terribly seriously by the retail stock brokerage industry. But as trading volume in futures steadily picked up, so did the resentment. And some of this resentment on the part of the brokerage industry was surely understandable. Nobody likes losing business to lower-cost competitors.

As long as total combined volume, stock and futures, was increasing, however, the resentment simply smoldered. But when the market crashed in October of 1987, and retail trading volume dropped off, a firestorm of attacks on the index futures broke out.

The role of the futures markets in that crash has been studied by academics, by the exchanges, by the regulators of both the futures market and the stock market, and by one special presidential commission, chaired by Nicholas F. Brady, who later became the U.S. Secretary of the Treasury. The Brady Commission was particularly critical of the part played in the crash by certain futures-related strategies such as so-called portfolio insurance, but subsequent academic research has not fully supported or endorsed that view. Portfolio insurance *was* surely part of the picture; but not all or even most of it. The panic selling by small investors, for example, was five times that traceable to portfolio insurance. Furthermore, stock markets fell all around the globe on that fateful day, with some of the biggest declines coming in countries with no index derivative markets whatever—including, alas, Mexico. And as for index arbitrage, or program trading as it is usually mistakenly called, and which became the new villain after portfolio insurance died in 1987, the weight of academic research has been virtually unanimous: despite the charges repeated almost daily in the financial press in both the United States and Japan, index arbitrage has not had, and indeed, cannot have any detectable effect on the overall volatility of the stock market. Volatility today is no higher than it was in 1960s or 1970s and is substantially lower than it was in the 1930s and 1940s.

Now, after years of bitter controversies, relations between the index futures markets and the cash market have finally settled down to an uneasy truce. Part of the traditional brokerage industry has made its peace with the futures industry by joining it, so to speak. Remember that stock index futures are still only ten years old and that when they were first introduced, many brokerage houses did not have the technical skills to win business away from the more specialized futures brokers. But those brokerage firms with a substantial institutional clientele have fully caught up and now offer a complete line of derivative products, both competitive to and complementary with exchange-traded futures.

At the same time, the more traditional wing of the retail stock brokerage community that still shuns futures trading has been appeased by the implementation of some of the recommendations of the Brady Commission. The futures exchanges, for example, in line with the Brady report, have installed "circuit breakers" which halt or delay further trading of futures on days with large market moves. Academic economists find it hard to believe that you can benefit people who want to trade by not letting them do so. The academics have tended to deride these circuit breakers as placebos. But they appear to have calmed the irrational fears of futures-induced crashes on the part of some small investors—and financial journalists. And that, after all, is what a good placebo is supposed to do.

The futures exchanges have also been driven to raise the margins or performance bonds for their retail index futures customers to levels that have virtually dried up retail participation in the market. That retail participation was always small relative to the institutional involvement, but it did at least add some liquidity to the market and make some useful contribution to the exchange's overhead. The current retail margin levels are not only far above those needed to protect the clearinghouse, given the present volatility of the index, but probably even above the levels needed to meet the Brady Commission's call for "harmonizing" stock and futures margins. The high retail margins were essentially the ransom the futures industry had to pay to the Bush Administration to prevent the transfer of regulatory jurisdiction over index futures (and possibly all futures as well) from a sympathetic futures regulator (the Commodities Futures Trading Commission) to a far from sympathetic stock market regulator (the Securities and Exchange Commission). This is what the Brady Commission had originally recommended and what Secretary Brady had proposed to Congress.

But, of course, the main reason for the recent dampening of criticism from the retail brokerage industry has surely been less the supposed reforms than the spectacular recovery of retail participation in the stock market. It is hard to complain that the futures markets are frightening away retail customers when retail share volume (and brokerage commissions) are running at near record levels (at least in the United States).

How long the current truce between the derivative products markets and the underlying stock market will last is hard to say. Much will depend on the political configuration when the next stock market crash comes, as it surely will. Stock market crashes, after all, of varying degrees of severity, have been occurring at more or less regular intervals for as far back as our records go.

About all we can be confident of at the moment is that equity derivative products are here to stay; if not on the exchanges, then in the over-the-counter market. And if not in the United States, then in London and Paris and eventually Mexico City. I look forward to welcoming Mexico to the club of countries with active derivative product exchanges, and I hope that it can avoid the unproductive quarrels between the old and the new ways of doing business that have so blighted relations between the derivative markets and the cash markets in the United States in recent years.

An address given at the Third Convention of the Mexican Securities Market, April 28–29, 1992, in Mexico City, Mexico.

10

Risk and Return on Futures Contracts: A Chicago View

I'm delighted to be here for your ninth birthday party of the Singapore International Monetary Exchange. At such occasions it's inevitable, of course, for some elderly relative to remark on how much you've grown and to brag over how much of your good looks or brains you seem to have inherited from his or her side of the family. That admiring relative role is the one I intend to play today, reminding you of your substantial inheritance from Chicago. I don't just mean from the Chicago Mercantile Exchange, or CME, on whose board I happen to serve currently as a public director. On that score, everyone here surely recognizes the mutual offset agreement with the CME as what began Simex's transformation from the modest little Gold Exchange of Singapore to the leading financial futures market in East Asia today.

But mutual offset is only the most direct and obvious Simex-Chicago connection. Simex has other important connections to Chicago and to me indirectly via the University of Chicago. Research and teaching by economists at the University of Chicago over the years, by identifying and explaining the important social contributions of futures markets, has helped create the favorable climate of opinion futures now enjoy throughout the world. The list of Chicago economists who have defended the futures exchanges against furious attacks from competitive vested interests and the regulators they have captured—like the Ministry of Finance in Japan—is far too long for me to review in detail. I will focus instead on just two members of the Chicago School, one very prominent and familiar to all of you; the other, a much less well-known figure, very influential in the

1920s and 1930s whose work has considerable relevance for current controversies over risk and returns in futures trading.

MILTON FRIEDMAN

Let me begin then with Milton Friedman, who is, and has long been, the leading figure in the Chicago School of free market economics. He is also, in my view, the leading economist of the twentieth century. But, of course, this has not been a particularly great century for economists, as was always quickly added by my colleague, the late George Stigler, himself a leading figure in the Chicago School, and who fully shared my views of Friedman's stature in the profession.

What is perhaps less well known about Milton Friedman is that he has long been an ardent and articulate champion of futures markets. In fact, the International Monetary Market of the Chicago Mercantile Exchange, from which Simex is descended, was inspired by Milton Friedman. Some of you, I'm sure, have heard the story—perhaps many times—but it's so good that it's worth a brief retelling, just in case someone may have missed it.

The story starts in the late 1960s when the Bretton Woods fixed-exchange rate regime, which the world had lived by for twenty-five years, was showing signs of increasing strain, similar in many respects to those of the European Monetary System in 1992. Milton Friedman believed that the British pound was substantially overvalued in the late 1960s and could not much longer maintain its fixed parity (which, if I remember correctly, was $4.00). Seeking to short the pound, he went to his local bank and asked them to sell pounds "forward" for him. When they stopped laughing, they told him that banks didn't do that sort of thing for *retail* customers. The forward market in currencies was for commercial transactions only. They probably also told him that even if they could do it, they wouldn't do it. Forward transactions were too risky for a college professors. Don't laugh. Forwards and futures in those days were also considered too risky for women; women were not allowed to open accounts with futures brokers.

Turned down by his bank, Milton Friedman fired off a letter to *The Wall Street Journal* on the idiocy of the rules that kept him from shorting the pound with his own money. Leo Melamed and others at the CME saw that letter and said to themselves: "If shorting a foreign currency is the problem, we have the solution. Just set up a futures market in currencies." Which they did.

But setting up a new futures market is not easy. Before you can even get started on the hard details of contract design, trading rules, or clearing and settlement procedures, you have to run everything by the regulators, whose natural response is to say no to any proposed financial innovation that competes with established interests, let alone one with the generally raffish image of the futures exchanges. And here again, in helping Leo Melamed and the CME to overcome, or at least bypass, the regulatory roadblocks in Washington, Milton Friedman once again played a major role.

For one thing, the CME commissioned him to write a position paper on the national benefits from a futures market in foreign currencies. That paper is still very much worth reading, even today, if only for making the important point, still not fully understood by some central bankers, that floating exchange rates need not be disruptive of trade flows as long as exporters and importers have adequate means of hedging their exchange transactions.

But there was another, somewhat more indirect channel of Milton Friedman's influence on our Washington power structure at the time. The International Monetary Market, it will be recalled, was being proposed in the early 1970s during the first Nixon Administration. Several of that administration's most influential people on matters of economics, notably Treasury Secretary George Shultz, were also members of the Chicago School as well as close personal friends of Milton Friedman. Can you imagine what might have happened if the Secretary of Treasury had been the Bush Administration's Nicholas Brady? The CME would still be waiting, or more likely, foreign exchange futures trading would have moved to London.

But if the International Monetary Market was Milton Friedman's great success as an inspirer of successful futures markets, he also had one great failure that I know rankles with him to this very day. Milton Friedman had complained in both his academic writings and his letters to newspaper editors, that there was no easy way in the United States to borrow and lend or to make contracts in real terms, as economists say; that is, contracts with correction for inflation. You could do that in some other countries, of course. The British government for one has some inflation-linked bonds, though like most things British it's unnecessarily complicated. It's the Jaguar of government bonds. And other countries have them, too, but not the United States. Don't ask me why. There *is* no good reason as Milton Friedman has argued again and again.

If the government won't do it, said Milton Friedman, why not the private sector, and in particular the futures industry? He and a number of other well-known economists thereupon wrote up the position papers that inspired the cost-of-living futures contract introduced by the Coffee, Sugar, and Cocoa Exchange in about 1983, if I remember correctly. Using that contract you could, in principle, lock in real rates of interest and hedge any cost-of-living clauses in your wage agreements. I say you could. But nobody actually did. The contract died of neglect after about a year.

The conventional postmortem was that the contract was developed too late; that it should have been brought out in the late 1970s just before inflation and interest rates in the United States really took off. By 1984 or so, inflation was no longer a serious problem in the United States and it's even less of a problem today. But if inflation does come back to the United States, we're ready at the CME with our Goldman Sachs Commodity Index contract. And for many other countries in the world today such as Russia and China, where the inflation monster has yet to be tamed, something like Milton Friedman's cost-of-living futures contract might still make sense, at least as a temporary expedient until they get their money supply under better control. (Author's note: Milton Friedman's hopes for inflation-protected U.S. Treasury securities were finally realized in January 1997. The overwhelming success of the U.S. Treasury's first inflation-protected ten-year note seems to have caught almost everyone in Washington and Wall Street by surprise. But not Milton Friedman.)

HARDY AND KEYNES

Clearly, Milton Friedman's contributions to futures have been very important. (I wish I had time to tell you about his simple and elegant defense of the social value of speculation, a defense so neat that it's been driving his critics crazy for forty years trying to find the flaw in it.) But there is another member of the Chicago School who also deserves mention, a scholar very influential in the 1920s, though much less well known today, whose views on risk and returns in futures trading are being rediscovered in this era of commodity trading advisers, commodities as an asset class, and pension funds getting into futures.

This too-long neglected member of the Chicago School is Charles O. Hardy, whose book *Risk and Risk Bearing*, published more than seventy years ago, was the first serious exposition of what today we would call the "risk management" industry. The book covers not just risk management with forwards and futures, but with insurance contracts and securities as well. He didn't discuss traded options, of course, or swaps (which didn't exist yet in their modern form), but I don't think he'd be surprised at how people have come to use them.

One of the issues that concerned Hardy and other academic economists during the 1920s was what kept futures markets viable. That is, since a futures contract is a zero-sum game—meaning that for every winner there must be an equal and opposite loser—what keeps the process going? Actually, the puzzle was even worse. Since commissions and other charges had to be paid, futures markets were actually *negative* sum games for the players. Yet the exchanges somehow managed to grow and prosper. How could that be?

One answer was offered by the great British economist J. M. Keynes. In fact, some economists, particularly what we call salt-water economists located near the oceans in Boston and Stanford, as opposed to the fresh-water economists located in Chicago on Lake Michigan, would put him ahead of Milton Friedman as the number one economist of the twentieth century. They're wrong about that, of course, as they are about so many things, but it's at least arguable.

Like Milton Friedman, Keynes too was an ardent fan of futures markets, much more so than stock markets. Keynes had made a huge pile of money in the 1920s both for his own account and for King's College, Cambridge, where he served as treasurer. Since he wrote so knowingly about commodity futures, we students of economics in the 1930s and 1940s always assumed he made it trading commodities or foreign currencies. But he didn't. As you can learn from biographies of Keynes, Keynes never made money on forwards or futures and even had to turn to family members to make up some of his margin calls. The big money he made seems to have been in stocks, which perhaps helps to explain some of his oft-quoted remarks about the irrationality of stock prices.

For explaining the viability of zero-sum futures markets, Keynes came up with an ingenious solution that I'm sure will seem like second nature to most of you, but it was all new back then in the 1920s. The Keynes view is sometimes called the hedging pressure view or insurance premium view. The processors accumulated inventories at harvest time—remember that futures in those days were almost entirely agricultural, grains, cotton, wool, and such—and the processors then sold futures against these inventories to protect themselves from price falls during the processing cycle.

The futures contracts they sold in such huge quantities were bought by so-called "speculators" who got them cheap on average by cost-of-carry standards and who rode them out at a profit. Not every time of course. Sometimes the speculators lost money. But on the average they made money. And that's what kept *them* in the game.

Because the game was zero-sum, the profits the speculators made on average, of course, were losses on average to the hedgers, but not economic losses, Keynes argued. The hedgers were still ahead in the same sense that you and I are ahead when we buy fire insurance. We have to pay a load fee to the insurance company over and above strict actuarial value. But it's more than worth it to shed the risk of major loss. The speculators' average profits, according to Keynes, are just the hedger's average insurance load factor.

Although Keynes may well have overemphasized short-hedging as opposed to long-hedging or combination strategies of one kind or another, his basic insurance-market interpretation made a lot of sense then and still does. When we talk about new contracts at the CME or the CBOT we know they couldn't hope to succeed on the basis of speculative interest alone. There must be a real, underlying hedging interest to keep a market going.

Charles Hardy of the Chicago School had no quarrel with Keynes's notion that hedgers were the key to the market. It was the other side of Keynes's story he wouldn't buy: the idea that speculators, as a class, made money on average at the expense of the hedgers, as a class. Hardy, I might add, wasn't just an ivory tower professor. He had spent much time at the Board of Trade, observing and talking with people at all levels of the industry. His observations led him to a view on the relation between hedgers and speculators that was very different from Keynes. Let me quote a key passage from his book.

> No statistics bearing on this question are available, but it does not seem probable that, as a matter of fact, speculators are more expert than the dealers, with whom they trade. Grain dealers, millers, and others who habitually hedge probably stay in business much longer on the average than do speculators, and, therefore, accumulate more experience. The speculative group includes a certain number of professional large-scale operators who do succeed in staying in business year after year, and presumably are making satisfactory profits, but these are the survivors of a large number whose financial strength is exhausted, or whose taste for speculation is satisfied before they attain the dignity of professionals. A few speculators make very large profits, but in all probability the business of furnishing hedging contracts belongs in the list of services which, as a whole, are rendered for society without compensation.

The profits of the successful speculators, in sum, come not from the hedgers, but from the other, less skillful speculators, who stay in the game presumably for its entertainment value. Add the returns of the two classes of speculators together and speculators as a class break even financially, with hedgers, in effect, getting their insurance for free.

Hardy was by no means dogmatic about his belief in zero returns to speculators as a class. You may recall how he starts the above passage: "No statistics bearing on the question are available." To the Chicago School, economics is an empirical science, not just a body of theoretical doctrine. For Hardy, the issue of whether speculators did in fact make or lose money on average was one that only the data could settle.

Hardy himself never actually carried out any statistical work on the subject but others at Chicago and elsewhere have done so. In fact, there are mountains of studies on the risk and returns from futures trading. Despite them, however, I fear we still don't have a definitive answer to Hardy's question. If you look at particular, individual commodities it's very hard to say whether average returns to nonhedgers are positive, negative or zero. There's just too much variation in returns to get a precise estimate of the average. You can increase the precision of the estimate by lumping together several contracts at a time, that is, by simulating a commodity pool. And when you do, you frequently find statistically significant positive average returns, even after adjusting for risk. But the results, as the statisticians say, tend to be very "sample dependent." Add or subtract a couple of years to your data, and the results can flip-flop entirely.

It is not possible to say, then, with any strong degree of confidence that the average return on speculative positions in futures has been positive in the past or is likely to be so in the future. The same cannot be said, of course, for common stocks. The data collected by our Center for Research in Security Prices at Chicago shows that over long periods of time, the returns on stocks have exceeded those on low-risk securities like Treasury bills. Not in every year, of course, but over most five-year periods, and even more so over ten-year periods. And we have strong economic grounds for expecting that relation to continue in the future. We cannot yet say the same about futures. We can't say that speculators, as a class, have made or will make money on average, and we can't say that they lose. The Keynes-Hardy question of what keeps the zero-sum futures markets going is still an open one.

That's the skeptical note on which I usually end my remarks about risk and return. But the events of the European Exchange Rate Mechanism in the fall of 1992 and again in June of 1993 suggest some additional clues to the puzzle of why forward and futures markets remain viable.

You may recall Warren Buffet's famous remark that there is a patsy in every market, and if you don't know who it is, it's probably you. Well, there are certainly patsies in the currency markets. And I don't just mean overpaid corporate treasurers who don't bother to shop around for quotes for their hedges. I mean the central banks of this world who have been fighting losing battles to defend their currencies against market realities.

The amount of money the central banks lost in September 1992 and again in June 1993 is enough to support you and the rest of the private risk-management industry of the world, on and off the exchanges, for the next twenty years. In June alone, for example, the Bundesbank spent the equivalent of $90 billion to support the French franc. The franc lost 4% so the net losses to the Bundesbank (and hence the net profits to you in the private sector) came to $3.6 billion. The Bank of Japan has lost at least that much supporting the dollar against the yen in the last few weeks with more to come.

Many of you are probably beginning to wonder how you could have been so lucky to find a market with patsies like that. Most patsies, after all, run out of money sooner or later and drop out of the game, as Hardy observed in the above passage. But these central bank guys can't run out of money because they actually *print* the stuff. The central banks in the European Exchange Rate Mechanism felt they couldn't drop out of the game—that they *had* to engage in these costly and ultimately futile defenses of their currencies. They were futile because there is no way you can sustain narrow, 2 ½% bands for fluctuations among countries with substantially different rates of inflation and rates of real growth without forcing at least some of them to suffer politically intolerable deflationary pressure.

How much deflationary pressure is tolerable, of course, depends on a country's threshold for pain. On that score, Sweden probably holds the all-time record, having pushed its short-term interest rates up to an annualized 500% in September 1992 in a vain attempt to avoid a fall in the Swedish krona. A failure as gallant as the Light Brigade at Balaklava. But what else would you expect from a country like Sweden whose idea of fun is to lock yourself in a wooden hut out in the woods, turn up the heat, beat yourself with birch branches, and then roll around naked in the snow? Now *that's* a country with tolerance for pain.

The citizens and taxpayers of countries like Sweden or France or Spain were willing to take the risk of facing such painful episodes because they feared their governments might rob them of their life savings through inflation. To tie their governments' hands, therefore, they insisted that their currencies be linked to the mark, whose Bundesbank was supposed to have been their protector. Unfortunately for them, the Bundesbank had to face a domestic inflation of its own occasioned by the reunification with East Germany. Stamping it out in Germany forced all the others through the same wringer of deflation.

But if it hadn't been the reunification, it would have been something else. For the countries in the European Exchange Rate Mechanism, substantial differences in "convergence rates," as they are called, are pretty much inevitable in a continent as large and diverse as Europe. The turmoil in May and June 1993 over the French franc, however, seems finally to have introduced a new sense of reality to the proceedings. The Europeans have widened the permissible bands around their exchange rates from 2 ½% to 11%, converting the system for all practical purposes into a floating rate regime. That's not good news for private-sector currency traders and speculators, of course, because the old fixed-rate (or should I say, semi-fixed-rate) system gave you such a favorable reward-to-risk ratio. Once a currency dropped near its lower bounds, and rumors began to arise that it *might* be devalued, everybody in the market who sold or shorted the currency had a free put on the central banks. If the currency *was* devalued, you made a bundle on that put. But even if it wasn't, your loss was limited. You were protected by the upside of the 2 ½% band. With an 11% band, of course, you're much less protected. You're virtually back in zero-sum game country again, and you'll have to earn your money either by Keynes's way or by Hardy's.

But don't despair. The central bank patsies will be back. With the rules of the game now changed to wider bands, and the markets no longer facing self-fulfilling destabilizing prophesies, the volatility in the European currency markets will eventually drop off. After a few months with nothing but small changes in exchange rates, the Europeans will conclude that the crisis has past and that the old narrow, 2½% bands can now be safely restored, though, presumably at the new, rather than the old, parities.

That's the fatal trap in reading the record of risks and returns in foreign exchange rates and futures contracts. The distributions of returns are what the statisticians call "leptokurtic." That is, on most days, nothing much happens. If you're selling naked out-of-the money puts, you can pocket a little premium almost every day. Every once in a while, however, the market is *really* going to move and you'll give it all back and then some. Sooner or later, then, the European central banks will be tempted by the calm in the markets to try narrow bands once again and the game for you will go from zero sum to positive sum. For an audience of speculators and traders as patient as you have been today, I hope it's sooner rather than later.

(Author's note: Recognizing the futility of maintaining narrow bands, the Europeans are now seeking to bypass the problem altogether by adopting a single European currency, the Euro. Whether they will, in fact, be able to bring it off successfully was still far from clear in January 1997, the time of this writing.)

Keynote address given at the Ninth Anniversary of the Singapore International Monetary Exchange Limited (Simex), Singapore, September 10, 1993.

11

Do Futures Markets Have a Future?

Around mid 1995 the U.S. futures and derivatives industries were everywhere being given up for dead. And understandably so. Scandals and disasters were breaking out at a rate of one a month it seemed, with each loss seemingly bigger than the one before. Structured notes and exotic options with their fat commissions were disappearing rapidly; even plain vanilla interest-rate swaps seemed to be drying up. On the futures exchanges, volumes were off substantially in the main markets in the United States, though, ominously, volumes were continuing to rise abroad. London International Financial Futures Exchange (LIFFE) was even reported as having passed the CME in contract volume traded. Gloom was everywhere, magnified by the re-emergence of the transaction tax, that nightmare for the industry, given new life by the urgent calls for balancing the budget in seven years.

Some of us argued even then, of course, that things really weren't as bad as they looked, despite the pervading angst. The volume drop on the U.S. futures exchanges, for one thing, was far from uniform. Some sectors, notably corn, wheat, and some of the other agriculturals were actually up substantially. So were equity index products, especially the S&Ps. Even the Singapore International Monetary Exchange, or Simex, despite the torrents of bad publicity directed at it after Barings, had the best year of its history in 1995.[1]

The big flap over the surge in foreign futures volume, moreover, was also at least partly illusory. For reasons lost in history, the futures industry insists on measuring its output by the number of contracts traded, without regard to the size of the contracts. One corn contract, for example, has a notional value of $17,000 or so while one Eurodollar contract has a notional value of $1 million. Most of the foreign futures contracts that seemed to be overtaking the U.S. exchanges were at the small end of the size scale. Nevertheless, some substantial growth in both futures and derivatives generally very clearly *is* taking place in venues outside the United States. Countries everywhere seem finally to be recognizing what we have been saying here for years; that is, that derivatives trading, broadly interpreted, not only offers great profit potential for financial service firms, but also provides great benefits to individuals and firms seeking to mitigate their exposures to business and portfolio risks. Now that the lesson has been learned, we can confidently expect more such overseas growth in the years ahead until they eventually achieve a proportion of the total world industry commensurate with their share of world wealth.

But while some areas of the U.S. industry were still growing a year and a half ago, the flagship contracts of the derivatives trade, interest rate products, unquestionably took a big nosedive in 1995 and have only partially recovered in 1996. Will volumes in these interest rate products ever reapproach the levels reached in the heady months of 1994? I am skeptical.

For many economists, myself included, the single biggest and most decisive piece of economic news of recent months has been that inflation, at long last, seems to be thoroughly under control (at least in the United States). And that's important because movements in interest rates, particularly short-term interest rates, reflect primarily—note I say primarily, not entirely—changes in expectations about future inflation rates. As uncertainty about expected future inflation rates diminishes, therefore, so almost by definition does uncertainty about future interest rates. And, of course, uncertainty (or volatility if you prefer that term) is what both the hedging and the speculative demand for derivatives—assuming there is any real difference between the two—is really all about. Why pay good money to lock in favorable rates, if rates aren't going to move much anyway? Falling inflation volatility, in sum, means falling trading volumes in interest rate products. And the point carries through to foreign exchange derivatives as well, since exchange rates are driven largely by uncertainties in interest rates and inflation rates.[2]

Drops in inflation uncertainty will lower the volatility of interest rates and foreign exchange rates, but won't eliminate that volatility completely for at least two reasons. First, even after you extract the inflation-driven component, the so-called real or inflation-adjusted component of interest rates still remains. That component too can fluctuate, though data from other countries with inflation-protected bonds suggests that those business-cycle driven fluctuations have been substantially smaller than the inflation-driven ones. Thanks to the new purchasing power bonds recently announced by Treasury Secretary Rubin, incidentally, we'll soon be able to see that directly over here. And two new products will automatically be available to trade—the real interest bonds *and* the inflation rate (which can be approximated by a spread trade between the nominal bond and the purchasing power bond). But no surge in volume is likely on that front. The experience with the Coffee-Sugar-Cocoa CPI (Consumer Price Index) index futures in the late 1980s suggests that no trading bonanza in inflation futures should be expected unless inflation and inflation uncertainty (since the two are clearly related) takes off into the stratosphere once again.

Second, it's always possible, of course, that the next Federal Reserve chairman, or possibly even the current one if the administration pounds on him long enough, will conclude that now that inflation has been conquered, the Fed can safely gun the money supply to boost growth rates in the economy. Then we're off and running again on the classic stop-go rollercoaster. That scenario is possible, as I say, but not likely, because central bankers the whole world over have become increasingly disillusioned with the prospects for countercyclical monetary policy. Price level stabilization and inflation fighting is now the order of the day. For the derivatives industry that is both bad and good news. The bad news is that inflation uncertainty and hence interest-rate volatility is unlikely to rise much above present levels for the foreseeable future. The good news is that it's not likely to fall much either.[3]

With the era of steady annual double-digit rates of growth for the derivatives industry now probably over, the interesting question, which I propose to consider from here on out, now becomes how the shares in this no longer very rapidly expanding derivatives pie are likely to be divided between its two main claimants, the futures exchanges and the over-the-counter swaps dealers.

THE COMPETITIVE BOUNDARY BETWEEN THE FUTURES EXCHANGES AND THE OTC FIRMS

The futures exchanges with their centralized trading floors, clearing houses, and daily settlement rules rank with the telegraph, the telephone, the railroad, and electricity as among the major technological inventions of the nineteenth century. (Technically, the invention of futures exchanges dates to seventeenth-century Japan, but it died there without progeny, murdered like so many other financial innovations then and since by Japanese bureaucrats who can't accept free markets and the messages they send.) Ingenious as the innovation of the futures exchange was, however, and as valuable to society as were its by-products of price discovery and price transparency, other competing technologies were and still are available.

Travel between cities is a helpful analogy here. You can go from Chicago to New York City by plane, by train, by bus, or by car. Those for whom time is more valuable than money will fly; those for whom money is worth more than time will go by bus or by train. Each mode of transport has its natural customer base, as it were. But, and this is the key point, the intermodal competitive boundaries are not fixed and immutable for all time (although the late and unlamented Interstate Commerce Commission, which was essentially just the government arm of the railroads and their unions, fought long and hard to keep those boundaries fixed). As tastes and technology change—and they change constantly—the boundaries between the competing modes shift, sometimes in surprising ways. Who would have dreamed even five years ago that Southwest Airlines would virtually obliterate bus travel between Chicago and Des Moines? Southwest Airlines may not be elegant, but it sure is cheap.

What is true for intermodal competition in transportation is just as true for intermodal competition in derivatives and financial services generally. Futures exchanges may have been a technological breakthrough of the nineteenth century, but swaps are the breakthrough of the twentieth century. Each technological mode of offering derivatives products has its natural customer base, and the boundaries are not rigid. The bigger a firm or bank you are and the higher your credit rating, the more choices of supplier you have. Which one you use depends on cost, broadly construed to include not just spreads and commissions but susceptibility to fraud, exposure to counterparty default, and lack of transparency in pricing. It follows then that if the cost of using a sector falls relative to those of its rivals, that sector is likely to expand. And if its costs of doing business rise relative to its rivals, it will almost certainly have to contract.[4]

The likely future division of the derivatives pie between the exchanges and the OTC sector thus comes down to a matter of the rate of change of *relative* costs. The word relative must be emphasized because success in a competitive arena depends on more than just running a tight ship and keeping overheads from rising. Firms are actually on a treadmill. In the manufacturing sector, for example, they have to *cut* their unit costs by at least two to three percent a year on average just to stay even with their competitors. In the service industries, of course, for reasons still not fully understood, annual productivity gains haven't consistently reached that rate, which is why U.S. productivity growth as a whole appears so modest. But the exchanges shouldn't count on getting by with zero productivity gains indefinitely. The first signs of a possible productivity surge by their OTC competitors *are* already visible.[5]

Can the exchanges reasonably hope to match those productivity gains by reducing the costs of trading in their own current open-outcry environment? Certainly the recent tales of chaos in the grain pits at the

Chicago Board of Trade are not encouraging. But the costs of *any* operation can be expected to rise steeply whenever the demands on a system approach its effective maximum capacity, which seemed to be happening in the grain pits. (Some of us have argued, in fact, that just such a volume surge beyond the effective capacity of the NYSE [New York Stock Exchange] was responsible for much of the trouble during the stock market crash of October 19, 1987.)[6] Fortunately for the Chicago Board of Trade, however, the completion of its new trading floor should create more than enough capacity in its grain pits to prevent a recurrence of the recent and highly conspicuous congestion, even without allowing for the proposed $7 million of electronic enhancements for getting orders into and out of the pits.[7]

Adding capacity to the pits substitutes fixed capital costs for the high variable costs occasioned by demand surges, but will the long-run average cost over normal volumes be put on the kind of steadily declining path necessary to keep the exchange/OTC intermodal boundary from shifting against the exchanges? Given the structure of the trading floors, that question comes down to the likely path of average costs for the individual traders. Here, some clear possibilities for significant cost reductions can be described, but whether they can actually be realized in time to do the industry much good remains problematic.[8]

THE SCOPE FOR COST REDUCTIONS ON THE TRADING FLOORS

One obvious area of potential cost savings is in something as elemental as trade recording. Under present technology, trades are recorded by writing five or six characters on trading cards, which are later collected and subsequently entered into one or more computer data-processing systems. The procedure is not only slow and labor intensive, but prone to substantial error which shows up in "outtrades" that must be settled in early morning, face-to-face negotiations next day before the parties can resume trading. Additional costs are incurred in reconstructing the so-called audit trails (essentially the precise timing of transactions) needed for detecting violations of the exchange's trading rules.

One natural solution to the problems of trade recording and timing would be some sort of handheld, wireless, electronic instrument that could record the trades as they occur and transmit the information instantly to the appropriate computers. Outtrades could then be reconciled right on the spot while memories are still fresh and the reconstruction of the trading sequence would be automatic. Costs to clearing members of monitoring their floor traders would also fall because credit limits could easily be programmed in. Both exchanges, to their great credit, have in fact cooperated to develop just such handheld terminal technology, so far, alas, with no success, despite the investment of as much as $20 million to date in the project—yes, I said $20 million.

Much of the blame for this conspicuous waste of resources on implementing the handheld technology rests with the CFTC and their Congressional Agriculture Committee overseers who were pressing the industry severely on the audit-trail issue—an issue that is trivial for society,[9] but crucial to the public relations image of the regulators, particularly after the famous FBI "sting" operation of 1989. Threats of sanctions and retaliation from those regulators led the exchanges to gamble on a crash program for a near-perfect audit trail well before the technology was there to support it. Nor is the end of these unnecessary regulatory burdens in sight. The deadweight costs piled on exchange trading by an archaic and uneconomic regulatory structure has been likened to forcing the exchanges to run their competitive race against the far less minutely regulated OTC market with a fifty-pound bag of bricks tied to their backs.[10]

Additional costs of using the futures route are incurred, of course, in the so-called "back office" operations of both the exchanges themselves and the Futures Commission Merchants, or FCMs, who serve as intermediaries between the exchanges and the customers. Here, at least, the prospect of some substantial reduction in costs in the near future is currently looking better. The futures exchanges, for a variety of reasons, have lagged far behind other industries in adopting uniform industry technical standards.[11] In after-hours electronic trading systems, for example, the FCMs currently confront no less than three totally incompatible systems: the CME's Globex, the CBOT's Project A, and the Nymex Access. And there are more to come. Each exchange, moreover, maintains its own unique order-entry and position-reporting systems, a lack of compatibility that not only adds to FCM costs, but leads to wasteful duplication of computing facilities. The CME and the CBOT, for example, maintain between them no less than five separate mainframe computers each costing them over a million dollars a year, when with a relatively simple accommodation, the exchanges could make do with at most two mainframes, and possibly only one if they could arrange for a suitable, off-site backup for any emergencies.

The recognition, however belated, that the exchanges and their customers can (and for their own survival must) achieve substantial cost reductions by consolidating their essentially similar clearing and settlement operations and by adopting uniform standards for entering and confirming trades was the motivating impulse behind the recent formation by the CME and the CBOT of the Joint Strategic Initiatives Committee, or JSIC, on which I was asked to serve as executive director. The formation of the committee was greeted with considerable skepticism by the press and many outside observers, and understandably so, given the natural animosities between the members of two such long-time rivals. But the two exchanges have, in fact, managed to cooperate on many joint projects over the years (including the unfortunate handheld trading terminal great leap forward) and I was confident they could do so again if they could somehow manage to surmount the problems posed by their own internal governance institutions.

The futures exchanges, in the United States at least, are organized not as investor-owned corporations, like the Swedish options exchange OM, but essentially as "trader cooperatives." Only a very limited class of operating decisions is delegated to professional managers. For example, all key decisions of the kind facing the JSIC must be voted on first by the thirty or so members (plus some "disinterested" outsiders) serving on the board of directors of each exchange, and then, in any matter of major importance, by several hundred trader-members in what amounts to a plebiscite. Recognizing this need to gain the consent of the membership before undertaking any major consolidations, the two exchanges have each nominated parallel lists of twenty or more of "influential" members to the JSIC and its six subcommittees. Such a broad-based participation will surely help in the long run when concrete proposals are eventually presented to the memberships of each exchange for approval. But, in the short run, the sheer size of the group makes it extremely difficult even to arrange committee and subcommittee meetings.

Still, I remain confident that these institutional obstacles to agreement will ultimately be overcome. As an economist, I believe that if the efficiency gains are large enough—and I am convinced they are—private negotiation and contracting between the individuals affected will achieve them. Admittedly, the opportunity for compensatory side payments in cash or stock of the kind routine in ordinary corporate negotiations would vastly simplify matters and hasten agreement, but in its absence, the mounting competitive pressure on the exchanges from their OTC and foreign rivals can serve as at least a partial substitute. In the famous words of Dr. Samuel Johnson, nothing seems to concentrate the mind better than the prospect of being hanged.

A DIGRESSION ON ELECTRONIC TRADING

Fifteen years ago, the universal view was that the open-outcry pits would dominate trading in futures for as far as the eye could see. Electronic trading would be confined to the periphery of the industry—after-hours trading systems perhaps, and low-volume settings more generally. The conventional wisdom has now swung 180 degrees. The rapid improvements in computer technology and the adoption of electronic trading by the foreign exchange interbank community, and even by major futures exchanges such as the German Deutsche Terminbörse, have led many to believe that open-outcry will disappear in the very near future.

Rumors of the imminent, if not actual, death of open-outcry are greatly exaggerated, however. Technological displacements always seem more abrupt looking backward than they really were, or than they actually seemed at the time. (Author's note: Recall the steamship example in chapter 1.)

For reasons of comparative advantage, open-outcry trading will not easily or quickly be driven from its niche in markets where the demand for "immediacy" is highest. Where immediacy is critical, nothing in current electronic trading technology can yet match the *simultaneous* active bidding by literally hundreds of competing floor traders—for reasons familiar to anyone who has ever used a time-sharing computer.

But the open-outcry pit's greatest strength can sometimes become its greatest weakness. Having hundreds of traders reporting for work and standing ready to fill orders makes no economic sense unless a large and continuous flow of orders is waiting to be filled. Electronic trading in the United States has thus found its entering niche mainly in low-volume after-hours trading. In countries outside the United States, especially in East Asia where futures markets are just beginning to develop, electronic trading based on any of a number of prefabricated "turnkey" systems makes sense. The overhead cost burden of a new, small exchange can be kept small that way, and no need arises for training hundreds of skilled and specialized floor traders.[12]

Remember also that while high immediacy and liquidity may be the strong suit of open-outcry trading, transactors may not always be concerned with those attributes. When I'm selling my house, for example, I'm willing to forego the first offer if I think searching further might turn up an even better prospect. Housing prices, after all, are not so volatile that they might collapse while I'm still waiting for an eager buyer to up the bid; similarly if I want to unload a really large position in stocks or any other asset. I'm not going to just dump a market order into the crowd in the pit for whatever it will bring. I'm going to take it "upstairs" and "work" the transaction, even though several days may be necessary to complete the deal.

In sum, just as a shifting competitive boundary exists between the OTC dealers and the futures exchanges, so does one exist between the open-outcry exchanges and electronic trading. For the medium term at least, say the next ten years or so, the Chicago open-outcry exchanges can probably achieve a rate of average annual productivity growth sufficient to stay even with, or at least not fall too far behind, their major competitors. For the longer term, however, the picture is murkier, given the enormous and far-reaching technological development through which we are living, and which threaten the current structure not just of the exchanges, but of financial trading generally. Trading floors and trading screens, after all, serve mainly to permit traders and other financial intermediaries to bring buyers and sellers together and to overcome the problems posed by the lack of perfect synchronization of their demands. But thanks to the Internet and related developments, buyers and sellers are increasingly able to find each other directly without the services of intermediaries, and certainly without trading floors. The regulators, of course, will do what they can to protect the investments of their exchange and brokerage constituents, but if history is any guide, they can at best only slow, not stop, the propagation of new technology as revolutionary as that of the new information age we are presumably about to enter.[13]

The eventual disappearance of the trading floor, however, need not mean the disappearance of the futures exchanges themselves. Their main function will simply change from one of offering primarily transaction services, to one of offering primarily the services of clearing and settlement. That may seem an improbable outcome perhaps from today's vantage point, but technology often has a strange way of reshuffling otherwise familiar decks.[14] Who today remembers that steam engines were invented originally to pump water out of coal mines?

Keynote address given at the 1996 APFA/PACAP Finance Conference, Taipei, Taiwan, July 9, 1996. Forthcoming in Pacific-Basin Finance Journal 2 (1997). *An earlier version was presented at the Conference on Derivatives and Public Policy, Federal Reserve Bank of Chicago, June 6, 1996.*

REFERENCES

Grossman, Sanford and Merton H. Miller, "Economic Costs and Benefits of the Proposed One-Minute Time Bracketing Regulation," *Journal of Futures Markets*, Spring 1986.

Miller, Merton H., *Financial Innovation and Market Volatility.* Basil Blackwell, 1991.

Part IV

Corporate Finance and Corporate Governance

12

Japanese Versus American Corporate Governance

Are the investment horizons of U.S. firms too short? Yes, was the conclusion of *Capital Choices,* a report published in August 1992 by twenty-five academic scholars under the leadership of Professor Michael Porter of the Harvard Business School. The Porter report was widely acclaimed not only by the U.S. financial press, but by many Japanese observers. Mr. Katsuro Umino, for one, vice president of the Osaka-based Kotsu Trading Company, is quoted in *The Chicago Tribune* of August 24, 1992, as saying:

> It's interesting to see that somebody in America is finally waking up to the real culprit behind the decline of American corporate competitiveness. I think many of us in Japan have known for a long time that America's capital allocation system is inherently flawed.

The flaw seen by Messrs. Porter and Umino and ever so many others is the overemphasis on stock prices and shareholder returns in the U.S. system of corporate governance. By contrast, a survey of one thousand Japanese and one thousand U.S. firms by Japan's Economic Planning Agency, reported in the same story in *The Chicago Tribune,* finds that on a scale of zero to three, with three being most important, Japanese firms give "higher stock price" a rating of only 0.02, while "increasing market share" gets a reported rating of 1.43 in Japan, almost twice its rating in the United States.

Surveys must never be taken too literally, of course. Japanese managers surely cannot believe that increasing market share is an overriding corporate goal. Achieving a market share for your product of one-hundred percent is too easy: just give it away. Profitability must also and always be considered. And indeed, the Japanese firms surveyed did give a rating of 1.24 to "return on investment"—far less than the 2.43 rating given by the U.S. firms, but still much, much more than the virtually zero weight given to higher stock prices.

For all its technical limitations, however, the survey does, I believe, accurately reflect differences in managerial behavior in the two countries. U.S. managers *are* more concerned with current movements in their own stock price than are Japanese managers. And rightly so. But the emphasis that U.S. managers place on shareholder returns is not a flaw in the U.S. corporate governance system, but one of its primary strengths.

Some of my academic colleagues believe, in fact, that U.S. big-business management has been putting too *little* weight on stockholder returns, leading to massive waste of both shareholder wealth and of national wealth. Their argument, however, has not, in my view, been convincingly established. The billion-dollar losses of companies like IBM and General Motors in recent years, offered by the critics as evidence for their case, testify less to failures in the U.S. governance system than to the vigorously competitive environment in which U.S. firms must operate.

MAXIMIZING SHAREHOLDER VALUE AS THE PRIMARY OBJECTIVE OF THE BUSINESS CORPORATION

Let me begin my defense of U.S. corporate governance by emphasizing that managerial concern with shareholder value is merely one specific application of the more general proposition that in U.S. society the individual is king—not the nation, not the government, not the producers, not the merchants, but the individual, and especially the individual consumer, is sovereign. Certainly that has not been the accepted view of ultimate economic sovereignty here in Japan, though the first signs of change are beginning to appear.

The connection between consumer sovereignty and corporate governance lies not just in the benefits customers derive from the firm's own output. The customers are not the only consumers the firm serves. The shareholders, the investors, the owners—however one chooses to call them—are also consumers and their consumption, actual and potential, drives the shareholder-value principle.

To see how and why, consider the directors of a firm debating how much of the firm's current profits, say $10 million, to pay out as dividends to the shareholders. If the $10 million is paid as dividends, the shareholders clearly have an additional $10 million in cash to spend. Suppose, however, that the $10 million is not paid out, but used instead for investment in the firm—buying machinery, expanding the factory, setting up a new branch, or what have you. The stockholders now do not get the cash, but they need not be disadvantaged thereby. That will depend on how the stock market values the proposed new investment projects.

If the market believes the firm's managers have invested wisely, the value of the shares may rise by $10 million or even more. Stockholders seeking to convert this potential consumption into actual consumption need only sell the shares and spend the proceeds. But if the market feels that the managers have spent the money foolishly, the stock value will rise by less than the foregone dividend of $10 million, perhaps by only $5 million, or possibly not at all. Those new investments may have expanded the firm's market share and may have vastly improved the firm's image and the prestige of its managers. But they have not increased shareholder wealth and potential consumption. They have reduced it.

Current Market Values and Future Earnings

Using stock market response to measure the true worth of the proposed new investments may strike many here in Japan as precisely the kind of short-term thinking that has led so many American firms astray. Let it be clearly understood, therefore, that, in a U.S.-style stock market, focusing on current *stock* prices is not short-term thinking. Focusing on current *earnings* might be myopic; but not so for stock prices, which reflect not just today's earnings, but the earnings the market expects in all future years as well.

Just how much weight expected future earnings carry in determining current stock prices always surprises those not accustomed to working with present-value formulas and especially with growth formulas. Growth formulas, however, whether of dividends or earnings, rarely strike my Japanese friends or my Japanese students as very compelling. Many Japanese firms, after all, pay only nominal dividends, and the formulas themselves don't make sufficiently clear what investors are really buying when they buy a growth stock.

Let me therefore shift the focus from a firm's rate of sales or earnings growth to where it ought to be, namely to the competitive conditions facing the firm over meaningful horizons. And let me, for reasons that will become clear later, measure the strength of those competitive conditions by the currently fashionable market value-to-book value ratio (also known as the market-to-book or "price-to-book" ratio). The book-value term in the ratio, based as it is on original cost, approximates what management actually spent for the assets the market is valuing. A market value-to-book value ratio of one (abstracting from any concerns about pure price inflation) is thus a natural benchmark, signifying a firm with no competitive advantage or disadvantage. The firm is expected to earn only normal profits in the economists' sense of that term, that is, profits just large enough to give the stockholders the average, risk-adjusted return for equities generally.

To sell for more than an unremarkable market-to-book ratio of 1.0—that is, to have a positive "franchise value" as some put it—a firm must have long-term competitive advantages allowing it to earn a higher than normal rate of return on its productive assets. And that's not as easy to do as it may seem. Above-normal profits always carry with them the seeds of their own decay. They attract competitors, both from within a country and from abroad, driving profits and share prices relentlessly back toward the competitive norm. Investors buying into a firm are thus making judgments about whether the firm and its managers have produced a competitive advantage over their rivals, and especially a judgment about how long into the future that competitive advantage to earn above-normal returns can be expected to last.

Some specific numbers may help to fix ideas.[1] Consider a U.S. firm with a market-to-book ratio of 3.0—and there still are many of these. And suppose, further, that it will be plowing back its entire cash flow into investments expected to earn at *twice* the normal competitive rate of return. Then in paying three times book value for the shares, investors are in effect anticipating that the firm will expand and stay that far ahead of its competitors *for the next twenty years.*

That's *really* forward looking. Much too forward looking, some would say, in this highly uncertain world. And perhaps that's why so many Japanese managers are instinctively skeptical of using the stock market to guide or evaluate managerial decision making. They don't really trust the prices in the Japanese stock market where market-to-book ratios at the height of the stock market boom of 1989 were not just 3.0 but, even after adjusting for real estate and for other corporate shares in cross holdings, ran routinely to 5.0 or even 10.0, implying opportunities to earn above-normal, competitor-proof returns for centuries to come.

Prices and market-to-book ratios have fallen substantially since then, but are still hard to take seriously because they are not completely free-market prices. The values are not only distorted by the pervasive cross-holdings of nontraded shares, but the prices of the thinly-traded minority of shares in the floating supply often reflect the heroic scale of market intervention by the Ministry of Finance, or MOF. Japanese managers can be pardoned for wondering sometimes whether their stock market may be just a *Bunraku* theater, with the bureaucrats from MOF backstage manipulating the puppets.

MOF's notorious market support activities also interact in other ways with the issue of corporate governance in Japan. Many academic observers in the United States (myself, in particular) have attributed MOF's famous P.K.O. (Price Keeping Operations, and a Japanese pun on the country's participation in the U.N.'s Peace Keeping Operations in Cambodia) to its role as cartel manager for the Japanese brokerage industry.[2] Another motivation traces, however, to the Japanese banking industry. Japanese banks, unlike those in the United States, can hold equity positions in the companies to which they are also lending; a dual role, in turn, often cited as the real key to Japanese managerial success. The bank connection presumably reduces corporate agency costs, provides better monitoring of corporate decisions, and above all, allows management to undertake profitable but risky long-run ventures confident of having the continued financial support needed to carry projects through to completion.

But any gains to the Japanese economy on the governance front have come at a substantial cost on other fronts. Corporate equities can be great assets for banks when the stock market is booming as it was in Japan in the 1980s. The price appreciation then provides the banks with substantial regulatory capital to support their lending activities. But when the stock market collapses, as in Japan after 1989, the disappearance of those hidden equity reserves can threaten the solvency of the banks and the integrity of the country's payment system.

The prospect becomes even more frightening when we remember that shareholdings in Japan run in both directions. Not only do banks hold the firm's shares but, again, presumably with a view to better governance, the firms also hold the *banks'* shares. The result is a classic, unstable positive-feedback asset pyramid. No wonder MOF must keep supporting stock prices, and always seems to be running around like the proverbial Dutch boy on the dikes, plugging holes and leaks in its regulations.

Stock Prices and Information

To say that the stock market in the United States is much closer to the free market ideal than the Japanese stock market is not to suggest that valuations in the United States are always correct. But at least those investors with bearish opinions about particular stocks or about the market for equities as a whole can express their pessimism by selling, even selling short, without encountering the kind of anti-selling rules and taboos for which MOF has become notorious. Those pessimists may well be wrong, of course. And so in their turn may be those who are optimistically anticipating a rise in future earnings and prices.

No serious student of stock markets has ever suggested that stock prices always "correctly" measure the true "fundamentals," whatever those words might mean. The most claimed is that the prices are not systematically distorted, like those in Japan where MOF's heavy thumb often tilts the scales against selling. Nor are the prices in the United States just some artificial numbers driven by whims and fads, as some academics have argued (and quite unsuccessfully so, in my opinion). The evidence overwhelmingly supports the view that prices do reflect in an unbiased way all the information about a company that is available to the investing public.

The word "available" is worth stressing, however. The stockholders and potential outside investors can't be expected to value managements' proposed investment projects properly if they don't have the information on which management has based those plans. And management may well hesitate to disclose that information for fear of alerting competitors. This inevitable asymmetry in information, to use the fashionable academic jargon, is what many see as the real flaw in the shareholder-value principle. Projects with positive net present value, possibly even with substantial net present value, may not be undertaken because outside investors cannot value the projects properly and will condemn management for wasting the stockholders' money. That, essentially, is the Porter position. As one way to deal with it, he recommends that U.S. governance rules be changed to permit firms to disclose proprietary, competitively-sensitive information *selectively* to that subset of the stockholders willing to commit to long-term investing in the company.

Can investment be discouraged by inability to disclose selectively? Possibly. Has it happened? And on what scale? That is much harder to say. The main evidence cited for its pervasiveness in the United States is the supposedly superior earnings and growth performance of bank-disciplined Japanese manufacturing firms relative to their impatient U.S. stockholder-disciplined counterparts. Note that I stress Japanese manufacturing firms. No one has ever suggested that Japanese market-share oriented firms were superior in the service industries, notably retailing, or in commercial banking.

And I should say that manufacturing *was* the main evidence for Japanese governance superiority cited before the current recession hit Japan. That recession, painful as it has been and still is in its impact on the Japanese economy, has at least served to remind us that myopia is not the only disease of vision afflicting business managers. They may suffer from astigmatism (distorted vision) or even from hyperopia or excessive far-sightedness. Looking back over the last twenty years, cases may well exist where U.S. firms facing strong stockholder pressures to pay out funds have invested too little in some kinds of capital-intensive technology. But many Japanese firms, facing no such pressures, have clearly *overinvested* during that same period, in highly capital-intensive plants that will never come close to recovering their initial investment, let alone earning a positive rate of return. And I won't even mention the wasted trillions of yen poured into land and office buildings both at home and abroad.

No form of corporate governance, needless to say, whether Japanese or U.S., can guarantee 20–20 vision by management. Mistakes, both of omission and of commission will always be made. My claim is only that those U.S. managers who *do* focus on maximizing the market value of the firm at least have a better set of correcting lenses for properly judging the trade-off between current investment and future benefits than those who focus on maximizing growth or market share or some other trendy, presumed strategic advantage.

MANAGEMENT OBJECTIVES AND STOCKHOLDER INTERESTS

Glasses help you see better of course, only if you wear them. The complaint of at least one wing of U.S. academic opinion, especially in the field of finance, is precisely that U.S. managers don't always wear their stockholder-corrected lenses to work. Because ownership of U.S. corporations is so widely dispersed among a multitude of passive individual and institutional investors, managers, so the argument runs, are left free to pursue objectives that may, but needn't, conform to those of the stockholders.

Shareholders, however, are not powerless. Although neither able nor willing to perform day-by-day monitoring of management operating decisions, shareholders do have the right to elect the company's board of directors. And the board, in turn, by its power to unseat management and even more by its power to design the program for executive compensation, has command over important levers for aligning management's objectives with those of the shareholders.

Compensation Packages and Management Incentives

The board of directors has a toolbox full of levers, but not, alas, any simple or foolproof set of instructions for using them. In fact, academic agency theory suggests that *no* all-purpose optimal compensation scheme—no "first-best" as opposed to, say, second-best or even lower-best solution—really exists for aligning interests when success depends on luck as well as skill.

To see why, ask yourself how the directors could make the managers accept the stockholders' attitudes toward risk. Suppose, to be specific, that the directors try what may seem the obvious performance-based compensation strategy of giving the managers shares in the company. Will that make a manager act like a shareholder? More so, probably, than if the directors just offered a flat—and presumably high—salary supplemented with generous retirement benefits. Managers so compensated are more likely to be working for the bondholders than for the stockholders. Salaried managers clearly have little incentive to consider projects with serious downside risk.

Giving managers stock does at least let them participate in the gains from their successful moves, but still does not solve the problem of excessive managerial timidity—excessive, that is, relative to the best interests of the outside stockholders. Those stockholders are, or at least in principle ought to be, well diversified. They can thus afford risking their entire investment in the company even for only 50:50 odds because their stockholding is only a small part of their total wealth. That, after all, is a key social benefit of the corporate form with fractional and easily transferable ownership interests: more efficient sharing of the business risks. But the managers are typically *not* diversified. A major fraction of their personal wealth and their human capital is tied to the corporation. Caution, not boldness inevitably becomes their watchword.

The executive stock-option was invented in the United States in the 1950s precisely to offset the play-it-safe tendencies of underdiversified corporate managers (though tax considerations and accounting conventions have since blurred the original incentive-driven motivation for options).[3] Stock options, suitably structured, work by magnifying the upside potential for the manager relative to the down. A bet of $1,000 if a coin comes up heads and a loss of $1,000 if tails, would hardly be tempting to the typical risk-averse manager. But tossing a fair coin might well seem attractive if heads brought $5,000 and tails cost only $500.

Options and their many variations—including option-equivalents like highly leveraged capital structures—not only can reduce management's natural risk-aversion, but may overdo it and tempt managers into excessively risky ventures. If these long-odds strategies do happen to pay off, the managers profit enormously. If not, the bulk of the losses are borne by the shareholders and probably the bondholders and other prior claimants as well. Many observers feel that a payoff asymmetry of precisely this kind for undercapitalized owner-managers was the root cause of the U.S. savings and loan disaster.

The inability to align management interests and risk attitudes more closely with those of the stockholders shows up most conspicuously, some academic critics would argue, in the matter of corporate diversification. Corporate diversification does reduce risk for the management. But because stockholders can diversify directly, they have little to gain (except perhaps for some tax benefits, large in some cases, from internal offsetting rather than carry-forward of losses) when a General Motors, say, uses funds that might otherwise have been paid as dividends to buy Ross Perot's firm, Electronic Data Systems. In fairness, however, let it be noted that the stockholders, by the same token, would have little to lose by such acquisitions unless the acquiring firm were to pay too high a price for control—which certainly has been known to happen.

Stockholders could also lose if corporate diversification predictably and consistently meant sacrificing the efficiencies of specialization. Some evidence suggests that it does—although hardly enough, in my view, to justify claims by some academic critics of corporate diversification and corporate conglomeration that loss of corporate focus and related failures of governance by GM or IBM or Sears in recent years, has destroyed hundreds of billions of dollars of their stockholders' and, by extension, of the nation's wealth.

For those firms, certainly, aggregate stock market values have declined substantially. But to treat that decline as a national disaster like some gigantic earthquake is to overlook the distinction between social costs and private costs. Consider, for example, the story told in Figure 12.1, which pictures an IBM-type firm about to be hit unexpectedly with an antitrust suit (and let it be clearly understood that this is an illustration, and not necessarily a recommendation). The company's initial demand curve is $d_1 d_1$ and its long-run marginal cost is BJ (assumed, for simplicity, as constant and hence equal to its average cost). Because the firm had "market power," it set its product price at OC (that is, above average and marginal cost), earning thereby the above-normal profits indicated by the rectangle BCDF. Those anticipated, above-competitive profits will be capitalized by the stock market and the company will sell for a high market-to-book value premium.

Now let the government win its antitrust suit against the company and immediately force the company's price and output to their competitive levels (OB for price and OK for quantity). The abnormal profits will vanish, the stock price will fall and the market-to-book value premium will disappear. Yet no net loss in *national* wealth or welfare has occurred. Wealth has simply been transferred from the company's shareholders to its customers; producer surplus has been transformed into consumers' surplus. In the case pictured, in fact, society is better off on balance, not worse off. Because output increases to the competitive level, consumers gain additional consumers' surplus in the form of the ("Harberger") triangle DFN.

The social and private consequences are easily distinguished in this antitrust scenario. But what if the decline in stock market value is a self-inflicted wound? IBM, after all, did *not* lose its antitrust case. Its market value was eroded by the unanticipated entry of new firms with new technologies.

That kind of value erosion, however, surely cannot be the national disaster to which the governance critics are pointing. Why, after all, should society's consumers care whether the new products were introduced by IBM or by Intel or Apple? Or by WalMart or by Sears, or for that matter, by General Motors or by Toyota? The complaint of the critics may be rather that the managements of those firms have failed to downsize and restructure fast enough even *after* the new competition had penetrated the market. Entrenched managements, unchecked by the hand-picked

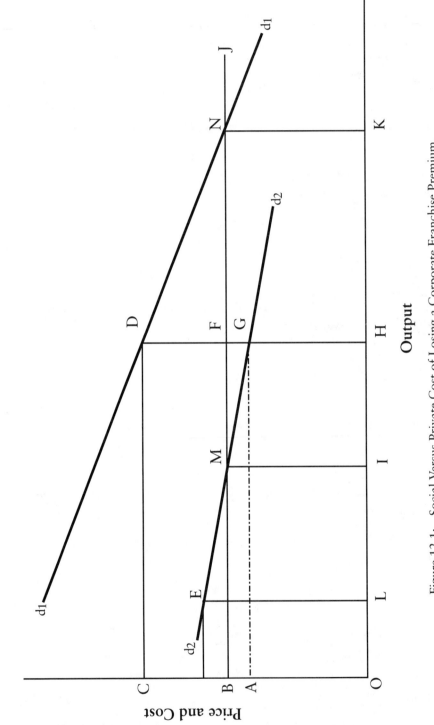

Figure 12.1: Social Versus Private Cost of Losing a Corporate Franchise Premium.

sycophants on their boards, kept pouring money into the old, money-losing lines of the firm's business rather than let their stockholders redeploy the funds to better advantage elsewhere.

But continuing to make positive investments in a declining industry—"throwing good money after bad" as the cliché would have it—cannot automatically be taken as evidence of economic inefficiency, and certainly not of bad management. Nothing in economic logic or commonsense suggests the best exit path is always the quickest one. A firm withdraws its capital by making its *net* investment negative, that is, by holding its rate of gross investment below the rate of depreciation. The marginal rate of return on that gross investment may well be high even though the average rate of return on the past capital sunk in the division or the firm as a whole is low or even negative. When the direct costs of exit (such as severance payments) are high, and when the firm is at least covering its variable costs (unlike many in Russia, so we are told), investing to reduce a loss can often be a most positive net present-value project indeed.

Suppose, however, for the sake of argument that some entrenched managers *were* too slow in downsizing. The losses reported by their firms still cannot be equated dollar for dollar with the social costs of bad governance. To see why, turn again to Figure 12.1, which represents our original firm, but after the entry of the new competition attracted by its earlier high profits. The firm's demand curve is now the much more elastic demand curve d_2d_2, and its new long-run equilibrium level of output will be OL, smaller than its earlier equilibrium output level OH.

Should the firm seek to maintain its earlier market share of OH, however, net losses of ABFG will be incurred, exactly as the critics insist. But only the triangle MFG represents the social cost of the failure to downsize. The rest, given by the area ABMG is, again, merely a transfer to consumer surplus. How much of the reported loss goes one way and how much goes the other cannot be settled, of course, merely from a schematic diagram. That requires specific empirical research of a kind not yet found in the recent academic literature so critical of U.S. corporate governance.

That the losses suffered in recent years by firms like IBM or Sears or General Motors may not be social losses will be of little comfort, of course, to those stockholders who have seen so much of their retirement nest eggs in those companies vanish. One can hardly blame them for wishing that the directors had somehow prodded management to abandon their formerly successful strategies *before* the success of the newer competitive strategies had been so decisively confirmed. Fortunately, however, shareholders whose personal stake is too small to justify costly monitoring of management, have another and well-tested way to protect their savings from management's mistakes of omission or commission: diversify. A properly diversified shareholder would have the satisfaction of knowing that his or her loss on IBM shares or Sears or General Motors shares was not even a *private* loss since it was offset in the portfolio by gains on Microsoft, Intel, Apple, WalMart, and other new-entrant firms, foreign and domestic, that did pioneer in the new technologies.

CONCLUSION

Summing up then, we have seen two quite different views of what is wrong with U.S. corporate management. One view, widely accepted in Japan and by the Michael Porter wing of academic opinion is that U.S. managers pay too much attention to current shareholder returns. The other view, widely held among U.S. academic finance specialists is that U.S. managers pay too little attention to shareholder returns.

Which view is right? Both. And neither. Both sides can point to specific cases or examples seeming to support their positions. But both are wrong in claiming any permanent or systematic bias for U.S. firms in the aggregate toward myopia or hyperopia, toward underinvestment or overinvestment relative either to the shareholders' or to society's best interests. There is no inherent bias because market forces are constantly working in the United States to remove control over corporate assets from managers who lack the competence or the vision to deploy them efficiently.

We saw those forces most dramatically perhaps in the takeover battles, leveraged buyouts, and corporate restructurings of the 1980s and more recently in many well-publicized board-led insurgencies. But, for all their drama, those events (which sometimes seem little more than struggles over how the corporate franchise premium is to be shared between the executives and the shareholders) represent only one part, and by no means the most important part, of the process of allocating society's productive capital among firms. The ultimate discipline for the managers of any one firm in the United States will always be the managers of other firms, including foreign firms, competing with them head to head for customer business. As long as we continue to have plenty of *that* kind of competition in the United States, I, for one, can't become terribly concerned about the supposedly fatal flaws in our governance system.

A talk given at the Second Symposium on Global Financial Markets on "Corporate Governance and Organization in Japan and the United States," sponsored by the University of Michigan School of Business Administration and Mitsui Life Financial Research Center, Tokyo, Japan, May 11, 1993. Thanks for helpful comments are owed to my colleagues Steven Kaplan and Anil Kashyap, and from Donald Chew.

REFERENCES

Miller, Merton H. and Franco Modigliani, "Dividend Policy, Growth and the Valuation of Shares," *Journal of Business,* Vol. 24, No. 4 (October 1961), pp. 411–433.

———, and Myron Scholes, "Executive Compensation, Taxes and Incentives," in *Financial Economics: Essays in Honor of Paul Cootner,* William Sharpe and Catheryn Cootner (Eds.), Prentice-Hall, Englewood Cliffs, NJ, 1982.

———, "The Economics and Politics of Index Arbitrage in the U.S. and Japan," *Pacific-Basin Finance Journal,* Vol. 1, No. 1 (May 1993), pp. 3–11. (Chapter 4 in this volume.)

———, "Japanese-American Trade Relations in the Financial Services Industry," Working Paper, Graduate School of Business, University of Chicago (September 1993).

13

German Bank-Driven Corporate Governance

I am often asked whether the successful recapitalization of Metallge-sellschaft, or MG, in February 1994 after a supposed narrow escape from bankruptcy offers lessons in corporate governance for the United States. I believe the episode *does* offer lessons about governance, but not the ones currently being drawn by some U.S. academics. They see the re-structuring of MG under the leadership of Deutsche Bank in February as a low-cost German substitute for the kind of lawyer-intensive Chapter 11 reorganization that might otherwise have been required in the United States. Perhaps so. But bankruptcy resolution is only a small part of cor-porate governance. For MG, moreover, focusing on the presumed low cost of the restructuring begs the key question: why was the restructuring nec-essary in the first place?

And here, I will argue, the role of German corporate governance was far from benign. I am not claiming, I hasten to add, that flaws in the Ger-man corporate governance mechanism actually *caused* the problem at MG—though that is certainly one plausible hypothesis, as we shall see. The real failure, as I see it, was not so much that German governance did *worse* when confronted with short-term cash outflows at MG than U.S. managements and boards might have done under the same circumstances, but that it surely didn't do *better.* And that's important because the gov-ernance should have been superior under those conditions if only to off-set the many other dimensions along which German bank-dominated cor-porate governance is *inferior* to the U.S.-British stockholder-driven governance model.

I know the statement that U.S. governance has *any* advantages over

German models may bring smiles to the faces of a German audience that has been seeing the value of the U.S. dollar fall so steadily recently relative to that of the Deutschemark. But the path of the dollar against the mark actually has nothing much to do with corporate governance. The exchange rate is a phenomenon of *macro*economics, not *micro*economics. And it is driven mainly by differences in national savings rates and monetary policies.

At the micro level, in fact, the corporate governance scheme for big business in Germany, and in Japan as well for that matter, has probably become a drag on economic growth rather than a contributor. Those two economies will be kept healthy during the 1990s and beyond not by their big bank-dominated firms, but by the smaller, independent firms that deliberately avoid too tight a link to the banks.

The defenders of German (and Japanese) bank-dominated governance focus too much on one of the two types of managerial errors and neglects the other. Just as in statistics we have type one and type two errors (the error of accepting a false conclusion and the error of rejecting a true one), so in management we have the error of overinvesting in low-return prospects and that of underinvesting in high-return prospects.

The positive case for German and Japanese governance has always been that the bank tie overcomes the underinvestment error by allowing the firm and its funders to take the long view on capital-intensive projects rather than overreact to short-term losses like stockholder-driven U.S. firms supposedly do. We learned recently, for example, from South Korea, which in governance generally follows the Japanese model, that the Samsung Corporation intends to enter the automobile industry and is fully prepared to put up with as much as ten years of losses before it becomes profitable. Twenty years ago it was the Russian gas pipeline that Deutsche Bank financed. That's the kind of deep-pocketed, far-sighted approach that German bank-driven corporate governance is supposed to provide. But in the MG case, it certainly didn't, as I will try to show.

Let me hasten to reassure you, however, that I am not going to walk you through the MG episode step by step. The story is much too complicated for that, and I have already written three articles on the case (some over twenty pages long with more than fifty footnotes), jointly with my coauthor Christopher Culp. Those interested in the fine details can find a good statement of our position in the February 1995 issue of the *Zeitschrift für Bankrecht und Bankwirtschaft.*

Reduced to simplest terms, MG's U.S. subsidiary MGRM sold forward delivery contracts for up to ten years at fixed prices for heating oil and gasoline in the central United States. MGRM's gross profit margin at the time the contracts were first entered was equivalent to about $3 a barrel of crude. MGRM, as virtually the sole such contractor in the market, could get deals that profitable because its customers were willing to pay a substantial premium for guaranteed price and delivery. But while the expected return on the contracts was substantial, MGRM was exposed to the risk that prices might take off sometime during the life of the contracts. During the Gulf War, for example, prices rose to nearly $40 a barrel.

So, quite sensibly, MGRM *hedged* that price level risk, allowing it thereby to concentrate on managing the so-called "basis risk" of its marketing/delivery business while remaining essentially "market neutral." The hedging strategy MGRM chose for neutralizing the overall market risk was a one-for-one "stack and roll" hedge based on short-term futures or their equivalents. That is not the kind of hedge likely to be recommended by your average U.S. professor of finance, of course, but contrary to what you may have been hearing from some of them, it was nevertheless a perfectly valid hedging procedure for a firm like MGRM.

U.S. finance professors typically see corporate hedging not as part of a basis management program, but as intended to *minimize* the cash-flow variability and hence the costs of possible "financial distress" for stand-alone firms with independent outside creditors. But MGRM, of course, was not a stand-alone firm with independent outside creditors. It was the U.S. subsidiary of MG AG, a firm in the classic, German bank-dominated, big business mold. The principal creditor *and* principal stockholder of MG AG was Deutsche Bank. No matter how hard and how often Deutsche Bank tries to deny it, MGRM was always regarded in the U.S. oil trade as bankrolled by Deutsche Bank. Otherwise, MGRM's futures and swaps counterparties would never have let it take on the positions it did.

Finance professors also insist MGRM should have done a so-called "strip" or maturity-matched hedge rather than a stack and roll. That would, indeed, have eliminated any basis risk, assuming, of course, that appropriate, low-cost futures and swaps of up to ten years tenor had been available (which they were not). But MGRM was trying to *manage* basis risk, not eliminate it. After all, if the requisite, low-cost long-term hedging vehicles were readily at hand, the customers wouldn't have needed MGRM. They could have hedged their delivery requirements directly!

An amusing sidelight on that point is that *current* MG management, anxious to show how much they have improved the way the company is being run, has cut the forward contract lives back down from ten years to the much shorter tenors for which strip hedges would be available via futures. Fine. That means their strategy will pass academic tests, all right. But they haven't yet found any *demand* for such short-term contracts. And they aren't likely to.

MGRM's stack and roll hedge did protect the company against price rises, even our most extreme critics accept that, but it also involved substantial cash drains for margin payments when prices fell, as they did in the autumn of 1993. By December 6, 1993, those cash drains had reached close to $1 billion and the governance machinery of MGRM faced its challenge.

Any of three rational management responses might have been taken at that point. First, the program could have been kept going with Deutsche Bank putting in whatever additional funds were needed. That, after all, is the presumed strength of the German bank-dominated governance system: it doesn't overreact to temporary, short-term difficulties. If the program is sound for the long run, you persist. You ride it out.

A truly farsighted management would have said at that point: oil prices have indeed been falling lately and that has required us to put up $1 billion or so in margin payments to maintain the stack. But we are *hedged*, after all. We have forward delivery contracts with our customers and those contracts go *up* in value when prices fall.

Admittedly, that offsetting increase in the value of the contracts is harder to see than the decrease in the value of the futures. You get a statement *every day* from the futures exchange telling you where you stand. Even a junior accountant can see that; he just adds up the bills. But for an MGRM-style combined delivery/hedging program, it takes farsightedness to see that the cash drains are only temporary and will flow back over time as deliveries are made on the forward contracts.

It's true, of course, that the hedge strategy used also involved substantial rollover costs—which were averaging about $20 million a month in 1993. But, once again, a truly farsighted management would have realized that always happens when prices fall and that rollover costs become rollover gains when prices rise. In fact, if you look over the whole history of oil prices, as a farsighted management is supposed to do, you would find that rollovers in oil don't just tend to average out to zero over time: the gains actually predominate. And there are good economic reasons for that asymmetry—for the so-called "backwardation" in oil prices.

The current management claims now that they didn't ride it out in December because they decided it wasn't a sound long-run program. But I'm afraid that won't wash. If the program wasn't sound in December, it wasn't sound in June either when a new supervisory board took over. If they believed the program was unsound, it should have been ended at that point. The new supervisory board says *now* that the program really *was* unsound in June as well, but that they were deceived about its true prospects by the previous management board. That won't wash either, however. Unless a German supervisory board is just so much symbolic window dressing, its job is *not* to be deceived.

Just look, for example, at what happened at Barings when the Dutch bank ING took over. They fired the whole top management, not because those managers were directly responsible for Nick Leeson's actions. ING recognized that top management didn't know what Nick Leeson was up to. But they *should* have known. And because they didn't know or try to find out, they're gone.

One possibility, then, was to continue the combined hedging/delivery program, but I know how hard it can be, psychologically, for any new management that had not fathered the program initially to have to report losses, even temporary losses. That's why I expect most U.S. managements, in the same circumstances, would probably have tried to sell off MGRM, or at least to sell its portfolio of forward contracts, which were worth a lot of money in December 1993 after spot prices had fallen by another $5 or so. By then the gross profit margin in those contracts would have been roughly $8 a barrel or more. At 150 million barrels, that comes to a sizeable amount.

The current management, of course, insists there were no buyers for the firm at any reasonable price. But there never are if you try to unload something in a hurry. You have to take your time to search out the best-positioned buyers and you have to work out the terms carefully. That's what good, responsible managements are paid to do, after all, especially the supposedly ultra-patient German managements we've heard so much about.

But how could the new management buy time when oil prices might fall even further and increase the cash drains for margin payments? Actually, a fairly simple and straightforward strategy was at hand that could have stanched the cash drain and bought time: buy put options on oil. That might have cost a couple hundred million dollars or so—roughly what they had to put in later for the restructuring—but would at least have eliminated any risk of further price declines while negotiations to sell the business were going on. There is evidence, in fact, that just such a suggestion was made to the new management by the old derivatives staff at MGRM. But the new management dismissed it out of hand.

Another possibility for ending the program, rather than funding it for the long term, would have been to do a piece by piece unwind, as is normally done when liquidating a swap book. That is, MGRM could have gone to each of its long-term customers in turn and said: because prices have fallen, you are now substantially out-of-the-money on your delivery commitments. We'll let you buy yourself out of the deal at essentially the present value of those commitments. Then, as each customer bought itself out, the proportionate fraction of the hedge would be liquidated. I'm not arguing here, of course, that they *should* have adopted that strategy. It would have taken a lot of costly negotiation, particularly since the customers would know MGRM was under pressure to unwind. I personally think that they would have been far better off to have sold the whole firm outright. But the piece by piece unwind was surely one of the three rational possibilities facing the firm.

Instead, of course, MG did none of the above. They adopted the worst strategy possible. They liquidated more than half the hedge in December at the bottom of the market. And then in January and February when prices started to go back up, they suddenly realized that they were now exposed on the forward contracts. So to bring the forwards and the hedge back into line, they *canceled* a big chunk of the outstanding contracts. That is, they demanded no compensation whatever from their out-of-the-money customers who they let walk away from their contracts. In U.S. finance jargon, we call that "leaving money on the table" whereas in Germany they call it "throwing money out of the window." But it's the same thing.

That's not the end of the tale. Once the current management realized they were vulnerable for having canceled contracts without compensation, they came up with the story that the contracts canceled were really not worth anything. They were just the so-called firm-flexible contracts, and they were valued, in the recent "independent" auditors special report not just at zero, but *at less than zero*. The stockholders, according to the company, thus actually benefitted from canceling these worthless contracts, though if they continue to argue that way, they may someday have to answer to our regulators for peddling what looks like toxic waste to their customers.

Whether the so-called independent auditors who provided these estimates really were independent and unbiased is something I don't intend to go into further here. Suffice it to say only that their figures for the value of the firm-flexible contracts (and of the firm-fixed contracts as well) are presented without any calculation or documentation. They are simply given *ex cathedra*.

Surely, one can always imagine *some* set of assumptions that would justify the auditors' figures. Perhaps we will get to see them and scrutinize them in the course of one of the MG trials now pending in the United States. But one would never see them in Germany in the normal course of events. The banks have no interest in having their mistakes discussed in public. Which brings me to what I see as the real, and ultimately fatal flaw in bank-dominated German corporate governance: whatever the original good intentions, the German governance system seems to have evolved into what electrical engineers call a closed-loop system—a system that runs entirely on its own internal momentum with no outside direction or correction whatever.

Many have recognized the dangers in this kind of purely self-contained corporate governance system, but have accepted it in the belief that entrusting the management of big business to the banks is the only way to solve the underinvestment problem—the problem of financing big projects with great long-run potential, but difficult short-term prospects. The development of German heavy industry in the nineteenth century is always cited in defense of the German governance model, but that development took place a long time ago and in a very different environment.

The more serious current problem in a mature economy like Germany these days is likely to be less MG-type problems than the *overinvestment* problem in which entrenched managements, subject to little outside scrutiny, continue to squander vast sums of capital on low return projects to maintain the size of their fiefdoms rather than return the funds to the market.

In the United States, we have that problem too, needless to say, but we also have a variety of mechanisms for keeping that kind of waste under some control—ranging from pressures on the management by pension funds and other large shareholders to hostile takeovers in which the managers are displaced. But no such solutions exist in Germany, thanks to the scheme of corporate governance and especially to the system of cross-holdings of shares and bank holdings of shares that have been allowed to grow up around it. In the case of MG, for example, Deutsche Bank directly held 10% of the shares. But another big chunk was held by Daimler Benz of which Deutsche Bank holds a big chunk and so on through Allianz and right down the line to individual shareholders who deposit their proxies with Deutsche Bank. That's why Christopher Culp and I have always used the words MG AG and Deutsche Bank interchangeably in our papers even though that has led some in Germany to claim we don't really understand how a German supervisory board is supposed to work.

A supervisory board, we are told, even if it does hold virtually all the shares, cannot legally intervene in the day-to-day operation of the firm. That is the exclusive domain of the management board. So even if the supervisory board, that is, Deutsche Bank, wanted to fire the old management of MG AG, it couldn't. Unless, of course, there was a crisis requiring urgent intervention by the supervisory board.

But if it takes a crisis for the controlling shareholder to replace its own chosen management people, then you don't have to be a cynic to believe that "crises" are going to be a fairly common by-product of German corporate governance. In fact, some people believe that is precisely what happened in the MG case. Deutsche Bank, for whatever reason, wanted to replace the previous management board, and precipitated a crisis to do it.

Despite all the legal hairsplitting, the big banks in Germany really do have *de facto*, if not literally *de jure* control over German corporate management. The corporate governance question thus ultimately comes down to who governs the banks. And, on that count, I must tell you of one of my German students who is currently writing a paper on the subject of German cross-holdings of corporate shares. To find out who really owns what, he has been constructing and solving sets of simultaneous equations in which Deutsche Bank owns part of Daimler and Daimler owns part of Deutsche Bank and so on.

He came in one day last week very agitated, and said: "I think I have finally figured out who owns Deutsche Bank. It's Deutsche Bank!" I can't say at this point whether that's literally true or not. Student calculations always have to be checked, several times in fact. But it's certainly true in principle. The ultimate control of the hundreds of billions of German wealth lies in the hands of a small, self-selected and self-perpetuating group of bankers accountable really only to themselves.

If that system really does somehow select the best and the brightest bankers for the job and if they perform their supervision effectively, then the country will prosper. For the sake of German big business, I certainly hope so. But Germany is leaving itself woefully overconcentrated in management styles and in access to resources. In the United States, at least, we've never been ready to take those kinds of risks with *our* economic future. We trust markets and competition more than bankers. And I don't think the MG case is going to lead us to change our minds.

A talk given at the University of Munich, June 12, 1995.

14

Alternative Strategies for Corporate Governance in China

Reforming the large state-owned enterprises in China is, in my view, essential to the country's long-run development, not just for reasons of microeconomic efficiency of the kind I'll be discussing later, but for reasons of macroeconomic stability as well. Much of the net cash drain currently incurred by unprofitable state enterprises—and the reports we get suggest there are many—shows up as part of the central government's fiscal deficit. To the extent that loans from the central bank are used either to finance that deficit or to finance the company losses directly, higher price inflation is the inevitable consequence.

Given the revenue-raising options available to the central government currently, of course, inflation may well be the lowest-cost strategy for filling the fiscal deficit gap. But it is not a low-cost strategy in any absolute sense. It can lead to substantial waste of national efforts and resources—wastes that will be compounded if the authorities succumb to the temptation of imposing price controls. Price controls not only won't succeed for any length of time in holding inflation in check, but will actually make matters worse by weakening incentives to produce and by fostering corruption.

Reform and restructuring of the state enterprises is thus essential for reducing inflationary pressures, but will certainly not be easy, given that many of what we think of as the large, money-losing state enterprises are really *cities*, not business firms. The purely business parts of the enterprise must somehow be separated from the schools, housing, and other municipal services now provided so that each piece of the enterprise can be managed and financed separately. How to achieve the separation is a task I must leave to the other speakers at this conference. I propose to focus instead on another class of problems related to reform and re-structuring, but closer to my own specialty area of financial economics. Reform amounts essentially to choosing a strategy for what economists call "corporate governance." How do you make sure that the enterprise managers get the funds they need for sound, *profitable* projects, but not more funds than that? What standards or criteria should the managers follow in running the business? Who will decide whether the managers really are being successful in their use of the corporate resources, and if not, who replaces them with better managers?

To avoid getting your expectations too high, however, let me assure you immediately that no universally accepted solution to this corporate governance problem yet exists. The topic is currently the focus of much controversy, not just in the United States, but in many other countries as well. On this occasion, I can really do little more than sketch out for you in very broad brush strokes some of the main lines of that huge volume of research. Think of my remarks then, not as a comprehensive survey, but as more in the spirit of an ancient Chinese watercolor in which just a few bold lines and dots seek to describe a bird perched on the branch of a willow tree.

The current lack of consensus about the best form of corporate governance may actually be good news on the whole for China. At this early stage of the reform process, China may still be able to pick those governance features that best suit its current needs, without locking in features that may become a drag on the economy when it reaches maturity.

In highlighting corporate governance, moreover, I do not mean to suggest that deciding on a governance strategy is the *only* major hard problem you have to look forward to. You will also have to develop efficient, low-cost procedures for speedily reorganizing bankrupt firms or recycling their useable assets when the firm must be liquidated. And you will have to develop a system of corporate profits taxation that does not distort investment and financing incentives. None of these are easy or already-solved problems, alas, and you will have a bewildering variety of conflicting models from which to choose. But choose you must, and the sooner you start exploring your options, the better.

THE MAIN CORPORATE GOVERNANCE MODELS

When it comes to governance, you will find in Western economies, if you will pardon my oversimplification, two main governance model types: the Japanese/German bank-driven model and the U.S./British stockholder-driven model. Under the Japanese/German model of big-business governance, a large bank typically serves both as a leading creditor *and* a major, if not actually a controlling, shareholder. Because the bank provides so much of the funding and owns so much of the stock, the lead bank, for all practical purposes, picks the senior management. And while usually giving the managers considerable autonomy over day-to-day operating decisions, the lead bank maintains a close general supervisory role over the entire business.

Under the U.S. system, by contrast, banks cannot hold equity stakes, and certainly not controlling stakes, in ordinary corporations, except temporarily, when they receive some equity in exchange for their loans in the course of a reorganization in bankruptcy. And even then, they must quickly get rid of the equity thrust upon them. Although creditor banks can surely exert some influence over management, the responsibility for selecting and replacing managers rests with the board of directors, who are technically the representatives of the stockholders and are elected by them.

Despite the impressive records of growth by both Japan and Germany in the years since World War II, and despite the seemingly slow growth of the United States recently, China would be well advised to survey the strengths and weaknesses of each approach before committing irrevocably to either one. The presumed great strength of the German/Japanese system has always been that it solves what has come to be called the *underinvestment problem.*

In corporate governance we are concerned with the problems of underinvesting in high-return projects and of overinvesting in low-return prospects. Because the bank in Germany and Japan is an insider, not an outsider, and because the bank participates from the outset in setting the firm's strategy, the managers of the firm can presumably take a long-term view of capital-intensive investments promising high, but deferred payoffs. American firms, of course, could, in principle, obtain the same amount of funds by selling securities on the public capital markets. But in convincing outside investors of the project's profitability, they run the risk of disclosing key elements of their strategy to their competitors. And if the project, once it gets under way, runs into temporary, short-term difficulties, the outside investors may misinterpret the events. The company's stock price may plunge and lead to a change in management. In the face of these risks, plus the ever-present possibility of bankruptcy if outside financial support dries up, the high-return project might never be undertaken and the valuable opportunity would be lost. That, of course, is precisely why we speak of an "underinvestment" problem.

The literature is filled with examples of how Japanese and German governance supposedly overcomes this underinvestment problem. During Japan's glory years, in particular, we heard over and over again that big projects require deep pockets and especially the assurance that funding won't be suddenly cut off in midstream.

THE OVERINVESTMENT PROBLEM

But even if the close bank tie does help German and Japanese firms to overcome the underinvestment problem, the seemingly unlimited access to funds that the bank tie seems to offer can often give rise to the opposite, or overinvestment, problem. As is now all too painfully clear in Japan, many firms there have invested in overly capital-intensive factories that will never come close to recovering their initial capital, let alone show a positive rate of return. I won't even mention the trillions of yen poured into land and office buildings both at home and abroad. Japanese firms, during the heyday of the 1980s, sometimes almost seemed to be proceeding as if their cost of capital were zero or close to it. And if the interest rate you use for discounting future values is low enough, almost any scheme, no matter how harebrained, can seem like a sure winner.

To suggest that the German/Japanese governance model is particularly vulnerable to overinvestment is not to say, of course, that the U.S. model is completely safe from the same flaw. It clearly is not. In fact, the overinvestment problem was first identified in a classic study of U.S. corporate governance by Adolph Berle and Gardiner Means in the 1930s. Berle and Means called attention to the gap between ownership and control that had developed in big U.S. business corporations especially during the 1920s (a period of rapid economic growth, much like China is currently experiencing), and during which most of the now familiar, but then newly formed U.S. business giants, like IBM, General Electric, and General Motors, sold huge quantities of common stock to the public. (I might mention, in this connection, that the Ford Motor Company, another well-known automobile giant, was an important exception to the standard, shareholder-owned model. Ford was a *family-owned* corporation until well into the 1960s with relatively few outside shareholders. (Henry Ford also disliked bankers as much as he disliked outside shareholders. He successfully financed his firm's growth entirely from internal cash sources, but like many other great entrepreneurs, he failed to solve the problem of managerial succession.)

Although sales of shares to outside investors proved a major source of growth capital for firms like General Motors in the 1920s, Berle and Means pointed out that the sheer multitude of such investors, and their dispersal around the country—around the world, in fact—meant that a self-selected and self-perpetuating group of managers and not the stockholders really controlled the corporation. The managers had virtually complete and uncontested discretion over how to use the cash flows generated from the company's operations. And it was this control that could lead to overinvestment. Rather than pay the funds as dividends (and raising any capital for new investment by floating new securities on the market), the managers could and did simply reinvest the proceeds in the firm as they saw fit.

Though Berle and Means in the 1930s, and many academic critics since then, have seen managements' right to divert the firm's "free cash flow" away from dividends as potentially harmful to the shareholders who supposedly own the firm, it is important to remember that this needn't always be the case. If the investments funded by the earnings not paid out in dividends had earned returns higher than the opportunity cost of capital—that is, higher than the stockholders could have earned on their own investments—then the shareholders needn't have suffered any financial loss at all. The profitably retained earnings would show up in higher stock prices—in capital gains, as they are called—which would actually have been better than cash dividends for many shareholders given the normally very favorable treatment of capital gains under U.S. income tax laws. (Incidentally, a decision about how to treat capital gains under the income tax is another one that China will eventually have to make.)

Although the capital gains from the reinvested earnings *might* offset the reduced dividends if management had invested the funds wisely, Berle and Means and subsequent critics pointed out that nothing guaranteed that outcome. Managers really had little incentive to make the best possible use of the shareholders' funds. Why take chances and risk losing your job and your corporate perrequisites when the benefits of your boldness would mostly accrue to others? Risk aversion and mediocrity, in sum, become the order of the day when ownership is separated from management. Or worse: the managers might simply divert the free cash flow to build up their own private kingdoms, using the profits on any winning entities in the conglomerate to subsidize the losers—earning just enough in the aggregate, perhaps, to keep the shareholders from revolting, but far from enough to represent maximum shareholder value. The stockholders, and the country as a whole, would thus be better served if entrenched, mediocre managers kept for their own firms less of the cash proceeds generated, returning those proceeds instead to the capital market via dividends or share repurchase where the funds could be recycled to higher-return ventures.

MANAGERIAL INCENTIVES
AND THE OVERINVESTMENT PROBLEM

Although this problem of corporate overinvestment and cross-subsidization of low-profit potential lines of business was first identified by studying U.S. corporations, it is a universal managerial problem found in China's own state-owned enterprises, and, as I indicated earlier, in Germany and Japan as well. In fact, I would argue that it's actually worse in Germany and Japan than in United States. The board of directors of U.S. corporations, thanks to the vigorous stock market environment in which U.S. big-business firms must operate, have more "control levers" at their disposal than their German and Japanese counterparts for rewarding managers who can (and for punishing managers who can't) earn returns on their investments greater than the opportunity cost of the funds invested. Thanks to craftily constructed stock options tied to relative stock market returns, managers' incentives in the United States can be much more precisely fine-tuned to performance than under competing system of governance.

Under the German, bank-dominated system, it is true, the managers have less opportunity to waste the company's cash flow. The banks directly and indirectly supply more of the client firm's capital and collect more of the client firm's cash flow via interest payments. The bank then reallocates the cash flow to one or another of its client firms, acting in effect, as a very personal substitute for the impersonal judgment of the market.

Of course, if a country has smart enough and dedicated enough bankers, the system might work tolerably well. But what if they weren't smart? And how would anyone in Germany ever know? The controlling German bankers, after all, are a closed society. The banks all own each others stock. The bankers serve on each other boards; they all know each other personally and, like the close friends they are, they all stand ready to cover up each others mistakes. Because they never have to face an outside judgment, no one can ever tell for sure how good or bad their investment decisions really are.

The Japanese system has many of the same, unfortunate, closed-loop control features as the German one, though the stock market plays a somewhat larger role in Japan than in Germany. The role is only somewhat larger, however, because the frequent market interventions by the Ministry of Finance impart a significant arbitrariness to stock prices as a basis for compensation. Rewards for superior performance are thus hard to structure.

But what is worse, the German and Japanese systems serve to insulate banks and their managers from what many observers regard as the most potent challenge incumbents can face: the hostile takeover. Thanks to the extensive cross-holdings of corporate shares—which act like mutual exchanges of hostages—hostile takeovers are virtually unknown in both Germany and Japan. They are actually not as frequent in the United States as some foreign observers seem to believe, but at least the threat is always there. And despite anti-takeover devices of various kinds, not even giants like IBM or General Motors can consider themselves safely immune from ultimate outside discipline. Both companies, in fact, have been forced by takeover threats (and by intense product-market competition) into major downsizing and restructuring in recent years.

Such then, as I see it, are the two main approaches to governance: relying on the capital markets, and especially on a free and vigorous stock market, for evaluating, rewarding and punishing big business managers, or bypassing the capital markets and leaving the task to a closed and self-perpetuating community of bankers and managers.

Because I think you know by now where I stand on the issue, I will end my remarks on that note. I am sure that many of you will feel that, like most economic theorists, I have spent too much time talking about purely imaginary worlds—without telling you how to get there. Fortunately, others at this conference who you will be hearing from *are* concerned with how you get there.

Keynote address given at the Conference on Reformability of the State Sector in China, sponsored by the Chinese Economic Association and the Shanghai Academy of Social Sciences, Shanghai, China, July 19, 1995.

15

Leverage

Under the terms of Alfred Nobel's will, the Prizes were to be awarded for an "important discovery or invention." Let it be clear from the outset, therefore, that my case must be one of the former, not the latter. Contrary to what you may have read in some press accounts following the announcement of the 1990 Nobel Prizes in Economic Sciences, I am not the coinventor of the leveraged buyout—the transaction that perhaps more than any other has come to symbolize the supposed financial excesses of the 1980s. Leveraged buyouts (LBOs), in which the younger, active managers of a firm borrowed the funds to buy the controlling shares from a firm's retired founder (or from his estate) were an established feature of the corporate landscape long before Franco Modigliani, the 1985 laureate, and I published our first joint paper on leverage and the cost of capital in 1958. The LBOs of the 1980s differed only in scale, in that they involved publicly held rather than privately held corporations and in that the takeovers were often hostile.

That Franco Modigliani and I should be credited with inventing these takeovers is doubly ironic since the central message of our M&M Propositions was that the value of the firm was independent of its capital structure. Subject to one important qualification to be duly noted below, you couldn't hope to enhance shareholder value merely by leveraging up. Investors would not pay a premium for corporate leverage because they could always leverage up their own holdings by borrowing on personal account. Despite this seemingly clear prediction of the M&M analysis, the LBOs of the 1980s were routinely reporting premiums to the shareholders of more than 40%, running in some cases as high as 100% and all this, mind you, even after the huge fees the deal-making investment bankers were extracting.

The qualification to the M&M value-invariance proposition mentioned earlier concerns the deductibility of interest payments under the unintegrated U.S. corporate income tax. That deductibility can lead, as we showed in our 1963 article, to substantial gains from leveraging under some conditions, and gains of this tax-driven kind have undoubtedly figured both in the rise of corporate debt ratios generally in the 1980s and in some recent LBOs and voluntary restructurings in particular. But after netting out the offsetting tax costs of leveraged capital structures (such as those discussed in my 1977 paper "Debt and Taxes" and its follow-up literature), tax savings alone cannot plausibly account for the observed LBO premiums.

CORPORATE LEVERAGING

Leveraged Buyouts: Where the Gains Came From

The source of the major gains in value achieved in the LBOs of the 1980s lies, in fact, not in our newly recognized field of finance at all, but in that older, and long-established field of economics, industrial organization. Perhaps industrial reorganization might be an apter term. Mikhail Gorbachev, the 1990 Peace Prize Winner, may have popularized the term *perestroika*, but the LBO entrepreneurs of the 1980s actually did it, and on a scale not seen since the early years of this century when so much of what we think of as big business was being put together by the entrepreneurs of consolidation like J. P. Morgan and John D. Rockefeller.

That the LBO entrepreneurs have achieved substantial real efficiency gains by reconcentrating corporate control and redeploying assets has been amply documented in a multitude of academic research studies. (See Kaplan 1989.) But this basically positive view of LBOs and takeovers is still far from universally accepted among the wider public. Some are reacting to the layoffs and factory closings that have sometimes followed hostile takeovers, although far more of both have occurred in our automobile industry which has so far been immune from takeovers. Others worry that these short-run gains may represent merely the improvident sacrifice of opportunities for high, but long deferred future profits—an argument presuming among other things that the market cannot properly compute discounted present values. Even more fear that the real efficiency gains, if any, will be more than offset by the collateral damage from the financial leveraging used to bring about the restructuring.

The Problems of Corporate Leveraging: Real or Imagined?

These fears will be the main focus of this lecture. The statutes of the Nobel Foundation stipulate that the subject of the Nobel Lecture "should be on or associated with the work for which the prize was awarded," which, in my case means the M&M propositions. Rather than simply reviewing them, however, or discussing the subsequent research they have inspired (a task already undertaken in Miller 1988), I propose here instead to show how those propositions bear on current concerns about overleveraging—concerns that in some quarters actually border on hysteria. In particular, I will argue, first, that the highly visible losses and defaults on junk bonds do not mean that overleveraging did in fact occur; second, paradoxical as it may sound, that increased leveraging by corporations does not imply increased risk for the economy as a whole; third, that the financial distress being suffered by some highly leveraged firms involves mainly private, not social costs; and finally, that the capital markets have built-in controls against overleveraging—controls, moreover, very much in evidence at the moment. Recent efforts by our regulators to override these built-in market mechanisms by destroying the junk bond market and by imposing additional direct controls over leveraged lending by banks will thus have all the unintended consequences normally associated with such regulatory interventions. They will lower efficiency and raise costs (in this case, the cost of capital) to important sectors of our economy.

That the current emphasis on the evils of overleveraging may be misplaced does not mean, of course, that all is well. My message is not: "Relax. Be happy. And, don't worry." Worry we should, in the United States at least, but about the serious problems confronting us, such as our seeming inability to bring government spending under rational control or to halt the steady deterioration of our once-vaunted system of public education. Let us not waste our limited worrying capacity on second-order and largely self-correcting problems like financial leveraging.

I hope I will be pardoned for dwelling in what follows almost exclusively on examples in the United States. It's just that a particularly virulent strain of the anti-leverage hysteria seems to have struck us first. Perhaps others can learn from our mistakes.

THE PRIVATE AND SOCIAL COSTS OF CORPORATE LEVERAGING

The charge that the United States became overleveraged in the 1980s will strike some as perhaps too obvious to require any extensive documentation. What could offer more compelling evidence of the overissuance of debt than the defaults of so many junk-bond issuers in late 1989, with news of additional or pending defaults now almost a daily occurrence?

Junk Bonds as Just Another Risky Security

To argue in this all too natural way, however, is to put too much emphasis on the word "bond" and not enough on the word "junk." Bonds are, indeed, promises to pay. And certainly the issuers of the bonds hoped to keep those promises. But if the firm's cash flow, for reasons competitive or cyclical, fails to cover the commitments, then the promises cannot be kept, or at least not kept in full.

The buyers of the junk bonds, of course, also *hoped* that the promises would be kept. But they clearly weren't counting on it! For all save the most hopelessly gullible, the yields *expected* on junk bonds (in the Markowitz sense of yield outcomes weighted by probability of occurrence) were below the nominal or promised yields. The high promised yields that might be earned during the good years were understood as compensation for the possible bad years in time and bad bonds in the total junk bond portfolio. The high nominal yields, in short, were essentially risk premiums. In 1989, for many of the junk bonds issued earlier, the risk happened.

Although the presumption in finance is that defaults represent bad outcomes *ex post*, rather than systematic misperception of the true *ex ante* odds, as seems to be the conventional view, that presumption cannot yet be established conclusively. The time series of rates of return on junk bonds is still too short for judging whether those returns are indeed anomalously too low (or perhaps even anomalously too high) relative to accepted asset-pricing models like those of my colaureate William Sharpe and his successors. Few such anomalous asset classes have so far been identified; and nothing in the nature of high-yield bonds strongly suggests that they will wind up on that short list.

Some may question the fairness of my treating these realized risks on junk bonds as essentially exogenous shocks, like earthquakes or droughts. Surely, they would contend, the very rise of corporate leverage that the junk bonds represent must itself have increased the total risk in the economy. On that point, however, modern finance in general and the M&M propositions in particular offer a different, and in many respects, a counterintuitive perspective.

Does Increased Corporate Leverage Add to Society's Risk?

Imagine that you, as a venerable academic professor of finance, are in a dialogue with an equally grizzled corporate treasurer who believes, as most of them probably do, that leveraging *does* increase total risk. "You will surely concede, Professor," he is likely to begin, "that leveraging up the corporate capital structure will make the remaining equity riskier. Right?" "Right," you say. A company with a debt/equity ratio of one, for example, earning a 20% rate of return on its underlying assets and paying 10% on its bonds, which, of course, have the first claim on the firm's earnings, will generate an enhanced 30% rate of return for its equity holders. Should the earning rate on the underlying assets decline by 25%, however, to 15%, the rate of return on equity will fall by an even greater extent (33 ⅓% in this case). That, after all, is why we use the graphic term leverage (or the equally descriptive term "gearing" that the British seem to prefer). And this greater variability of prospective rates of return to leveraged shareholders means greater risk, in precisely the sense used by my colleagues here, Harry Markowitz and William Sharpe.

That conceded, the corporate treasurer goes on to ask rhetorically: "And, Professor, any debt added to the capital structure must, necessarily, be riskier debt, carrying a lower rating and bearing a higher interest rate than on any debt outstanding before the higher leveraging. Right?" "Right," you again agree, and for exactly the same reason as before. The further a claimant stands from the head of the line at payoff time, the riskier the claim.

Now the treasurer moves in for the kill. "Leveraging raises the risk of the equity and also raises the risk of the debt. It must, therefore, raise the total risk. Right?" "Wrong," you say, preparing to play the M&M card. The M&M propositions are the finance equivalents of conservation laws. What gets conserved in this case is the risk of the earning stream generated by the firm's operating assets. Leveraging or deleveraging the firm's capital structure serves merely to partition that risk among the firm's securities holders.[1]

To see where the risk goes, consider the following illustrative example. Suppose a firm has ten securities holders of whom five hold the firm's bonds and the remaining five hold equal shares in the firm's leveraged equity. Suppose further that the interest due on the five bonds is covered sufficiently for those bonds to be considered essentially riskless. The entire risk of the firm must thus be borne by the five shareholders who will, of course, expect a rate of return on their investment substantially higher than on the assumed riskless bonds. Let two of the common stockholders now come to feel that their share of the risks is higher than they want to bear. They ask to exchange their stockholdings for bonds, but they learn that the interest payments on the two additional bonds they will get in exchange could not be covered in all possible states of the world. To avoid diluting the claims of the old bondholders, the new bonds must be made junior to the old bonds. Because the new bonds are riskier, the two new bondholders will expect a rate of return higher than on the old riskless bonds, but a rate still less, of course, than on their original, and even higher-risk holdings of common stock. The *average* risk and the average expected interest rate of the seven bondholders taken together has thus risen. At the same time, the risk assumed by the remaining three equity holders is also higher (since the two shifting stockholders now have taken a prior claim on the firm's earnings) and their expected return must rise as well. Both classes of securities are thus riskier on average, but the *total* risk stays exactly the same as before the two stockholders shifted over. The increased risk to the three remaining stockholders is exactly offset by decreased risk to the two former stockholders who have moved down the priority ladder to become junior bondholders.[2]

Leverage and the Deadweight Costs of Financial Distress

That aggregate risk might be unaffected by modest changes of leverage some might willingly concede, but not when leverage is pushed to the point that bankruptcy becomes a real possibility. The higher the leverage, the greater the likelihood, of course, that just such an unfortunate event will occur.

Actually, however, the M&M conservation of risk continues to hold, subject to some qualifications to be duly noted below, even in the extreme case of default. That result seems paradoxical only because the emotional and psychological overtones of the word bankruptcy give that particular outcome more prominence than it merits on strictly economic grounds. From a bloodless finance perspective, a default signifies merely that the stockholders have now lost their entire stake in the firm. Their option, so to speak, has expired worthless. The creditors now become the new stockholders and the return on their original debt claims becomes whatever of value is left in the firm.

The qualification to the principle of risk conservation noted earlier is that the very process of transferring claims from the debtors to the creditors can itself create risks and deadweight costs over and beyond those involved when the firm was a going concern. Some of these "costs of financial distress," as they have come to be called, may be incurred even before a default occurs. Debtors, like some poets, do not "go gentle into that good night." They struggle to keep their firms alive, even if sometimes the firm would be better off dead by any rational calculation. They are often assisted in those efforts at life support by a bankruptcy code that materially strengthens their hands in negotiations with the creditors. Sometimes, of course, the reverse can happen and over-rapacious creditors can force liquidation of firms that might otherwise have survived. About all we can safely conclude is that once the case is in bankruptcy court, all sides in these often-protracted negotiations will be assisted by armies of lawyers whose fees further eat away the pool of assets available to satisfy the claims of the creditors. For small firms, the direct costs of the bankruptcy proceedings can easily consume the entire corpus (an apt term), but they are essentially fixed costs and hence represent only a small portion of the recoveries in the larger cases. In the aggregate, of course, direct bankruptcy costs, even if regarded as complete social waste, are minuscule relative to the size of the economy.[3]

The Costs of Financial Distress: Private or Social?

Small as the aggregate deadweight costs of financial distress may be, bankruptcies can certainly be painful personal tragedies. Even so generally unadmired a public figure as Donald Trump has almost become an object of public sympathy as he struggles with his creditors for control over his garish Taj Mahal Casino. But even if he does lose, the loss will be his, not society's. The Trump casino and associated buildings will still be there (perhaps one should add, alas). The only difference will be the sign on the door: Under New Management.[4]

The social consequences of the isolated bankruptcy can be dismissed perhaps, but not, some would argue, bankruptcies that come in clusters. The fear is that the bankruptcy of each overindebted firm will send a shock wave to the firm's equally overindebted suppliers leading in turn to more bankruptcies until eventually the whole economy collapses in a heap. Neither economics generally nor finance in particular, however, offer much support for this notion of a leverage-induced "bankruptcy multiplier" or a contagion effect. Bankrupt firms, as noted earlier, do not vanish from the earth. They often continue operating pretty much as before, though with different ownership and possibly on a reduced scale. Even when they do liquidate and close down their inventory, furniture and fixtures, employees, and their customers flow to other firms elsewhere in the economy. Profitable investment opportunities that one failing firm passes up will be assumed by others, if not always immediately, then later when the economic climate becomes more favorable. Recent research in macroeconomics suggests that much of what we used to consider as output irretrievably lost in business cycles is really only output postponed, particularly in the durable goods industries.

To say that the human and capital resources of bankrupt firms will eventually be reemployed, is not to deny, of course, that the personal costs of disemployment merit consideration, particularly when they become widespread. All modern economies take steps to ease the pains of transferring human resources to other and better uses, and perhaps they should do even more. But delaying or preventing the needed movements of resources will also have social costs that can be even higher over the long run, as the economies of Eastern Europe are discovering.

The successive waves of bankruptcies in the early 1930s may seem to belie this relatively benign view of bankruptcy as a matter essentially of private costs with no serious externalities, but not really.[5] Contrary to widely held folk beliefs, bankruptcies did not bring on the Great Depression. The direction of causation runs from depressions to bankruptcies, not the other way around. The collapse of the stock market in 1929 and of the U.S. banking system during 1931–1932 may well have created the appearance of a finance-driven disaster. But that disaster was not just the inevitable bursting of another overleveraged tulip bubble as some have suggested. (Actually, recent research has cast doubt on the existence of even the *original* tulip bubble, but that is another story; see, for example, Garber 1989.) Responsibility for turning an ordinary downturn into a depression of unprecedented severity lies primarily with the managers of the Federal Reserve System. They failed to carry out their duties as the residual supplier of liquidity to the public and to the banking system. The U.S. money supply imploded by 30% between 1930 and 1932, dragging the economy and the price level down with it. When that happens even AAA credits get to look like junk bonds.

That such a nightmare scenario might be repeated under present day conditions is always possible, of course, but, until recently at least, most economists would have dismissed it as extremely unlikely. The current chairman of the Federal Reserve Board himself, as well as his staff, are known to have studied the dismal episode of the early 1930s in great depth and to be thoroughly aware of how and why their ill-fated predecessors had blundered. The prompt action by the Federal Reserve Board to support the liquidity of the banking system after the stock market crash of October 19, 1987 (and again after the mini-crash of October 13, 1989) is testimony to the lessons learned. The fear of some at the moment, however, is that both the willingness and the ability of the Federal Reserve to maintain the economy's liquidity and its credit system are being undermined by regulatory overreaction to the S&L crisis—an overreaction that stems in part from underestimating the market's internal controls on overleveraging.

THE SELF-CORRECTING TENDENCIES IN CORPORATE LEVERAGING

Just what combination of demand shifts and supply shifts triggered the big expansion in leveraged securities in the 1980s will eventually have to be sorted out by future economic historians. The main point to be emphasized here is that whether we are talking automobiles or leveraged equity or high-yield bonds the market's response to changes in tastes (or to changes in production technology) is limited and self-regulating. If the producers of any commodity expand its supply faster than the buyers want, the price will fall and output eventually will shrink. It's the same in the financial markets. If the public's demand for junk bonds is overestimated by takeover entrepreneurs, the higher interest rates they must offer to junk-bond buyers will eat into the gains from the deals. The process of further leveraging will slow and perhaps even be reversed.

Something very much like this endogenous slowing of leveraging could be discerned in early 1989 even before a sequence of government initiatives (including the criminal indictments of the leading investment bankers and market makers in junk bonds, the forced dumping of junk bond inventories by beleaguered S&Ls, and the stricter regulations on leveraged lending by commercial banks) combined to undermine the liquidity of the high-yield bond market. The issuance of high-yield bonds not only ground to a halt, but many highly-leveraged firms moved to replace their now high-cost debt with equity.[6]

Junk Bonds and the S&L Crisis

To point out that the market has powerful endogenous controls against overleveraging does not mean that who holds the highly leveraged securities is never a matter of concern. Certainly the U.S. savings and loan institutions should not have been using government-guaranteed savings deposits to buy high-risk junk bonds. But to focus so much attention on the junk bond losses of a handful of these S&Ls is to miss the main point of that whole sorry episode. The current hue and cry over S&L junk bonds serves merely to divert attention from those who expanded the government deposit guarantees and encouraged the S&Ls to make investments with higher expected returns, but alas, also with higher risk than their traditional long-term home mortgages.

Some, at the time, defended the enlargement of the government's deposit guarantee as compensation for the otherwise disabling interest-rate risks assumed by those undertaking the socially desirable task of providing fixed-rate, long-term mortgages. Quite apart, however, from the presence even then of alternative and less vulnerable ways of supplying mortgage money, the deposit guarantees proved to be, as most finance specialists had predicted at the time, a particularly unfortunate form of subsidy to home ownership. Because the deposit guarantees gave the owners of the S&Ls what amounted to put options against the government, they actually encouraged the undertaking of uneconomic long-odds projects, some of which made junk bonds look safe by comparison. The successes went to the owners; the failures to the insurance fund.

More is at stake, however, than merely assigning proper blame for these failed attempts to overrule the market's judgment that this politically powerful industry was not economically viable. Drawing the wrong moral from the S&L affair can have consequences that extend far beyond the boundaries of this ill-fated industry. The American humorist, Mark Twain, once remarked that a cat, having jumped on a hot stove, will never jump on a stove again, even a cold one. Our commercial bank examiners seem to be following precisely this pattern. Commercial banking may not quite be a cold stove at the moment, but it is, at least, a viable industry. Unlike the S&Ls, moreover, it plays a critical role in financing businesses, particularly, but not only, those too small or too little known to support direct access to the public security markets. Heavy-handed restrictions on bank loans by examiners misreading the S&L experience will thus raise the cost of capital to, and hence decrease the use of capital by, this important business sector.[7]

Whether regulatory restrictions of these and related kinds have already gone so far as to produce a "credit crunch" of the kind associated in the past with monetary contraction is a subject much being argued at the moment, but one I prefer to leave to the specialists in money and banking.

My concerns as a finance specialist are with the longer-run and less directly visible consequences of the current anti-leverage hysteria. This hysteria has already destroyed the liquidity of the market for high-yield bonds. The financial futures markets, currently under heavy attack for their supposed overleveraging, are the next possible candidates for extinction, at least in their U.S. habitats.

Many in academic finance have viewed these ill-founded attacks on our financial markets, particularly the newer markets, with some dismay. But they have, for the most part, stood aside from the controversies. Unlike some of the older fields of economics, the focus in finance has not been on issues of public policy. We have emphasized positive economics rather than normative economics, striving for solid empirical research built on foundations of simple, but powerful organizing theories. Now that our field has officially come of age, as it were, perhaps my colleagues in finance can be persuaded to take their noses out of their data bases from time to time and to bring the insights of our field, and especially the public policy insights, to the attention of a wider audience.

Nobel Memorial Prize Lecture presented at the Royal Swedish Academy of Sciences in Stockholm, December 7, 1990. © The Nobel Foundation 1990; published in the Journal of Finance, *Vol. XLVI, No. 2, June 1991. Thanks for helpful comments on an earlier draft are owed to my colleagues Steven Kaplan and Robert Vishny.*

REFERENCES

Garber, Peter, "Tulipmania." *Journal of Political Economy* 97 (June 1989): pp. 535–560.

Kaplan, Steven N., "The Effects of Management Buyouts on Operations and Value." *Journal of Financial Economics* 24 (June 1989): pp. 217–254.

Miller, Merton H. "Debt and Taxes." *Journal of Finance* 32 (May 1977): pp. 261–275.

———, "The Modigliani-Miller Propositions after Thirty Years." *Journal of Economic Perspectives* 2 (Fall 1988): pp. 99–120.

Modigliani, Franco, and Merton H. Miller, "The Cost of Capital, Corporation Finance and the Theory of Investment." *American Economic Review* 48 (June 1958): pp. 261–297.

———, "Corporate Income Taxes and the Cost of Capital: A Correction." *American Economic Review* 53 (June 1963): pp. 433–443.

Part V

Questions I'm Often Asked

16

Can China Make It?

As economists look to East Asia these days, they have to be wondering about the true growth potential for mainland China and what that growth might portend for the future of the world economy. If mainland China, for example, could duplicate over the next fifty years the progress that Taiwan has already made in the last fifty years, then mainland China would become far and away the world's leading economic power. Japan, even if it managed to stay prosperous, would become just a small and rapidly aging island country playing a role roughly comparable that of Switzerland in today's world.

Don't laugh. Remember that anything that *has* happened, *can* happen. Remember that at least until late Ming Dynasty times (1368–1644) China *was* far wealthier than the rest of the world combined. China boasted several thriving megacities larger than anything in the West, and supporting a much more intricate division of labor. Chinese technology then was leading in virtually every field of human activity and such flow of technology as was occurring in those days went primarily from East to West. Obviously, over the succeeding centuries China lost its once overwhelming lead, though the reasons why Chinese economic development seems to have hit a brick wall are still the subject of much controversy. Some of the blame can surely be placed on the cycle of wars, invasions, and political instability throughout the nineteenth century (including a virtually brain-dead imperial household and bureaucracy), followed by more invasions, civil wars, and cultural revolutions in the twentieth century. But all that is behind us now, and, we can begin seriously at last to consider whether China really *can* regain its former position as the world's leading economy. Clearly China *could*, by duplicating the amazing and still too little appreciated growth record of Taiwan over the past fifty years. But is that likely? What are the essential differences and similarities in the two cases?

As for the similarities, Taiwan and the mainland surely have in common what, for want of a better term, might be called their human and cultural base, especially the great emphasis they place on what we in the United States have come to call "family values." The Chinese, of course, are by no means the only people to put such heavy stress on family values and continuity, but there aren't many other cultures that put *more* emphasis on it. On the mainland, the emphasis on family values may well have weakened somewhat during the cultural revolution, but with the dissolving of the communes after 1979, the traditional family attitudes have re-emerged with a vengeance.

The stress the Chinese put on family values shows up, among other things, in the pressure for academic and professional achievement that Chinese parents typically put on their children. To use some economics lingo, Chinese families, even with modest incomes, are prepared to make big investments in the *human capital* of their children. And both the private and social payoffs on that kind of investment are high.

As an aside on the premium on education in the Chinese tradition, I always note with wonderment every time I visit Taiwan that virtually everybody in the government, from President Lee on down is a Ph.D. Is this the modern-day counterpart of the ancient tradition of government by learned mandarins? The mainland is still far behind when it comes to administrators and industrialists with serious academic credentials, but over the last ten years the flow to western universities of talented young people—the country's future leaders, I remind you—has been quite remarkable. According to press accounts the number of mainland Chinese students, many of them in economics and business I'm happy to say, has now reached 50,000.

Critical as has been the human capital tracing to the Chinese family pressures for educational and professional achievement, we must not overlook the role of the family in the accumulation of *financial* capital as well. A society, after all, grows basically by *saving*—that is, by consuming less than its total output and by devoting those resources diverted from immediate consumption to *investment* in factories, machinery and other forms of productive capital—investments that lead to higher output and income in the future. Other things equal—and I'll be expanding on some of the necessary qualifications shortly—the larger a country's ratio of savings to income, the higher the rate of growth in the country's per capita national income—that is, essentially, the growth in its standard of living. (And the reverse is true, as well, as we have been learning in this country.)

The classic example of high saving-propelled growth is Japan, of course, but rates of saving have been of comparable magnitude in Taiwan over most of the last fifty years. The savings rate on the mainland, although perhaps not up to the 40% rate sometimes cited, is surely high even after discounting the official figures and is likely to stay that way if the country continues to grow rapidly. Nature has been kind in some ways to countries striving to grow: they must use savings to grow, but growth doesn't use it up. Successful growth creates more saving for further growth in a virtuous circle, as opposed to a vicious circle.

High domestic saving, then, is one element in the growth equation, but only one. The savings must be invested wisely and profitably, which requires entrepreneurship and, here again, the Chinese human and cultural pool is well provided. The Chinese talent for successful entrepreneurship is visible not only in Taiwan, and in Guangdong province and in the township enterprises springing up all over China, but in such nominally non-Chinese countries as Thailand, Vietnam, Singapore, and Indonesia. Most of the economic development in those countries actually traces to Chinese entrepreneurs and bankers, though that fact is not always apparent, thanks to local assimilationist laws. Businessmen in that part of the world have business cards with their names in the local language on one side and in Chinese on the other.

In fact, if the wealth of the ethnic Chinese *outside* mainland China could somehow be made into a single country, it would rank about eighth or ninth in the world, and much higher yet as a source of the foreign investment on the mainland. While the big-name U.S. firms get most of the publicity about investing in China, the real foreign investment story is the thousands of small and medium-sized factories set up and managed by the overseas Chinese. Most of their wealth, of course, traces originally to family savings, invested wisely in family banks and businesses, and with profits reinvested steadily year by year.

Family business ties, however, for all their occasional uglier side, may actually also have a further saving grace for economic growth. Unlike Hong Kong, neither Taiwan nor the mainland share the British/American "rule of law" tradition, with a well-developed system of courts offering reasonable prospects that the terms of contracts, validly entered, will in fact be enforced. The lack of such assurances vastly magnifies the risks in business and inevitably acts as a damper on sustainable economic growth. The web of interfamily business connections, however, can substitute to a considerable extent for the impersonal, and reasonably corruption-free, government-run court system that we in the West look to for settling contract disputes. (I should add that not until well into the nineteenth century was it really very different here in the West.)

Relying on private family ties rather than public-sector courts for monitoring contract performance may well be a less efficient solution, but at least it's better than the mafia-style, private-sector approach to conflict resolution that has sprung up as a substitute in Russia and which, for centuries, had been the costly alternative to public law in Sicily and the backward areas of southern Italy.

To sum up, then, Taiwan and the mainland certainly share a common pattern of cultural and family values, very conducive on the whole to economic growth. But those patterns are only *necessary* conditions for growth, not sufficient conditions. That is why it's still unclear whether the mainland can hope to duplicate Taiwan's growth.

Taking over on Taiwan fifty years ago, the Kuomintang of Chiang Kai-Chek was in some ways luckier than the government standing at the threshold of growth in Beijing today—though I'm sure it didn't seem like such good luck back then in the 1950s. But it was indeed a blessing for them to be writing on what was essentially a blank page. There was virtually no industrial or manufacturing base on the island. Taiwan was almost entirely agricultural. Mainland China too, of course, was also basically agricultural when Deng Xiao Ping began the push to growth in the late 1970s and early 1980s, but with an important difference.

In addition to agriculture, Deng and company *did* also inherit a significant industrial and manufacturing sector. Much of this sector, for course, contained old technology and was incapable of competing in the international market (or, in the worst cases, of even generating enough sales revenue to cover cost of materials). Mainland China may have had a smaller number of these surviving dinosaurs than the republics of the former Soviet Union have today, but it still had plenty of them.

The bloated state-owned enterprises, despite improvements recently, cannot be expected to contribute much to future growth. Nor is the obvious solution to be found in privatization, that word so beloved to Western economists, myself included. Quite the contrary. Remember that the big state-owned enterprises are more than just factories: they are *cities*. The factory complexes provide their labor force with schools, hospitals, roads, housing, utilities, and virtually every other social amenity. Remember also that these iron rice bowls, as they have sometimes been called, with thousands of people standing around or sweeping the floors, are also the Chinese equivalent of our Social Security and Medicare systems. For the government to start laying off millions of these pensioners—and I mean millions—is like their singing that old Country and Western parody: "You've worked for me all these years, mother dear. Now go out and work for yourself."

That's no way for a government to maintain its mandate from heaven, as they say over there. No private buyers are going to volunteer to pick up those liabilities.

For those great, hulking iron rice bowls, the urgent need in the short run is actually the opposite of privatization. Responsibility for the safety net and for the civic services must be transferred away from the conglomerates and back to the public sector. Otherwise, rational economic calculations in the business sectors of the enterprise becomes impossible. Worse yet, the tremendous budget deficits of these combined firms and cities may lead their managers to demand (and to get) protection from the competition of the newly created private sector and township enterprise firms not burdened with so much additional baggage. If so, the mainland will find it difficult to match the benign Taiwan solution, in which a nongovernment sector, growing rapidly relative to a state public sector, absorbs the huge stream of manpower flowing out of agriculture.

This process of growth by the influx of small firms—as in the Taiwan experience—is already well underway on the mainland with one curious difference. Many of the firms are technically owned by the townships or municipalities; and even more would be occurring if only the central government would get off their backs.

Are these municipal and township enterprises *public* or *private* institutions? That's hard to say. Things in China don't always fit neatly into rigid Western categories. But the key point is this: they do seem to respond to what we would call economic incentives. We are not dealing here with classic Communist command-and-control style management, like that responsible for the famous collapse of the town hall in the city of Smolensk in the early 1970s. The building collapsed because the big chandelier installed in the lobby was too heavy. Why? Because the production goals for the chandelier factory were based on the weight of the chandeliers produced. Clearly the plant manager thought he was solving a whole year's worth of his production problems by building the mother of all chandeliers. Don't laugh. We can often be just as idiotic here when we use management criteria other than economic value added.

The firms in China owned by townships and municipalities are fully aware of the problems of inappropriate business objectives that Bennett Stewart has written about at such length. (Last summer, for example, I toured one of Shanghai's textile factories and I was struck by the presence of some large and obviously very expensive German textile printing machinery. Does this make sense? I asked the factory manager. After all, China is an economy with low labor costs and high capital costs; why are you using all this labor-saving machinery? Well, he said, we *used* to be an area with low labor costs, but not any more. The really cheap labor areas are now in the countryside. We have to automate in order to stay competitive.)

The growing fringe of modest-size Chinese enterprise, even technically government-owned (though by local governments), is very concerned with economically rational management calculations. So much so, in fact, that to my surprise, the Chinese economists who have invited me to a conference in China this summer (for the third year running) have told me they want the Western economists to do something different this year. Instead of the usual conference where we just read learned papers to each other, they want us this year to speak with a group of real plant managers in Guandong province about the latest techniques of economic management—including especially economic value added, or EVA. Yes, they *have* heard of EVA and they were delighted to learn that I'm actually on the board of EVA. They told me to be sure to bring plenty of materials with me and to try to persuade Joel Stern, Bennett Stewart, and the rest of the EVA board to begin thinking of setting up a China branch.

Let me conclude by returning to my original question: Can China make it? My feeling is that if you mean make it over the next fifty years, that may be a bit optimistic. The problems are just too immense even without factoring in any of the accumulating social unrest being occasioned by the huge internal migration going on from the countryside to the cities. Sooner or later the Chinese authorities, whether they like it or not, will have to allow these growth-induced pressures to dissipate through electoral politics rather than through lavish resort to the police powers and conflicts in the streets. But they're likely to try everything else first.

Fifty years then may be an unlikely target date for China to catch up to where Taiwan is today, but a *hundred* years is probably not. To my Chinese friends and students I know that may seem pessimistic; but it's not really. You cannot witness, as I have, the spectacular transformation taking place in Shanghai and Beijing (and even deep in the interior at places like Kunming) without realizing that China, at last, is firmly on the road to modernity. It will just take fifty years or so longer than it took Taiwan. But what's a mere fifty years, after all, in the life of China?

An address to the EVA Association Meetings, La Quinta, California, February 18, 1996.

17

What's Really Going to Happen to Interest Rates?

I am sure I speak for my fellow Laureates in Economics when I say that the question we're asked most frequently these days is: "What's going to happen to interest rates?" Not "What's going to happen to stock prices," mind you; but what's going to happen to *interest rates.* As to the former perennial question about the stock market, apparently thirty years worth of academic research on the difficulty—some of my colleagues would say the *impossibility*—of forecasting stock prices from publicly available information has finally taken hold. People now realize that we Laureates can't really forecast stock prices, or we'd all be too rich to spend our time talking to them. But for interest rates, the presumption seems to be that *any* economist—and certainly any Nobel Laureate economist—must have some special insight into where interest rates are headed—some private nugget of wisdom that he's only too delighted to share with others.

So much a ritual has the inevitable interest rate question become, and so many times am I asked it, that I couldn't resist playing a little practical joke recently on the chairman of one of the big Japanese banks to whom I was about to be introduced. The chairman came forward to greet me, surrounded by his customary large entourage of bowing flunkies and interpreters. And I knew exactly what they had coached him to say. So I decided to beat him to the punch and I said: "Ah, Chairman Kawamatsu, how delighted to see you. What do *you* think is going to happen to interest rates?"

I could see the look of absolute panic in his eyes. I had taken *his* question and he was turning in dismay for help from his equally flustered aides.

But I realized that was too cruel a trick to play on such an important and dignified gentleman so I decided to take him off the hook before any serious face was lost by saying: *"I think interest rates are going up,"* and in the rest of this talk I'll try to explain why. (Author's note: remember, this was in the fall of 1994.)

Let me begin by emphasizing that the simple phrase "interest rates" that we toss around so casually actually refers to two related, but quite distinct animals: one that economists call the "nominal" rate and one they call the "real" rate. The real rate is the nominal rate after correction for the expected rate of inflation, a proposition I'll refer to hereafter as Irving Fisher's law in recognition of the great U.S. economist (some would say the *greatest* U.S. economist) who enunciated it in the early years of this century. If you lend someone money for a year at a nominal rate of 20% and if you expect prices to be rising over that year by 15%, by Fisher's law your expected real interest return is only 5%.

I've deliberately made the numbers in my illustration unrealistic to force you to think about your own real rates. That's the rate that counts for economic decisions. If you have a house with a mortgage of 20%, that may seem prohibitively expensive. But if prices are rising at 20%, you are actually getting your housing free. And if prices were rising even faster than nominal rates, as sometimes happens in other countries when governments try to put ceilings on interest rates, then your creditors are actually subsidizing you.

Where do real interest rates stand in the United States at the moment? That's not easy to say because unlike many other countries in the world, notably Great Britain, our politicians have steadfastly refused to issue purchasing-power adjusted bonds. (Author's note: Refused, at least, until January 1997 when inflation-protected U.S. Treasury securities finally became available.) If they were available, of course, you could not only read off the real rate of interest directly, but by subtracting the real rate from the nominal rate, you could directly measure the public's expected rate of inflation. And that's the kind of very clear and personal report card on their stewardship that our politicians and our central bankers don't like to face up to.

But while we can't get an exact reading in this country on the real rate or the expected inflation rate, we can make some reasonably good estimates by leveraging off the results for those lucky countries that *do* have inflation-adjusted government bonds. After all, thanks to that much overused term "the globalization of world financial markets," we know that forces exist to keep real rates across the world from drifting far apart. Currently, real, default-free interest rates on thirty-year government bonds in Britain are running at close to 4%; so that with U.S. thirty-year government bonds at 7.8% nominal or so, the public is projecting inflation rates over the next 30 years to be averaging somewhere between 3.5 and 4.0% a year. If, therefore, I am correct in predicting that interest rates will rise, I must be predicting either that real rates will rise above 4% or that inflation rates will rise above 3.5 to 4%, or both.

Let me focus first on the inflation rate, which in some ways is the more problematic of the two, at least for the United States. The inflation rate is a lot easier to forecast in some other countries, however, especially in the newly industrializing countries, and even in some, like Turkey, that have already made substantial progress along the road of economic development.

When I visit those countries, especially those newly emerging from communism, like Vietnam, where few of the relevant government functionaries have previously been exposed to Western-style academic economics, I always enjoy stunning the locals there with my accurate estimates of their current inflation rates, even though I may have landed there only a few hours before. There's no great trick to it really, however. It's all in a simple formula we economists have been using for centuries now, and which we call the Quantity Theory of Money. I merely ask: "How fast is your money supply growing currently?" If they say by 30% a year, then I say in my best Sherlock Holmes manner: "Your inflation rate, I presume, must then be running currently at a bit over 20% a year." An elementary deduction, really, because the Quantity Theory tells us that in a world of fully anticipated ongoing inflation, the rate of price inflation is simply the difference between the rate of monetary expansion—their 30% figure—and the rate of real economic growth, which, in those rapidly growing economies can run as high as 8% a year or more, but rarely higher than 10% for any sustained interval, even in China. And, needless to say, 30 minus 8 to 10 comes to 20 or a bit more.

Parlor tricks like that are a bit harder to pull off here in the United States at the moment, unfortunately. Money growth has been running recently at about 12% a year; real growth has been about 3.5% which together should imply an inflation rate of 8 or 9% or so—a number, of course, far above what we're actually experiencing at the moment. Why is that? Where has the old reliable Quantity Theory gone wrong?

The answer is hidden in that qualifying phrase I used earlier, "a fully anticipated, ongoing inflation." The simple Quantity Theory formula I gave you works well only when the rate of inflation stays roughly steady from year to year—20% a year, or 75% a year as in Turkey between 1980 and 1990 or perhaps even zero percent over long stretches if any country should be so blessed. But the Quantity Theory doesn't work well when rates of monetary growth change abruptly from 20%, say, to 30%; or from 10% to zero. When changes like that occur, and while they are still working their way through the system, other terms enter the Quantity Theory equation and complicate the linkage between money growth, output growth, and price inflation.

Of the several transitional affects that kept prices from surging in re-

sponse to the Fed's gunning the growth rate in the monetary base from
near zero in 1991 to 12.5% in 1992 and 1993, three temporary factors
are perhaps worth some comment. One factor was the collapse of the
monetary systems of the former communist countries after 1991 (plus the
inflationary explosions in such noncommunist countries as Brazil and Argentina in that year), which created a huge demand for dollars as a re-
placement currency. Another factor absorbing the Fed's 12.5% monetary
growth rate was the cyclical recovery of the U.S. economy (a recovery that
reached a very strong 7.5% in the last quarter of 1993). I don't mind giving credit for a normal cyclical recovery to the Clinton Administration,
provided, of course, that they're prepared to take the blame when the next
cyclical downturn occurs, as it inevitably will. But if an administration
were to accept the blame, it would be the first time. Don't count on it.

The third temporary factor absorbing the Fed's monetary expansion
was the substantial fall in short-term interest rates in 1993, which reduced
the cost to firms and households of holding larger cash balances. That
fall in rates is always attributed to the Fed's deliberate policy efforts, but
rates normally fall when an economy slips into a recession. To the Fed's
credit, however, at least it didn't resist the fall by restricting monetary
growth, which is more than can be said for Japan's central bank.

But the temporary factors that have cushioned the price impact of the
rapid monetary growth the Fed initiated in 1991 when the economy was
sliding into recession, have by now pretty much run their course. From
here on out, monetary expansion, which was still proceeding at a fairly
brisk rate until a couple of months ago, is likely to have a bigger impact
on prices. Interest rates, which reflect the market's anticipations of future
inflation rates under Fisher's law, have already begun to rise and the current consensus expects them to keep rising even further.

How can I be so sure of a current consensus for rising rates? Do I have
access to some secret polling of informed opinion? Actually, I don't have
to go around asking people what they think will happen to interest rates.
Economists have a simpler way of divining the consensus view of which
way interest rates are heading. We just turn to the table labeled Treasury
Bonds, Notes, and Bills on the financial pages of our daily newspaper.
That table, which we call the "term structure of interest rates" lists the
current market prices and yields to maturity, or interest rates, on all government (and hence default-free) securities from Treasury bills with one
week to maturity to long-term bonds maturing in 2024, thirty years from
now. To deduce the consensus view from the entries in the table we check
the difference between the market interest rates on long term and on short
term Treasury instruments. If rates on long-term bonds are lower than
on short-term Treasuries, as was the case in the early 1980s, then the consensus is that rates are going to fall. But if long rates are substantially
above short rates (or, as we say, if the term structure is sloping upwards

as it is at the moment), then the market consensus is that interest rates are likely to rise. Why this way of finding the consensus works (I'm sure it will strike many of you as close to witchcraft) is something that will have to be left for another occasion. If you happen to get trapped in a plane next to an economist on a long flight, just ask him or her to tell you about the Expectations Theory of Interest Rates.

Like any other economic forecast in this very uncertain world, the consensus view can be wrong. In fact, during the 1930s, when I was first becoming aware of economics, the term structure consensus was wrong year after year for more than ten years running. It's record over the last fifty years has been substantially better, however. While the slope of the term structure is far from infallible as a forecaster, anyone strongly disagreeing with its prediction should be armed with a good reason why.

Many in the press, and especially in the Clinton Administration, reject the consensus forecast of rising interest rates and inflation because they believe the currently still high rates of unemployment, and slack in the economy generally, will keep prices and wages from surging. These critics see inflation as caused basically by a cost push rather than by a monetary pull, at least as long as the economy stays below some critical threshold called "full employment." These critics, apparently, have forgotten the days of so-called "stagflation" in the late 1970s and early 1980s when we had both substantial inflation *and* substantial unemployment. Despite that painful episode, however, the notion still persists that high unemployment means low inflation and, more perversely yet, that higher inflation means lower unemployment.

When stated that way, the implied tradeoff between changes in rates of inflation and changes in rates of unemployment is called a Phillips curve in honor of the British (actually New Zealand) economist who first traced it out in historical data some forty years ago. Since then literally hundreds of statistical studies have been conducted to pin down the precise Phillips-curve tradeoff between higher inflation and lower unemployment. But like the fabled Loch Ness monster, many claim to have seen it, but no one yet has brought back an authenticated photograph.

The view among economists, at least at the University of Chicago, is that they never will, because no reliable and consistent *long-run* tradeoff exists between changes in inflation and changes in employment. There may, and I emphasize may, be some short run, temporary tradeoff and that possibility is fueling, though if in a somewhat roundabout way, the current consensus view that short-term interest rates are likely to be rising.

Look at it this way. Suppose you believe that a sudden and unanticipated increase in the monetary growth rate by the Fed will lower short-term interest rates and make banks more eager to extend credit. On that point, at least, we can all agree. Now suppose that the added bank credit leads the borrowing firms to expand their output and employment. That, as I indicated, is more problematic. It certainly didn't work that way in the 1930s. But for the sake of argument, suppose it does; and suppose that output increases and unemployment drops off. So far, so good.

But now comes the cruel part. There is no *long-run* Phillips curve, which means that the effect on unemployment is only temporary. If the Fed does nothing more at this point, the initial monetary stimulus will work its way slowly but steadily through the economic system, raising prices and costs at each step along the way. As prices rise, unemployment creeps back up until it's right back where it was before the whole process got started. But it's not a wash. *Unemployment* is not *permanently* lower, but *prices* are permanently *higher.*

Were that the whole story, of course, it wouldn't be all that terrible. If you chugalug down a double shot of whiskey tonight, you may get a buzz for awhile, and possibly even a mild hangover as it wears off, but you'll be okay and ready to get back to work by morning. The trouble comes when you turn to the "hair-of-the-dog" approach, and try to cut the pain of the last hangover by downing another double shot.

Similarly for any central bank that puts controlling unemployment on in its policy agenda. The rise in unemployment as the initial monetary stimulus wears off may tempt it to try still another monetary injection in the hopes of keeping its unemployment-cutting ball rolling. And then they're really in a mess. For the second and any subsequent injections have to be larger and larger to have any effect on unemployment, so that even if unemployment does stay low (and as I indicated earlier, this is by no means assured) prices will be rising, not a once-for-all jump, but as a steady, and possibly even increasing, rate of inflation. And, thanks to Irving Fisher's Law, interest rates too will be higher and possibly even rising if still higher rates of inflation are anticipated.

That, in brief (and with my pardon to my academic colleagues for some inevitable simplifications necessary to make the essentials stand out starkly) is the mechanism that underlies the current up-slope of the term structure, and its consensus forecast that interest rates are likely to rise. The market believes apparently that when push comes to shove, and the Fed has to choose, or, at least thinks it has to choose, between maintaining price stability and reducing unemployment, or at least not increasing unemployment, it will inevitably choose the latter. And that choice, in turn, gives monetary policy the worst of both possible worlds: it won't have any long-run effect on employment, but *will* guarantee a long-run nonzero rate of inflation.

But, you'll say, Alan Greenspan, our current Fed Chairman, has stated repeatedly in recent months that price stability is the Fed's overriding goal, not unemployment control. And I'm sure he believes it. But does the public really believe him? And even if it did, his term, after all, is up in a couple of years. How do they know his eventual successor will share the same views? In fact, the recent remarks by Alan Blinder, the current vice chairman of the Fed, to the effect that the Fed must be as much concerned with unemployment as with price inflation set off quite a flurry in the bond market. Understandably so, as I hope I've helped you come to see.

So what can a poor central bank head like Alan Greenspan do to make the Fed's price stability promise credible? Not much in the short run, I fear. To gain credibility, you have to do it in the old-fashioned way: you have to earn it. You have to show by your actions that you will focus on controlling inflation, and won't allow yourself to be diverted from that task by political pressures to do something about unemployment or to do something to get the economy moving again. Earning that kind of a reputation can be done, though it's not easy and takes time. The German central bank, the Bundesbank has managed to do so, and its Deutschemark has, in fact, become the prototype of the stable, hard currency, a role our own dollar once played not that many years ago. Nowadays, of course, if someone says you're sound as a dollar, you should probably call your doctor.

Why have the Germans been more successful than we as inflation fighters? Both the Bundesbank and the Fed, after all, are independent central banks, which is certainly not the case in many other countries. In countries where the central bank is just another branch of the treasury, inflation at a fairly nontrivial rate is pretty much inevitable. That's how those governments finance themselves; that is, by printing money to pay their bills, which is a form of taxation, of course, but often a less politically painful one than direct taxation or drastic cuts in government programs. I know we don't usually think of inflation as a tax. But that's what it is. It's a tax on cash balances. Each night, while you're asleep, it's as if a little angel or devil comes silently into your bedroom and takes a little bit of the hard-earned money out of your wallet or purse, and turns it over to the government. That's why the inflation tax is so popular in weak governments around the world. If they tried to collect that money by ordinary taxes, the people would beat up the tax collectors.

It may make sense for some governments to use the inflation tax as their cheapest alternative but it *does* have costs, though they're indirect. They're the resources the public wastes in figuring out ways to thwart the midnight visits of the invisible tax collectors and the collateral damage, especially social damage, that inflation inflicts on the public. And that perception of the relative painfulness of inflation and its alternatives in Germany and the United States may hold the ultimate clue to the difference in attitudes. The Germans endured a catastrophic hyperinflation in the early 1920s—a tragedy that, among other things, destroyed public confidence in democratic institutions and paved the way for Hitler. Hyperinflation thus became the obsessive nightmare of German political and economic life. Other countries, too, notably Argentina and Brazil have suffered through hyperinflation of the German kind without becoming as obsessive as the Germans, but that has been changing substantially in the last few years. The public in those countries appear to have finally had enough. The mass of poor people in those countries—and that's the bulk of the population—have finally figured out that they're the ones being shafted by the inflation, not the bankers and the rich who have mastered the art of protecting themselves against the inflation tax. Both Argentina and Brazil have recently set up monetary stabilization programs (at least the fifth time for Brazil; three, at least, for Argentina) that are off to a surprisingly good start, and that have commanded widespread political support.

We in the United States have never experienced hyperinflation, not even reaching double digit (let alone triple-digit inflation) rates until the closing years of the Carter Administration. Our inflation problem, up to now, has been of the chronic, slow-creep kind rather than acute hyperinflation of the kind that leads to serious social unrest. Our collective and obsessive nightmare has been of the reverse kind, not inflation, but deflation and depression, especially the Great Depression of the 1930s, where prices *fell,* not rose but fell, 30% over three years, ripping the guts out of the economy in the process.

Even that episode was inflation-related too in a perverse kind of way. The inflation I have been talking about so far has been the inflation of prices of goods or services. But once the process gets under way, it also raises the prices of assets such as real estate and common stocks. Conspicuous price rises of that kind put great pressure on the monetary authorities to "do something" to put an end to all this immoral speculative activity—speculative booms or bubbles created, of course, originally by their own prior inflationary policies.

Sometimes, as in Japan after 1989, governments respond to the pressures by slamming on the monetary brakes and precipitating a crash of stock prices and real estate. In Japan, for example, the super tight monetary policies initiated after 1989 to end the so-called bubble economy led to a decline in real estate and stock prices of close to 50%. Think of that—50%. In the process the Japanese economy was forced through its worst and most prolonged recession in its postwar history. The Volker crunch of 1979–1982 was a similar episode, though much less severe.

It's not always the case, however, that a depression traces to the deliberate slamming on of the monetary brakes. The severity of the U.S. Great Depression of the 1930s was magnified many times over by the Fed's refusal to take its foot *off* the monetary brakes after the stock market crash of 1929 for fear of reigniting another stock market boom.

So that's the problem facing your average central banker. He's damned if he does and damned if he doesn't. How can he establish credibility as an inflation hawk without precipitating a depression?

For a country like the United States, I'm afraid he probably can't. The best he can hope for is to get a reputation of being sufficiently quick to start tapping the brakes *before* the inflation party gets under way. That's clearly what Greenspan is trying to do but hasn't succeeded yet in convincing all the skeptics, which is one reason why the market expects market rates to keep going up.

Up to now, I have been focusing on nominal rates and on inflation expectations that drive them. But what of real rates? Which way are they likely to go?

At first sight, it may seem inevitable that they're sure to rise substantially in the years ahead, if only because of the huge demands for capital investment coming from the newly awakening economies of Eastern Europe, and even more from East Asia, especially China. Among the many mega-projects the Chinese have on their drawing boards at the moment (and when it comes to thinking big, the Chinese are like the old Texans) are projects for the world's tallest building and the world's longest bridge, and especially the world's biggest dam, along the Yangtze River, bigger by far than the Nasser Dam in Egypt. If they ever get that underway, and most of us hope they don't (since like so many other of the world's prestige projects, the Yangtze Dam would be an economic loser), it would absorb most of the world's output of cement.

But even if they get sensible and go for a series of smaller dams, the demand for capital in China to build not only dams, but roads, bridges, houses, factories, railroads, airports, and everything else is staggering. By itself, of course, demand won't raise real interest rates. That will depend on the balance between demand and supply—between the demand for investment and the supply of saving. And here, when it comes to the savings side, there's an offset—a saving grace as it were.

It's not clear why God has been so good to us, but the fact is that growth generates its own savings to finance it (as was not explained by my long-time friend and colleague Franco Modigliani some forty years ago). What country today has the highest savings rate? China! Higher even than Japan at the height of its most rapid growth period in early 1970s. And that huge flow of Chinese domestic savings, assuming banking and other financial institutions can be developed to funnel that flow into productive investments, is what will drive the growth engine in China. Foreign inflows of capital will also be part of the story, of course; but they're as much or more important for the transfer of technology they bring than for the sheer flow of capital. For sustained, long-term growth, every country ultimately has to rely primarily on its own internally-generated sources of capital.

Thanks to this self-compensating feature of growth and savings rates, we won't see any huge upsurge in real rates in the years ahead. But there will almost certainly be some net rise. In fact, that may be contributing to the recent worldwide rise in interest rates.

Are higher real rates really so bad? You might think so if you listen to all the talk coming out of Washington these days about the importance of low interest rates for the health of the economy. That's a one-sided view, however. Whether you prefer high interest rates to low interest rates depends on whether you are a net borrower or a net lender. That, in turn, typically depends on where you stand in your life cycle. If you're a young person setting up your first home and worried about your credit-card balances, mortgage payments, car and furniture payments, then you want interest rates to be low. But if you're an elderly retiree, trying to maintain your standard of living with income from your investments, then you hope for high real rates. Putting it that way, needless to say, shows you where I stand in the argument.

But in a deeper sense, it doesn't really matter. The gains and losses will average out over a lifetime. What you should really be worrying about is not what will happen to interest rates, but how big a bite the government will be taking out of your income. But, surely, you didn't have to invite me down all the way from Chicago to tell you that.

A talk given at The Jacqueline Baldwin Dunlap Distinguished American Lectureship, University of Dubuque, October 19, 1994.

18

What Have We Learned From the Crash of 1987?

Did we *really* learn anything from the Crash of 1987? I think we did. We've learned so much, in fact, that I couldn't possibly hope to cover it all in a brief talk. So let me concentrate here on what I feel we have learned from the academic research on the crash and surrounding events—the *academic* work, as opposed to the polemical or special-interest pleadings like those of the Brady Commission or the Securities and Exchanges Commission.

Let me begin by making sure that we're all using the term crash in the same economic sense. What *I* mean by the crash is best illustrated by the story of the Wall Street money manager who boasted the day after the crash that he'd been able to reduce his clients' equity exposure by 20% on the day of the crash. And he didn't even have to do a single transaction.

There's actually more sense to that remark than you might think. After all, everyone *does* have a desired equity exposure at every point in time, whether they think about it in those terms or not. And if, for any reason, more people decide to reduce their equity exposure than to increase it, something has to give. Because the supplies of equity and debt securities are basically fixed in the short run, that "something" that restores the equilibrium can only be the price level of equities and the price level of debt instruments.

Yes, I did say also the price level of *debt* instruments; that is, bonds. All the accounts of the crash stress only the loss of wealth in the stock market. They rarely mention that the Chicago Board of Trade's 30-year Treasury futures market locked limit up on October 19. The London markets stayed open, however, and went up another 200 basis points or so. There was a "flight to quality" that day, as the press often puts it, or as we would say, a preference for lower risk securities. You have to add the increase in debt security values to the decrease in equity values to get the *net* change in real wealth due to the crash. Since the value of debt securities was substantially larger than that of equities, the net fall in wealth on October 19 was actually much smaller than people realize. Remember also that there were vast other components of wealth not affected by the crash, such as real estate and human capital.

I stress this wealth effect because the price change on the day of the crash gets all the attention. But the price change in equities is really *not* the problem. If anything, it's really part of the *solution* to a problem— the problem of a desired change in equity exposure. The price change is, in some senses, actually therapeutic. It not only adjusts the proportions directly, as my joke suggested, but it will keep adjusting them until the public no longer wants to change them.

Why then does the price fall get all the attention when all we're seeing is society's taking money out of its equity pocket and putting it into its debt pocket? I think the main reason is that a large price move is seen as anomalous—a sign that something is broken in the market or in the economy or both. Hence the term crash—like the Challenger crash or an airplane crash, followed by people coming out from Washington and sifting through the rubble looking for a broken O-ring.

We should have learned from Benoit Mandelbrot thirty years ago, however, that large, sudden movements in stock prices, whether of individual stock or equity levels as a whole, are not really something new or anomalous. We've had dozens of daily moves of 3% or more (in both directions, incidentally) in every decade as far back as the data go, and we'll presumably have them for the foreseeable future as well. It's the nature of the beast. Nothing in economics suggests that the economy or the stock market will grow at a steady, compound rate year after year. Long-lived assets like common stocks, long-term bonds, and real estate (especially commercial real estate) are inherently highly volatile. Their prices can, do, and always will change abruptly.

When we buy a common stock we're not buying *current* earnings or *current* dividends, though we often talk that way for shorthand as when we speak of the price to current earnings ratio or the current dividend yield. We're buying *future* earnings and dividends, not current ones. How far into the future? If the dividend yield is 3%—roughly what it was in the summer of 1987—and if the appropriate, risk-adjusted discount rate is 10%, then more than half the value of the share represents dividends from more than five years out—from year five to infinity. Needless to say, estimates of events that far into the future are very, very chancy.

Nor is it just a matter of year-to-year variations in earnings or dividends which might cancel out. Earnings and dividend flows, good or bad, tend to be persistent, like climate, and today's prices have to allow for that positive serial correlation. They have a saying over at the Chicago Board of Trade that when a cloud appears in the sky over La Salle Street in August, soybean futures prices lock limit down. Why such a big reaction to only a wisp of clouds? It's not as if it was actually raining heavily. A price drop then would be understandable because heavy rains mean a bigger crop and a bigger crop means lower prices. Yet this is only a cloud, not rain.

But weather patterns are persistent, as Mandelbrot emphasized. And the cloud may be signaling that the long dry spell of the summer may be coming to an end. The market, of course, had taken that dry spell into account. Every day without rain reduced the expected crop and raised the expected price at harvest time. The market not only reflected the accumulated rain deficiency to date, but was expecting it to continue even further, since weather tends to be persistent. The sudden appearance of the cloud means that extrapolation breaks down. That alone would cause a break in soybean prices. But it's even worse than that. The cloud may be signaling the start of a *rainy* trend which would call for even lower expected prices.

And similarly for the stock market. Because of persistence, it takes only a small change in the perceived economic climate to precipitate a major reduction in desired equity exposures, and hence a major move in equity prices. If you like to think in terms of valuation formulas, they're highly nonlinear. Even half a percent upward shading in risk-adjusted discount rates (and risk-adjusted is important because the adjustment won't always show up in quoted interest rates), combined with a half percent downward shading in dividend growth rates can produce a 20% drop in share prices.

What led to that upward shading of risk-adjusted discount rates (or downward shading of dividend growth rates) in October 1987 is still a matter of controversy, but I think my colleague at the University of Chicago Graduate School of Business, Mark Mitchell, and Jeffrey Netter of the University of Georgia may have put their finger on it. They point to the House Ways & Means Committee and its announcement on October 13, repeated and extended on October 15, that it hoped to eliminate the deductibility of interest in hostile takeovers and even to a substantial degree in voluntary corporate restructurings. That, they argue, was the straw that broke the market's back in the week before the crash.

The fall the tax proposal set off in the week before the Crash was in fact quite large and would have attracted much attention if it hadn't been overshadowed by the events of October 19. Nobody notices the moon when the sun is shining. So big in fact was the drop the week before that it seems to have led to major changes in desired equity holdings by foreign investors. As Richard Roll showed in his paper on the international aspects of the crash, the markets in East Asia opened first on October 19 and were way down. The selling wave spread from there to Britain and from there to the United States.

People always smile when they hear the Ways & Means Committee's tax proposals as the likely trigger for the crash. The taxes would have raised only a few hundred million dollars, after all, and equities declined by a half trillion or so. But remember, the tax bill was just the *trigger*. The firing on Ft. Sumter was the trigger for the Civil War, not the cause. It's not clear what the *cause* of the Civil War really was. Or even if the notion of causation has any meaning in a setting that complex. Similarly for the crash. The finger points to the Ways & Means Committee as the trigger—the snapping twig that set off the avalanche, so to speak—the event that led investors to change their expectations about future returns. Incidentally, they seem to have been basically correct in their expectations. Realized rates of return in the five years since the crash have been about the same as in the five years before the crash. The 20% drop, in other words, appears to have been an equilibrating adjustment and not simply a transitory panic, which would have implied above-normal returns post-crash.

Furthermore, as triggers for crashes go, the proposed tax changes were not that unusual. Remember the mini-crash of October 13, 1989? The takeover deal for United Airlines fell through and the market dropped 6% in less than two hours. The market, rightly, sensed that the great takeover boom of the 1980s finally was over.

Though it took scholars more than sixty years to locate it, even the Crash of 1929 had a regulatory trigger. George Bittlingmeyer (1992, 1993) finds the trigger for that crash in the then Attorney General's announcement on the Friday before Black Monday of new and more restrictive antitrust enforcement policies by the Justice Department. Like Mitchell and Netter, Bittlingmeyer follows the subsequent backing and filling by the Attorney General on the issue and notes the response of the stock market: always significant in the predicted direction.

Getting back to 1987, then, we find that the selling wave started on October 19 in East Asia and spread from there to the United States. Note that I said to the United States, not to Chicago. The selling wave actually hit both New York and Chicago simultaneously. It's just that the micro structure of the markets is different in the two cases, and that made it look like it hit Chicago first and went from there to New York. In Chicago the tidal wave of selling registered immediately in lower prices. The Chicago markets strive for maximal efficiency in price discovery. When the bell rings, trading begins even if that means the price has to gap substantially to find its new equilibrium. The New York market, on the other hand, puts price continuity ahead of price discovery. I'm not saying that's bad or good, it's just a fact. It's the way they run their business. You might ask, how can they do that? How can they maintain price continuity in a world that's fundamentally discontinuous? The answer is that they have a little man inside, called a specialist, and he smooths it out.

In New York when there is a major imbalance at the opening that would cause prices to gap, the specialist delays the opening while he tries to round up counterparties on the opposite side. But the quote vendors have to keep reporting last transaction prices and those were Friday's close.

A couple of graphs that I'm sure will be familiar to many of you will help clarify the issues for those who haven't looked at them recently. Figure 18.1 shows the relation between the Chicago index futures and the underlying index on a normal day—say, October 14, 1987, in the week before the crash. Note that except for two little pockets at the beginning and the end (on which more later) the futures price is normally above the cash index. That's because you don't actually have to put up the cash when you commit to the futures so you save the interest. But, of course, you lose the dividend. Since interest rates then were higher than dividend yields, the net effect finds the futures above the cash.

Figure 18.2 shows the markets on the morning of October 19. The little pocket at the opening has become a huge gap. The graph doesn't do it justice because you have to compact the scale to get it on the page. That's a 7% gap—a huge gap by any past standards. If you don't know how to read that graph (and all too many don't) it looks for all the world like the futures is pulling the cash market down, which is basically what the Brady Commission concluded.

But, of course, that's not what was happening. The tidal wave, as I noted, struck both markets simultaneously. How could it be otherwise? Firms like Salomon Brothers are active in both markets (and in London and the Far East too). Do you think they didn't know that stocks would have to open down, when they finally began trading? And that's the clue: when they began *trading*. But the big ones, like IBM, *didn't* open for trading. So the vendors were reporting the Friday close prices. There was no way you could arbitrage that gap because there was no way you could trade on Monday at Friday's prices.

The specialists, having delayed the opening as long as they could in a search for buying interest—something that usually takes only a few minutes on a normal day—finally gave up and opened the stock at its trading level, which was, of course, the 7% down level already discovered in the free-trading futures market. They didn't open them all at the same time, however. They opened one by one. And as each one opened, the cash index, which is just an average of Friday's prices for the closed ones and Monday's prices for the open ones, moved that much closer to the futures level. By an hour and a half, when the last major stock finally opened, the two series had converged to their normal relations.

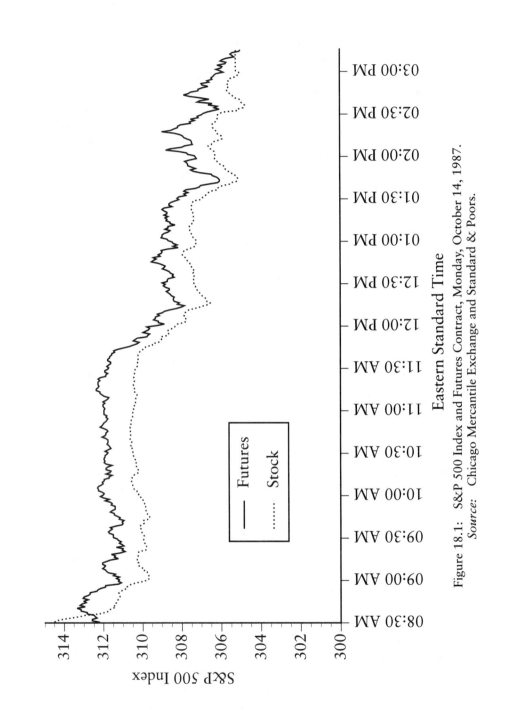

Figure 18.1: S&P 500 Index and Futures Contract, Monday, October 14, 1987.
Source: Chicago Mercantile Exchange and Standard & Poors.

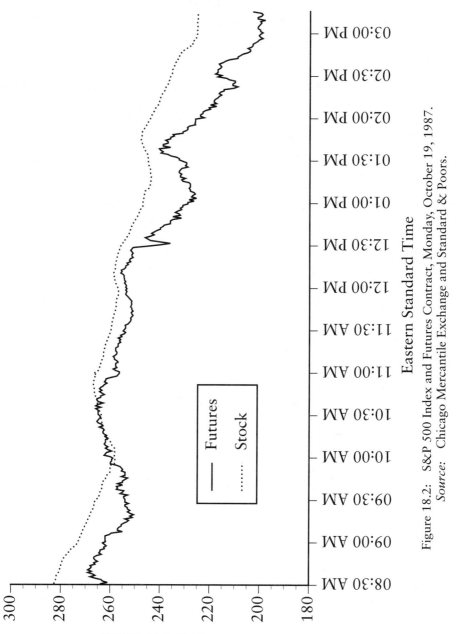

Figure 18.2: S&P 500 Index and Futures Contract, Monday, October 19, 1987.
Source: Chicago Mercantile Exchange and Standard & Poors.

We can conclude very definitely, then, that the crash was not caused by some failure in the futures market that was communicated via arbitrage to the cash market—what I call the Brady-Breeden theory of market mechanisms and the crash. Remember, that was the official title of the Brady Commission: The Presidential Committee on Market Mechanisms. In fact, subsequent academic research, notably by Allen Kleidon of Stanford, suggests that such serious market mechanism failures as occurred—the broken O-rings, so to speak—were actually at the NYSE.

Look again at the behavior of the two series on October 19 and note that they did resume their normal relations at about 10 A.M. or so, Chicago time. But subsequently, the futures once again fell below the cash market and stayed below for the rest of the day. In fact, the longer the day wore on, the wider the gap became. Of all the many strange phenomena on that day, this one poses some of the most serious intellectual challenges to the market microstructure profession.

Why wasn't that gap arbitraged out? You've all heard the efficient-market jokes about twenty dollar bills lying on the ground, but this is ridiculous. We're talking here about *thousand* dollar bills. These inter-market gaps are so large that if you actually *could* do the arbitrage at those prices, you could retire for life. Why then was so much money being left on the table?

My first inclination, when I was working on the CME's blue ribbon academic panel on the crash along with Myron Scholes and Burt Malkiel, was that it might be essentially the same mechanism as at the open, namely non-trading. The specialist not only has the option of delaying the open, but of halting trading if the imbalances are too severe to prevent gapping. That wasn't it, however. Larry Harris of the University of Southern California checked it out in a very careful study, and he showed that while there were some trading halts, there were nowhere near enough of them to account for the gap.

So we looked for other things. We thought it might possibly be due to the so-called uptick rule which prevents short sales except at a price higher than the previous transaction. And when the market is falling, there won't be many of those. But that couldn't be it. True, you can't sell short except at an uptick, but at least until the NYSE's recent Rule 80A you *could* sell your long position in shares and buy futures. General Motors pension fund, which holds $35 billion of equities, is run by some of the most sophisticated investment professionals in the world. They knew all about futures markets and arbitrage opportunities. But still the gap persisted? Why?

That's what Allen Kleidon of Stanford finally figured out. It turns out that the ultimate problem was the common one of having the parts of an organization, in this case the NYSE, upgrade their internal infrastructure at different speeds. The NYSE set itself a target of a one billion share per day capacity by the end of the 1980s. Unfortunately, the crash came *before* the end of the 1980s.

The NYSE's first step toward its billion-share goal was to put in its electronic order entry system, the justly celebrated Superdot system. And a fabulous system it is. Instead of the old routine of telephone calls and paper trails, just pushing a button on a computer routes the order directly to the specialist, and just as routinely sends the confirmation back. In fact, in some ways, the Superdot was *too* much an electronic marvel. One of its features was an innocent looking command labeled "list," which lets you send sixteen separately designated orders out simultaneously. Thus, though Superdot was designed with the retail customer in mind, it turned out to be of greatest value to the program traders and arbitragers. One button did it all, and the program traders flocked aboard to the dismay of the NYSE authorities.

But powerful as the Superdot was, it covered only market orders, not limit orders. They were still handled the old-fashioned way: call to the floor, get a ticket printed up, walk it over to the specialist, and put it in his book. Limit orders were scheduled for upgrading, too, in due course. (Now they are fully automated. The specialist's book is no longer a physical book with two pockets, but a screen.) But by October 19, 1987, only 20% or so of the limit orders were automated; it was the manual ones that caused the trouble.

The process of entering and removing limit orders was so slow that queues built up at the printers for some of the stocks. Furthermore, the volume was so heavy by normal standards that all sorts of mechanical breakdowns occurred. Printer ribbons got shredded and had to be replaced. The software at some stations developed bugs (as it always seems to), and you couldn't withdraw some limit orders after you had entered them.

Though the troubles were widespread, not all stocks were affected equally. Some stocks would work through their queue and then, after trading for a while at current prices would find another queue building up. The price couldn't catch up to where it should have been until that queue in turn had been worked through. Stocks stuck in the queue would register on Larry Harris's database as not closed; and in the strict technical sense they weren't. But in a practical sense they *were* closed. And their effect on the arbitrage gap illusion was exactly the same as what had happened at the opening. The reported index was a moving average of past and current prices. The *current* prices *were* in line with the futures. Or, to put it a bit differently, the futures price was marginal to the average represented by the index. And when the marginal is below the average, the average falls.

That's important not just as a matter of intellectual curiosity, but because it also puts the whole issue of circuit breakers in a different light.

The serious case for circuit breakers, after all, rests in substantial part on this supposed de-linkage of the two markets. A temporary trading halt would give the slower-moving stock market a chance to catch up, or so the argument goes. But Kleidon shows that the problem was created by a shortage of capacity at the NYSE—a shortage that has since been remedied.

You won't ever again see the prolonged gaps between the two indexes unless you mandate them by so-called collars like the NYSE's Rule 80A which makes intermarket arbitrage more costly after big market moves. If your concern is with preventing the kind of chaos we had on the floor of the NYSE on October 19, you really don't need circuit breakers of the kind both exchanges have installed. But we have them, and there's no way we are going to get rid of them. The world, and especially the financial press, thinks they are a great success—the one great thing to come out of the whole sorry episode. They have prevented a recurrence and they have defanged the ferocious program-trading monster. If they want to believe that, why should we academics disillusion them? Placebos, after all, are a perfectly standard and accepted part of the practice of medicine.

Let me conclude by reviewing briefly one further area where academic research has helped clarify our interpretation of crash-related events, and that has been in the matter of volatility. The conventional wisdom (what I call the Brady-Breeden view) was that introduction of low-margined futures in 1982 had led to a substantial increase in market volatility. A crash was inevitable. It just happened to come in 1987. Bill Schwert's monumental and classic studies of volatility put that one to rest, however. Schwert extended the time series data on volatility not simply back well before the crash, but back well into the nineteenth century—150 years of volatility. You only had to look at the full time series, spread out on a graph, to see that there was nothing particularly remarkable about the 1980s. The average level of volatility in the 1980s was in fact far, far below that routinely experienced in the 1930s.

It's true, of course, that there was a big spike of volatility in October of 1987. But if you looked closely at the graph you could see an average of two or more spikes in volatility per decade in every decade going all the way back to the early nineteenth century. The 1987 spike in volatility was bigger, but so was the price fall. One of the few things we know about volatility is that it always goes up after a crash. The 1929 and 1987 crashes were both big crashes, and both led to surges in volatility of very close to the same size. It's just that after 1929, the money supply imploded, the banking system collapsed, and the economy along with it. Little wonder then that volatility in the 1930s didn't decay quickly back to its long-run, permanent level as it did after the 1987 crash. Or, to put it a little differently, 1987 was a normal crash; 1929 was an exceptional one.

In a deep sense, of course, that is why the 1987 crash attracted so much attention at the time. At the back of everyone's mind was the fear that it was all going to happen again—that a 1930s style great depression was on the way. But, of course, it didn't come; and anyone who had actually studied the monetary policies of the early 1930s knew it wouldn't come unless Alan Greenspan and company had taken complete leave of their senses.

Oh, I know a lot of people were arguing during the 1992 campaign that a 1930s style depression was actually happening. But I knew the 1930s. Believe me, the early 1990s were not the 1930s. And even those who thought we really were in a depression didn't connect it with the Crash of 1987. (With Ronald Reagan, perhaps, but not the crash.) The connection of the two events in the public mind has finally been broken. And if that's all we have learned from the Crash of 1987, that's all to the good. Because we can all stop worrying about imaginary problems, and start worrying about the *real* problems facing our society and our economy.

A keynote address given at The Inaugural International Conference on Financial Management, Department of Finance, Suffolk University School of Management, Boston, Massachusetts, November 12–13, 1992; published as "The 1987 Crash Five Years Later: What Have We Learned?" in New Directions in Finance, Eds. Dlip K. Ghosh and Shahriar Khaksari, Rutledge, 1995.

REFERENCES

Bittlingmeyer, George, "The Stock Market and Early Anti-Trust Enforcement," *Journal of Law and Economics* 36, 1, Pt. 1, April 1993, pp. 1–32.
———, "Stock Returns, Real Activity and the Trust Question," *Journal of Finance* 47, 4, December 1992, pp. 1701–1734.
Harris, Lawrence, "The October 1987 S&P 500 Stock-Futures Basis," *Journal of Finance*, 44, 1, March 1989, pp. 77–99.
Kleidon, Allan W., "Arbitrage, Nontrading and Stale Prices: October 1987," *Journal of Business* 65, 4, October 1992, pp. 483–507.
Roll, Richard W., "The International Crash of October 1987," *Black Monday and the Future of Financial Markets,* Robert W. Kamphuis, Jr., Roger C. Kormendi, and J.W. Henry Watson, eds., Irwin 1989.
Schwert, G. William, "Business Cycles, Financial Crises and Stock Volatility," Working Paper, Simon School of Business, Rochester University, 1990.

19

Do the Laws of Economics Apply to Japan?

Although the theme of this symposium is "translating culture," my contribution will actually emphasize the opposite. Translation may indeed be necessary for cultural achievements in literature, in the arts or in films. But not in economics. No uniquely Japanese (or U.S.) economics exists, any more than a Japanese physics or a Japanese chemistry. The fundamental laws of economics apply everywhere, and nothing illustrates that universal applicability better perhaps than Japan's current recession and the accompanying banking crisis.

Those twin crises have, at least in broad outline, relatively straightforward explanations in economic terms, though professional economists, a notoriously contentious group, may well quarrel over the details. Most serious economists, moreover, and certainly those of the Chicago variety, like myself, would agree on the broad outlines of policy appropriate for Japan at this rather difficult point in its economic history. We say to Japan now, as we have said so often over the past ten to fifteen years, that you cannot treat a twentieth-century (soon to be twenty-first-century) economy as if it were a seventeenth-century rural estate run for a daimyo by a swarm of bailiffs. You should rely more on impersonal market forces, especially in the area of capital markets, broadly understood, for directing the flow of resources in your economy and less on administrative guidance of one kind or another by the graduates of Tokyo University Law School who run the Ministry of Finance, or MOF for short. Otherwise, you will simply keep blundering from crisis to crisis, destroying, in the process, not just vast amounts of your national wealth, but much of the civility in interpersonal relations that so many of us in the West have come to admire and envy.

Why have we had such a hard time convincing you of what seems so clear to us? Part of the answer, surely, is your past success. Japan came from virtually nowhere in the years after World War II to become the second largest economic power in the world today. And throughout that period of spectacular growth, the Japanese economy seemed to be guided by what has come to be caricatured as Japan Inc.—a combination of political monopoly by the Liberal Democratic Party, the industrial policies of the Ministry of International Trade and Industry, and the detailed micro-management of the financial markets by MOF. Whenever one criticized Japan Inc. one got the obvious response: it may not be pretty, but you have to admit it works.

To argue that way, however, is to commit one of the oldest of logical fallacies. It's so old, it's usually referred to by its ancient Roman name: the *post hoc, propter hoc* fallacy. Mere association in time must not be confused with causation. The rooster crows and the sun comes up. But surely the sun would have come up anyway even if the rooster had been put into the cooking pot.

Similarly with Japan Inc. To credit the bureaucrats and politicians with Japan's success is in many ways a libel on the Japanese people. The spectacular growth of Japan traces to the ingenuity, the craftsmanship, the work ethic, and the entrepreneurship of the Japanese people; and especially to their remarkable willingness to save, that is, to forego immediate consumption in favor of future, sometimes distant future, benefits. Those are the real sources of the success. A strong case can be made, in fact, that Japan's success has been achieved *despite* its politicians and bureaucrats.

That the bureaucracy of Japan Inc. may actually have been counterproductive on balance seems accepted now for Ministry of International Trade and Industry. But recognition of the negative influence of MOF has been much longer in coming, partly because finance is too abstract for most people. Any time the subject of financial policy comes up, the eyes of many immediately begin to glaze over. In a way, therefore, the current banking and related disasters may actually be a blessing in disguise by focusing the attention of the Japanese public on matters of finance and getting them to understand that MOF and all it stands for is the *problem* not the solution.

But while it is easy to fault MOF, the Bank of Japan, and the Japanese political establishment generally for the policy blunders over the last fifteen years—blunders that in almost any other country might have found the politicians and bureaucrats hanging from the lampposts—it is not so easy to draw up any complete blueprint for reform. Certainly no foreigner should even try. I propose here instead to focus on a few broad, but still relatively simple, long-range reforms that have so far received little attention in the press and in public discourse.

I know that approach will disappoint many in the audience who will say: Isn't that just like an economist; the house is burning—that is, the banking system is in distress—and he's talking about the decorations in some mansion to be built in the future, assuming we ever get there. In the United States we often refer to my kind of talk, derisively, as rearranging the deck chairs on the Titanic. But in my own defense, let me reassure you at least that your current banking problems are painful, but not really very complicated.

Simple economics—accounting, really—tells us that if a bank has 100 of assets and 80 of deposits, it has 20 in capital, net worth, or equity. But if the value of those assets falls to, say, 70, while the deposits stay at 80, the bank will now have no capital. It will, in fact, have negative net worth. It will be technically insolvent.

That a bank is insolvent doesn't mean, of course, that it can't actually continue to function as a bank in many of its activities. People can continue to make their regular daily deposits and withdrawals (which will roughly balance out); they will continue to pay off their installment loans and mortgages and the bank can relend the proceeds of those payoffs in the form of new loans and mortgages. What the bank can't do, however, is contribute to economic growth by *expanding* its portfolio of loans to business and industry.

That's easy enough to see when the value of the assets falls to 70, so that the bank's net worth becomes –10. But a more insidious problem, in some ways, arises when the value of the assets falls not all the way down to 70, but only to 82, say, leaving a thin sliver of capital and avoiding a technical insolvency. Under those conditions, the bank's owners and managers have powerful incentives not just to keep lending, but to take on huge risks, far beyond normal prudent bank lending policies. If these highly risky ventures actually do succeed, the bank is saved. The profits earned will restore the bank's capital, and the fortunes of the owners will be more than restored. They will balloon. If the venture fails, most of the losses will fall on the depositors, which in practice means on the general body of taxpayers. That's what happened in the U.S. savings and loan industry collapse.

The regulators, of course, which in Japan means MOF, face a similar "moral hazard" problem when bank assets dip down to or below the value of bank liabilities. Like a gambler who doubles his bets hoping to recoup his previous losses, MOF may avoid taking the necessary therapeutic actions in the hope that the current distress in asset prices is temporary and that the banking crisis will solve itself in the not too distant future as the economy revives. Sometimes, of course, doubling up the bets in this fashion will succeed. But sometimes it won't, and the eventual losses are magnified.

That is also, of course, what is clearly worrying much of the Japanese public at the moment (as well as worrying many foreign creditors to the

Japanese banks). It is important to emphasize, therefore, that while bank shareholders, debenture holders, and the general body of taxpayers may well ultimately suffer substantial losses, the *depositors* as such probably will not. No modern government, whether it has a formal system of government deposit insurance or not, is going to allow its citizens to lose the substantial portion of their life savings they hold in bank deposits. The British claim they would not automatically pay off all the depositors and that the public understands that their deposit guarantee is severely limited in amount. They point to the BCCI collapse as proof of their rejection of the "too big to fail" doctrine. But I think it's more than a coincidence that the victims in the BCCI case were mainly foreigners and immigrants rather than part of the normal British electorate. And, in any event, BCCI (and Barings) were single isolated failures of relatively small banks, not system-wide failures.

For obvious political reasons, therefore, something like the U.S. savings and loan bailout can be confidently expected if concerns over bank insolvency lead to massive withdrawals of deposits from many beleaguered banks at the same time. And that could happen, thanks to some very special and peculiar Japanese financial institutions. A Japanese bank depositor these days could well ask himself or herself, why should I take a chance on a government guarantee of my bank account? Even if there's only a very small chance that they will follow the British example and not pay off, delays and paperwork hassles are almost inevitable in getting my money back. Why take chances? Let me just transfer the deposit to the state-owned Postal Savings System. The interest rates paid are virtually the same and the guarantee is built in from the outset. This easy alternative for the public will remain a long-term competitive threat to your commercial banks until the postal system is finally privatized. With its potential for generating runs, it will remain a short-term threat as well until bank capital gets restored, and with it, confidence in the health and viability of the commercial banking industry.

How to do that is a subject on which the economics profession has much to say, but, as I indicated earlier, I prefer to leave to the specialists the details of how to deal with the current problems and concentrate instead on some of the deeper structural reforms needed to keep the next banking crisis from happening. Those reforms, as you will see, are aimed at reducing dramatically the role of MOF in the Japanese economy.

STRATEGIES FOR LONG-RUN REFORM OF JAPANESE BANKING AND FINANCIAL MARKET REGULATION

When the subject is reducing the role of MOF in Japanese financial life, one hardly knows where to begin. Virtually every rule and regulation on MOF's books imposes a deadweight cost of some kind on the Japanese public at large, though often benefiting handsomely the relatively small number of firms and individuals for whom MOF is really working. Think of MOF, I've often stressed, as a cartel manager not a regulator in the Western sense of that term. (Western regulators, I hasten to add, are often just as concerned as MOF with protecting the competitive interest of those they regulate, but they are more constrained politically. The New York Stock Exchange surely hoped to enlist the power of the state in hobbling the futures exchanges in MOF-like fashion, but the futures exchanges had enough independent political power of their own to beat back the attack. U.S. regulators, moreover, like the SEC or the CFTC, must come to Congress each year for appropriation of the funds needed to support their staffs and their programs. MOF never has to bother; MOF decides its own budget, along with that of everyone else in the government.)

As a first step toward cutting back MOF's all-encompassing influence over the economy once and for all, I propose to take away completely MOF's jurisdiction over the banking industry. The *micro* side of banking regulation, covering such things as audits, inspections, and ensuring that internal controls meet international standards (something we can no longer take for granted in light of the Daiwa scandal) should be transferred to a specialized, separate agency. That new bank examination agency, however, should not be just the same old sections of MOF under a new name. The long-standing relations between the bureaucrats of MOF and the MOF-tans in the banks have made Japanese banking "supervision" suspect. Why not entrust the task of monitoring the safety and honesty of the banks to people from the tax-collecting services, who have proven more reliable as watchdogs?

The *macro* side of banking, having to do with the level and growth of bank reserves and other components of the monetary base, should be transferred to the Bank of Japan. And now a key point: the Bank of Japan should become completely independent, not simply independent of MOF, but independent of both the executive and legislative branches of the government itself, much like the Bundesbank in Germany.

I know this recommendation will strike many as strange, for at least two reasons. First, because a country's central bank must always be the lender of last resort during a liquidity crisis, shouldn't that bank be the natural one to maintain supervisory authority over the banking system? Not necessarily, I and many other economists insist. Detailed supervision over commercial bank operations is, or should be, focused on questions of solvency and possible mismanagement at the micro level, not with liquidity, which is basically a macro issue. A central bank, in principle, could handle both responsibilities—like our U.S. Federal Reserve System does—but Japan has already suffered enough from gigantism in its regulatory structures. U.S.-style bank regulation, which I am very definitely *not* recommending for Japan, has the opposite problem of excessive duplication of regulatory supervision, with sometimes as many as five separate agencies examining a single bank. Better to set up a single, stand-alone supervisory authority, which will not only make for better accountability when things go wrong, but will permit the micro and macro regulators each to specialize more efficiently on carrying out their primary responsibilities.

Others may object to giving independence to the Bank of Japan because the Bank of Japan certainly didn't cover itself with glory either in its handling of events leading up to the so-called bubble economy of the 1980s, or in the aftermath of the collapse of that presumed bubble in the 1990s. In fact, many students of those events actually fault the Bank of Japan for not heeding the advice of MOF to moderate its overly deflationary monetary policies sooner and more vigorously in 1991 and 1992. But whether MOF was right or the Bank of Japan was right on some particular past decision is beside the point. As long as the operations of the Bank of Japan are seen as a standard part of government economic policy (that is to say, of MOF economic management) trouble is inevitable, particularly when you factor in the interservice rivalries between the two agencies, intensified by the five-year cycle of revolving Bank of Japan chairmanships.

The seeds of your current troubles were planted, after all, in the mid-1980s during MOF's five-year tour of duty. Under the Plaza Accords of 1985, and again, and even more so, under the Louvre Accords of 1987, the Japanese government, pressed hard by the U.S. government, agreed to slow its accumulation of dollar assets and let the yen rise against the dollar. Fearful, however, that a higher yen might damage the Japanese export industries and precipitate a domestic recession, the Bank of Japan pressed down hard on the domestic monetary gas pedal. Over the next few years, broad-based measures of the Japanese money supply grew by more than 10% a year. The banks, flush with cash and reserves, were eager, to put it mildly, to lend money to both their business and individual customers.

Normally, when central banks pump in money in such vigorous fashion, prices and wages begin to rise and public concern soon arises over the erosion of the real values in past accumulated bank deposits, bonds, and other assets denominated in nominal terms. As public awareness grows about the central bank's continuing inflationary policies, rising nominal interest rates serve to warn the monetary authorities that serious adverse political consequences may be ahead, as the Carter Administration in the U.S. learned to its sorrow in 1979. But the classical inflationary scenario did not occur in Japan in the mid-1980s, for reasons still not fully understood by students of the episode. Part of the answer was surely that the much feared recession never actually did happen; growth continued at a fairly high rate, by Western standards (and real growth, of course, offsets a proportional part of the impact monetary expansion would otherwise exert on prices). The rising yen, moreover, though it might seem initially to hurt export prices and profits, serves by the same token to lower import prices, and hence the consumers cost of living in Japan. That effect was masked in the late 1980s, however, by the inefficiency in the Japanese retail distribution system. The inflation showed up not as rising prices, but as prices not falling as fast as they should have given the rising yen.

Whatever the reasons, the facts are clear. Despite the rapid monetary growth, retail price inflation in Japan during the 1980s was minimal— so much so that even an inflation hawk as zealous as Milton Friedman was loud in his praises of the Bank of Japan. In all the many statistical tests by academics of price inflation and the degree of central bank independence, moreover, Japan, at least in the years after the oil shocks of the 1970s, always turns up as an outlier: close to the bottom on the bank independence axis, and also close to the bottom on the inflation axis.

The money the Bank of Japan was so assiduously pumping into the Japanese economy in the mid-1980s didn't blow up consumer prices, it is true, but it had to show up somewhere. And that was in a construction boom and rising asset prices—stock prices, of course, but also housing prices, commercial real estate prices, and even golf course memberships, all financed with generous helpings of relatively low-cost bank loans.

The asset price inflation set in motion by the easy credit policies of the Bank of Japan was intensified by some well-meaning but ultimately unfortunate interventions by MOF. During the U.S. stock market crash of October 1987 the value of U.S. equities fell by some 20%. Strong downward pressure was also felt in the Japanese equity market, but MOF stepped in quickly with one of its famous PKOs—Price Keeping Operations. The price drop in Japan was kept to only 7 or 8% and I remember the comments by the MOF bureaucrats at the time that we in the United States just didn't seem to understand any better how to manage our stock market than we did how to manage automobile companies.

But price supports along MOF lines, if they are seen as successful, can actually backfire. If the public believes MOF will leap in whenever stock prices start to sag, then owning Japanese equities no longer has downside risk. The stock market is transformed into a call option market, for all practical purposes, and prices have nowhere to go but up. And up they did go, to levels that now seem almost absurd.

Real estate and stock prices continued their upward spiral virtually unchecked, until the regular five-year alternation of Bank of Japan chairmen replaced a MOF man with a more traditional banking type. He immediately set out to burst what he dubbed the "bubble economy," which he did starting in early 1990. The asset boom came to an abrupt halt, and turned into an agonizing slide over the next five years in which more than 60% of the previous gains vanished into thin air.

Many wonder whether the whole disastrous up-and-down episode could have been avoided if a more traditional central banker, like Chairman Mieno, had been put in charge much earlier, say in 1984 rather than 1989. My answer is that it's possible, but not likely unless the Bank of Japan had been far more independent of the government than it actually was.

We do know, at least, that asset inflations, once they have built up a head of steam, are hard for a central bank to control, thanks, in part, to the absence of any obvious victims who can generate enough political pressure to bring the process to a halt. In an asset inflation, *everyone* seems to be benefiting: the firms who get cheap and easy access to capital, the banks who see a surge in the capital base they need to expand their loan business, the brokerage industry earning huge commissions from the stock transactions of their customers, and the customers themselves who see the value of their net worth climbing steadily, sometimes almost day by day. In sum, as one U.S. central banker once put it, no central banker likes to be in the position of removing the punch bowl just when everyone at the party is having such a wonderful time.

The pressures on the central bank not to intervene are further reinforced by an absence of obvious monetary tools for dealing with what are called "sectoral" problems. Targeted credit controls don't work any more reliably than any other kinds of controls; people quickly invent ways around them. The U.S. Federal Reserve System, in the aftermath of our 1929 stock market crash, put great faith in margin requirements for dampening stock market movements, but finally gave up after many years of conspicuous lack of success. Margin requirements for stock purchases have remained absolutely unchanged for the last twenty years. A central bank confronting an asset inflation thus feels it faces a cruel choice: let the boom keep on rolling; or slam on the monetary brakes and risk plunging the whole economy into a tailspin.

A truly independent central bank, however, might well be prepared to take the risk of stepping on the brakes earlier in the process than if it were part of the government. But even independent central bankers, needless to say, are not supposed to lock themselves in a dark room and block out all sensations coming from the real world out there. They must also recognize when to take their foot off the brakes and resume normal driving patterns. The Bank of Japan failed to maintain the necessary flow of liquidity to the banking system out of an almost obsessive fear of rekindling the asset inflation. Eventually, of course, the Bank of Japan (and the Federal Reserve before it) brought the process of monetary contraction to a halt, but not before much unnecessary damage had been done to the balance sheets of the banks and the general public.

Nothing can guarantee, of course, that a central bank, however strongly insulated from short-run political pressures, will eschew the kind of stop-go monetary policies that have plagued both Japan and the Western economies for so long. The best we can hope to do is to reduce or eliminate distractions keeping them from focusing exclusively on providing stability and predictability of monetary growth. Independence helps by cutting away pressures to respond to each change in exchange rates or in unemployment levels. But at least one other current distraction can and should be removed. I refer to the profitability and capital adequacy of the banking system as a whole (as opposed to that of individual banks which, in any event, is a micro matter better left, as noted earlier, to the bank examiners). The macro distraction to the central bank's task posed by bank capital and profitability problems generally, can be much reduced with a relatively simple and straightforward change in the rules governing bank portfolios.

BANK OWNERSHIP OF CORPORATE SHARES

Specifically, I propose that Japanese banks no longer be permitted to own the common stock of other corporations (except temporarily, when stock is received in exchange for bank debt in a corporate reorganization in bankruptcy, and when the shares are those of a operating subsidiary of the bank itself). Distasteful as it is for me as a committed Chicago free-market type to have to recommend legislative restrictions on a bank's portfolio decisions, this particular restriction offers too many long-run and short-run benefits to be passed over on purely ideological grounds.[1]

If nothing else, the restriction would contribute to my primary objective of reducing MOF's role in the economy by removing a key motivation for its frequent interventions in the stock market, *viz.*, keeping falling stock prices from wiping out the capital cushions of the banking system. Remember that under the BIS rules, 45% of the unrealized appreciation of stocks held can be counted as Tier II capital. Once the banks no longer own stock, therefore, MOF can be more easily persuaded to abandon its huge arsenal of price-propping weapons, like the banning of new common stock issues and the hobbling of equity derivatives—weapons that don't really work to keep prices up, as we've seen over the last five years, but which undermine the efficiency of the financial markets in allocating capital.

But even more immediate benefits would flow from a forced divestiture of stock by Japanese banks. Many of those banks, as noted earlier, are now skating close to the edge on their primary or Tier I capital and not just their Tier II capital. Additional Tier I capital could be raised, in principle, by plowing back profits (if indeed the banks were making profits), or from sales of new bank equity (if indeed the original shareholders were willing to accept the massive dilution of their ownership those sales would entail).[2] To restore bank capital, how much simpler merely to sell off the stock held in the portfolio, treating the now *realized* gain on the 55% not already included in Tier II as a profit that would boost both Tier I capital *and* the cash in the till available for supporting the banks' now stagnant lending programs?

In principle, of course, the banks could choose this route to raising capital on their own without a forced divestiture rule. But at least two major obstacles stand in the way of any such voluntary solution. First, of course, MOF would be absolutely horrified at the prospect of the huge equity sales that would be involved—as if there were some way to get massively more equity to recapitalize the banking system without price pressure in the equity markets.[3] MOF would clearly prefer propping up bank capital with no real change in any part of the current banking system and especially its own dominion over it. One way MOF could accomplish those objectives would be by something along the lines of the Reconstruction Finance Corporation set up by the U.S. government in the 1930s that pumped capital into the ailing banking system by buying special issues of preferred stock newly created for that purpose.

A second obstacle to forced divestiture of bank-held equities is that sales of stocks held even at today's depressed prices would expose the bank to heavy capital gains tax liability on stocks purchased long ago for sums that are trivial by today's standard. Fortunately, however, a simple solution for that problem exists: set the tax rate on capital gains for banks and other corporations to zero, as it now is for individuals. That is the third, and in some ways ultimately the most important, component of my program for getting MOF to let go of the banking sector.

Distancing MOF from the banking sector is no more, of course, than a first step toward the ultimate goal of substituting the impersonal judgments of the market for the dictates of the bureaucracy. Even shorn of its banking arms, MOF would still be an enormous concentration of virtually unchecked power, thanks to its control over the budget and taxes.

The many beneficiaries of MOF's administrative guidance can be persuaded to sacrifice privileges they have long enjoyed only when they come to accept that the costs of maintaining those benefits are becoming too high. Many in Japan have already reached that conclusion and I hope that many more will soon opt to throw off the stifling blanket of bureaucracy in which they have been wrapped for far too long in favor of a more open, market-based system in which their ingenuity and creativeness can come to fuller flower.

An address given at a symposium entitled "Translating Cultures" sponsored by the University of Chicago in the Keidanren Kaikan Conference Center, Tokyo, Japan, November 28, 1995.

20

Japanese-American Trade Relations: Can Rambo Beat Godzilla?

My views on Japanese-U.S. trade relations, though shared by most of the academic economists in United States, will disappoint many of you. So much so, in fact, that I propose to begin by stating what my three main points will be.

Point one: The U.S. merchandise trade deficit with Japan, about which you've heard so much, is in no sense a crisis—one of the Clinton Administration's all-time favorite words. And, what's more, the administration *knows* it's not a crisis. The administration is purposely (and frankly, somewhat cynically) exploiting the deficit, to whip up American public opinion against Japan, and in support of its own so-called, market-opening agenda.

Second point: those highly-touted market opening initiatives will have no more than a temporary and trivial effect, even by the administration's own calculations. And the reason is simple: restrictions maintained by the Japanese government, for all the horror stories, actually have very little to do with their export surplus or our import surplus. The administration's program, if it succeeds, will benefit, at best, a few U.S. firms. But if it fails, and leads to trade sanctions, it will impose huge costs on the rest of us, and the rest of the world. The administration's Rambo-style tactics are thus the classic bad investment: a low payoff on the upside, but a big risk of loss on the down.

My third and final point is that even if the administration's reckless threats to impose sanctions do force a weak and insecure Japanese government to back down now and accept numerical targets for our products, those threats erode what little credibility we still have as the leading proponent of multilateral freer trade. They expose us as mercantilist hypocrites, every bit as determined to foist our exports on others as we claim the Japanese to be. We're just turning ourselves into another Godzilla, and this, mind you, at a time when increasing numbers of Japanese are coming to realize that Godzilla policies are not really in a country's best interests. To reclaim the moral high ground at this point we should agree, in our negotiations with Japan, to get serious about opening our market by scrapping our antidumping laws and all the many remaining "voluntary" and involuntary import restrictions—such as the sugar quotas and the multi-fiber agreements—rather than just phase some of them out slowly over ten years under GATT. But don't hold your breath.

THE ADMINISTRATION'S CAMPAIGN TO INCREASE OUR EXPORTS TO JAPAN: BENEFITS AND COSTS

The administration's case for strong-arming the Japanese has gained much plausibility because, let's face it, the Japanese do so often seem to be blocking U.S. products, and on the flimsiest and most laughable of pretexts. Everyone's favorite story, I'm sure, is that of Tsutomu Hata, the former Minister of Trade and Industry, who kept out U.S. beef for being incompatible with the smaller Japanese intestines. But while we smile, we should remember as well that Japanese tastes frequently *do* differ from ours, and that U.S. firms do not always adapt their products accordingly. The classic example, of course, was that of Chrysler Corporation. When Lee Iacocca was complaining at his loudest of being excluded from the Japanese auto market, the Chrysler Corporation was in fact producing no cars with right-hand drive. Now they *do* produce them, and the Jeep Cherokee is selling briskly there, just as here.

Remember also that many Japanese restrictions and regulations we complain of are not really import restrictions. They apply equally to Japanese firms, though, of course, from long practice, the Japanese firms are often nimbler at getting around them. But not always. A recent study of the Japanese Retail Trade Law showed that contrary to widely held views in the United States, repealing that law could actually *reduce* imports from the United States. The retail law, in practice, was a greater burden on small Japanese suppliers than on U.S. exporters.

Adding up all the pluses and minuses, then, no major and permanent change is to be expected in our overall trade deficit with Japan in the immediate future even if Japan dismantled every one of its disputed regulations. And note that I said overall deficit, because some part of any reduced bilateral deficit with Japan will surely show up as bigger bilateral deficits with China, say, or Indonesia, as Japanese firms, pushed out of their home market, make it up by increasing their sales to those countries, or even to us. Have you ever tried to get a dent out of an underinflated volleyball?

The administration's economists know that no great change in our aggregate trade balance can be achieved by these bilateral negotiations with Japan, no matter how many successes Mickey Kantor and the lawyers proclaim. Why then is the administration pressing ahead with a program that most academic economists see as reckless in the extreme? The answer is that political decisions in this country are not taken by polling the members of the American Economic Association. They're not even taken by polling the economists within the administration. The function of administration economists, as I remember well from my own days as a government economist, is to come up with clever debating points rationalizing positions already taken by their political superiors. And believe me, the economists in this administration have responded particularly well to that challenge.

The decisions they must rationalize are made in response to polls all right, but polls in the form of congressional and presidential elections. In those polls, producer interests can often deliver votes (and the financial means of getting even more of them) in quantities sufficient to carry the day. In the case of our trade posture toward Japan they clearly have. The pressure to get tough with Japan is coming not from U.S. consumers, but from *some*—and I emphasize the word some—U.S. producers, notably the auto parts manufacturers, the big construction companies, the Silicon Valley crowd, and some big Wall Street investment banks like Morgan Stanley. They want Bill Clinton to be the new Commodore Perry, which suits this administration just fine. The administration will be doing favors for politically powerful business interests for which, needless to say, it will be expecting favors in return. Just watch which firms line up in the Rose Garden when a new administration policy initiative is announced.

On that score, surely, this administration is no worse than any of its recent predecessors. Remember that the so-called "voluntary" quotas on Japanese car imports were introduced under that great free trader Ronald Reagan. And remember that George Bush himself personally led a delegation of U.S. auto executives to demand that the Japanese government let them do more business in Japan. But the only pressure he brought to bear was throwing up on Prime Minister Miyazawa's shoes. This president, however, is actually threatening trade sanctions against Japan, and that is very definitely something not to laugh about.

Japan, after all, is far and away our biggest trading partner. Sanctions that reduce the flow of imports from Japan would inflict huge losses on American consumers and would destroy generations of successful diplomatic and trade initiatives by this country. Why risk it for the miserable pottage of an increase in sales by a handful of U.S. corporations?

The answer I suspect, is that the administration felt it wouldn't actually have to invoke those sanctions. The mere threat would be enough. The Japanese would cave at the last minute, as they always do, because they have even more to lose from a trade war than we do. They can't even count on feeding themselves anymore. A spell of bad weather and they now must import rice, let alone all the oil, coal, iron ore, and other industrial raw materials they have to import every day to survive even when the weather is good.

But while the administration's calculations are certainly rational enough as far as they go, you can't always be sure the other side will follow the script. Dozens of academic studies have shown that settling out of court is almost always better for both sides than incurring the expense of a trial. But the court calendars stay clogged. Using the same reasoning as our administration, you can prove that World Wars I and II could never happen. But they did. There are no sure things in law or diplomacy.

You must always allow for your bluff being called, and that the Japanese this time will either reject your demands or, more likely, judging from recent events, will agree, with much fanfare, to some meaningless and trivial concessions. Now what do you do? If you accept purely cosmetic concessions—whether in Japanese trade or in Chinese human rights—you lose your credibility as a player in the future. The other side will crow that your threats are empty and will start kicking sand on your blanket all over the world. In fact, the more rational and calculating you seem— and certainly Bill Clinton, that great policy wonk comes across that way—the more international leverage you're going to lose. A Richard Nixon could credibly use threats of retaliation because you could never be sure he wasn't just crazy enough to do it. A Ronald Reagan could do it, as the air traffic controllers learned. Even a George Bush could do it as he did in the Gulf. But not a Bill Clinton.

The lesson in all of this is the familiar law of the old West: never draw your gun unless you mean to shoot. Don't make threats unless you're really prepared to carry them out. And what worries me is that some of this administration's politically powerful constituents may actually be hoping that we *do* carry out the threat. What a perfect excuse and occasion for "saving American jobs" by stanching the flood of Japanese cars, steel, and cameras once and for all.

These fears could be dismissed, the administration insists, if only the Japanese would stop stonewalling and "return to the negotiating table." But the administration uses the term "negotiating" in a very strange sense indeed. The only discussable issues are how much they are to concede and how fast. The *quid* we are to provide in return for their *quo* is simply not to bash them—the same "bargain" one makes with a mugger. This is not only dumb policy on our part, for reasons I've indicated, but it brands us as hypocritical as well. God knows that we have plenty of market-closing regulations of our own that *we* aren't prepared to give up unilaterally. Multilateral, mutual concessions as in the Uruguay Round GATT negotiations may be a slower way of eliminating trade barriers, but they are a surer and safer way of expanding world trade than the bullying policies of this administration.

Let me add a brief cautionary comment on GATT at this point. The GATT agreements were signed with great fanfare in Morocco in early April 1994, but the legislation to implement them here is not yet on the congressional docket. The momentum GATT built up in 1993 is ebbing away and the protectionist forces, recovering from their NAFTA defeat in November 1993, are regathering their strength. They are preparing to make a big issue of GATT in the upcoming congressional elections. A further complication is the need to come up with $20 billion or so in offsetting revenue or expenditure cuts to maintain budget neutrality for GATT. Ultimate passage is probably still likely, but it's by no means a sure thing.

THE REAL SOURCE OF THE JAPANESE TRADE SURPLUS AND ITS FUTURE PROSPECTS

The administration's politically-motivated Japan-bashing rhetoric is a particular irritant to many academic economists because they know Japan's vaunted trade surplus is not some deliberate beggar-my-neighbor policy foisting unemployment on the rest of the world, as so much administration propaganda contends. Their surplus traces mainly to the very high level of savings by Japanese households and firms, reflecting in turn both cultural and especially demographic features of Japanese society, but even more, the very rapid and sustained rates of per capita income growth achieved there over the last thirty years, at least until recently.

The Japanese families that save so much must put those savings somewhere, of course. At first, they put them into bank savings accounts, life insurance policies, and Japanese government and corporate securities. But they were saving more than the Japanese economy could employ locally at high returns. So they, their banks and insurance companies did what American families have been doing lately in this period of low interest rates: they reached out for higher yields. And they sought to reduce their investment risks by diversification, especially international diversification. For them, in the 1970s and 1980s that meant buying U.S. securities—both the corporate securities financing our plant and equipment and the U.S.

government securities financing the great rearmament push of the 1980s that led ultimately to the implosion of the old Soviet Union.

But the Japanese save in yen and we sell our corporate and government securities in dollars. Where can the Japanese get those dollars to buy our securities? Only by selling us more automobiles, cameras, and fax machines at the current exchange rate than the automobiles, timber, and grapefruit we sell to them. And that's the Japanese trade surplus or U.S. trade deficit that all the shouting is about.

When you get rid of all the emotional terms like deficits or unfavorable balances you can see that we as a country, especially we as consumers—and we are everyone of us consumers, however varied our occupations—have been benefiting hugely from this arrangement. I used to tease my Japanese friends back in the 1980s whenever they took to boasting about their trade surpluses with us, that we were actually playing a cruel trick on them. We had conned them into sending us all those wonderful autos, cameras, and machine tools they were busting their backs to produce. And what were we getting them to take in exchange? Pictures of George Washington.

How long can this game go on? Until either Japanese savings rates fall or U.S. savings rates rise. The administration has been working hard on both ends of that equation, but its proposals, as usual, are at cross purposes and serve mainly to exacerbate political tensions both at home and abroad.

In the matter of increasing our domestic savings, the Clinton Administration, like the Bush Administration before it and the Republican opposition in the Congress, was surely correct in pushing for reduction in the federal deficit. That will increase net domestic saving by reducing government *dissaving*. But for that to affect the trade deficit, given that you want to maintain the level of productive domestic investment, you must reduce either government consumption or private consumption. The administration proposed originally to do the former, at least partly, merely by relabeling some government consumption as government investment, and to do the latter—not by broad-based taxes, which *would* reduce consumption—but instead by raising taxes on the upper income groups and corporations. That may have been politically convenient, but taxes like that fall mostly on savings, which is presumably what the administration was trying to increase.

As for Japanese saving, the administration can't affect that directly, but hopes to do so indirectly by forcing the Japanese government to adopt the kind of massive deficit spending that our own Congress and public opinion wouldn't tolerate even when we too were suffering through our own recession. Nor is the Japanese reluctance to follow what we say rather than what we do merely an emotional reaction to our hypocrisy. There is genuine skepticism within the economics profession—though you'd never guess it from reading the reports of *this* Council of Economic

Advisers—about the real efficacy of the fiscal steps proposed for lifting Japan out of its recession, and in the process, boosting Japanese purchases of consumption goods in general and U.S. products in particular. Our administration's position on this matter is strictly 1960s Keynesianism—I'd call it naive Keynesianism, but that might imply there's some other kind.

Nowadays, economists don't believe that fiscal stimulus is anywhere near as automatic as administration spokesmen maintain, particularly in a country with Japan's recent history. Japanese households have just seen a terrifyingly large fraction of their accumulated wealth disappear in the fall of stock prices and even more so in the fall of real estate values. Given a big income tax cut, Japanese households are less likely to rush out and spend it than to save it, so as to restore the desired balance between their income and their net worth.

Japanese household saving may well increase even further, for precautionary reasons, as the Japanese see the yen rise against the dollar, and attribute that rise to malevolent intervention by the United States. I am not saying that the U.S. actually *is* intervening, but that really doesn't matter. Here, as so often, it's the perception that counts. Their belief that we're driving up or at least talking up the yen leads Japanese firms to repatriate their U.S. profits faster, and Japanese banks and investors to sell off their U.S. holdings and bring the funds home which, of course, just pushes the yen even higher. And to the Japanese, a rising yen, the dreaded *endaka*, has important emotional overtones. The *endaka* is a portent of hard times to come. Nor is that fear mere superstition because while exchange rates don't matter much in the long run—the economy's internal price and wage levels will simply adjust to keep the real or inflation-adjusted exchange value at the level warranted by the fundamentals—that process of internal price and wage adjustment can be a painful one indeed in the short run. Layoffs and shutdowns are likely in many export-oriented or import-competing industries. Remember the trauma of our own rust belt firms back in the early 1980s when the dollar was soaring against the yen and the mark.

For the near future then, I see little prospect that Japanese saving rates will fall enough to make a major dent in their trade surplus and hence in our trade deficit. Their trade surplus will surely drop some as they come out of their current severe recession. And they could probably accelerate that process somewhat by a less restrictive monetary policy. The Bank of Japan still seems inhibited by its memories of the middle 1980s, when its last attempt to offset *endaka* by easy money policies fueled an explosive boom in stock prices and land values. But assuming the administration is just bluffing in threatening massive retaliation against imports from Japan, no major change in our Japanese trade balance can be expected before our next presidential election.

Over the longer haul, however, the picture is likely to change dramatically. By a generation from now, say twenty to twenty-five years, the current and recent past trade surpluses of Japan will seem just a golden memory for them. The huge flows of household savings that supported those surpluses will have largely dried up by then, partly because many of the cultural forces that fed those saving habits will have vanished along with the kimono and the daily two-hours-each-way commutes. But mainly it will be because the age structure of their population will have changed so dramatically. The country will be graying and its annual growth rates and saving rates will have fallen back to the levels of mature societies like ours. With lower savings rates, their trade surpluses will not only be down, but turned very likely into trade deficits, like ours. And how will they finance that excess of imports over exports? The same way we do: by collecting interest and dividends on our past overseas investments and by selling securities to the savers in more rapidly growing economies. In Japan's case probably China. This turnabout will surely be very distressing to any of their still surviving old mercantilist bureaucrats who see trade deficits as a crisis. But at least they won't have to waste time dreaming up new arguments and policies for eliminating trade deficits. They can always recycle the tired old material from the Clinton Administration in the 1990s.

A public lecture given at the University of California, Santa Barbara, California, April 21, 1994.

21

Do the M&M Propositions Apply to Banks?

Addressing the question of whether (and how) the M&M Propositions apply to banking gives me the chance, at long last, to wrap up a discussion of that very topic I had with a group of bankers some fifteen years or so ago, but which I never actually got a chance to finish. The conference was hosted by Carter Golembe, a name I'm sure is familiar to many of you; he always liked to hold his conferences in exotic places, this time in the colonial town hall building in Williamsburg, Virginia. My particular panel was set up in a lovely room overlooking the well-manicured lawns of the village green and our subject that day was (what else?) capital requirements in banking. Some things never seem to change. The banker sitting next to me had just finished his presentation, the burden of which was that his bank was being forced to pass up profitable lending opportunities because it was bumping up against its capital constraint.

"Then, why don't you raise more capital?" I asked him.

"It's too expensive," he said. "Our stock is selling for only fifty percent of book value."

"That has no bearing on your cost of equity capital," I replied. "That's just the market's way of saying: look at these guys; you give them a dollar and they'll manage to turn it into fifty cents."

At that point, there was a rumbling noise from the audience of bankers, most of whom were selling for even less than fifty percent of book value. I happened to look up just at that minute and through the window I could see a platoon of soldiers in Revolutionary War costumes and muskets marching on the village green toward the town hall.

My God, I thought, they're sending for the firing squad.

They didn't actually shoot me, needless to say, but they didn't let me say much of anything else either. I never could seem to catch the moderator's eye.

Looking back now I can see that perhaps I hadn't handled it in the best way possible. Though my banker certainly wasn't making his point effectively, he *did* have a point. Equity capital *can* be an expensive form of capital to raise, especially for smaller banks, if only for the very substantial flotation and underwriting costs usually involved. Nor, as I hope I needn't remind this audience, does that statement contradict in any way the M&M Propositions, properly understood.

The M&M Propositions are *ex ante* propositions. They're concerned with *having* equity, not with *raising* equity. When a firm has substantial amounts of debt already in place, and when the original contract interest rate on that debt has not anticipated the new infusion of equity, or could not be renegotiated to reflect it, then a new equity issue clearly *would* be costly to the existing shareholders. The new equity serves mainly to blow up the value of the bonds. It's like pumping gas into another man's car, as Mickey Rooney used to say of his alimony payments.

And, sometimes, of course, the market may interpret a new equity issue as just the insiders' attempt to bail out at the top of the market. Nor can you always avoid these adverse information effects merely by cutting dividends to boost capital. The market might well read that as "pulling the red handle," to quote the then chairman of Continental Illinois, explaining his decision to maintain Continental's dividend in the teeth of the rumors, later confirmed, that it was about to go belly-up.

Raising *new* equity capital, external or internal, does present problems which I'll get to in due course. First let me shift away from these unanticipated changes in dividends or equity and focus instead strictly on *ex ante* bank capital ratios. Would the M&M Propositions apply there to the same extent as they apply to any other industry? Or is there something fundamentally different about banking? And if so, what?

ARE DEPOSITS LIKE OTHER SECURITIES?

The notion that the M&M Propositions might apply to banks often seems strange to some at first sight because demand deposits, which represent by far the major source of funds for banks, differ in so many ways from ordinary corporate securities. For nearly thirty years, in fact, banks couldn't even legally pay interest on those deposits, yet the public held them. Try that on corporate bonds and see how far you'd get. But the interest prohibition on deposits applied, of course, only to cash payments. Banks simply paid interest in less efficient noncash forms such as low-fee checking, convenient branches, and even toasters. In fact, I still have the free toaster my bank gave me in the early 1950s; it's actually lasted longer than the bank. And, though I hate to rub it in on some of the older bankers present, their classic price-fixing cartel began to come apart at the seams in the late 1960s when nominal interest rates began to surge, and collapsed utterly by the early 1980s. Nice try, guys, and my admiration for keeping your zero-interest scam going as long as you did.

But although demand deposits now pay interest like all other securities do, some argue that they pay much less interest than they "ought to," in some relevant sense that makes their cost lower to banks than any comparable source of financing to other businesses. Where does this free lunch supposedly come from? It can't just be that deposits are uniquely liquid instruments. Every security has liquidity to a greater or lesser extent, and there are clearly costs as well as benefits in supplying more of it in your securities with a view to lowering your financing costs. If there really were unique rents to be earned by issuing ultra-liquid, conveniently transferrable demand obligations, then surely more ordinary corporations would be fishing in those waters. And don't say that they can't, because one of them, but so far only one of them, already has.

I'm referring not to the money market funds which do issue demand obligations that compete with bank deposits, but which do not treat their demand accounts as a means of financing the regular business activities of, say, Merrill Lynch. I refer instead to the IBM Credit Corporation, no less; the lease-financing subsidiary of IBM, which issues, under an ongoing shelf registration, a security it calls a Variable Rate (that is, a floating rate) Book Entry Demand Note. That security, of which about $1 billion or so is currently outstanding, is functionally equivalent in every essential respect to a bank demand deposit. Why haven't more companies chosen to follow suit? I really don't know. Perhaps they will once they recognize the competitive advantages they have over banks in that kind of demand security: no reserve requirements, no bank examiners, no Community Reinvestment Act. (I am indebted to my colleague Geoffrey Miller, of the University of Chicago Law School, for calling my attention to the IBM demand notes. They haven't received much publicity and they probably won't until someone can think up a snappier acronym for them.)

In a capital market left to its own devices, then, it's hard to see anything so special about demand deposits as a security to rule out application of the M&M Propositions to the banking industry. When it comes to banking, however, the markets are not left to their own devices. The government repayment guarantees for bank demand deposits, found on no other corporate securities that I'm aware of, will surely affect the cost of capital from this source. But are those guarantees a net subsidy or a net tax?

Much of the academic literature on banking, particularly during the banking and S&L crisis years of 1990–1992, has routinely treated the insurance program as a net subsidy, enabling banks to obtain funds at less than an appropriately risk-adjusted cost. This advantage was said to lead banks to a corner solution in which their desired ratio of deposit liabilities to earning assets was as large as possible and their desired equity ratio as small as possible, much in the spirit of the M&M Tax Correction paper of 1963. Many bankers, however, believed in the 1950s and 1960s, and increasingly so even today, that the insurance premiums more than offset the benefits they draw from the guarantee. And both views may well be correct because selecting a uniform schedule of insurance premiums that would exactly match the value each bank derives from the guarantee is virtually impossible. The premiums are bound to be too high for some and too low for others, and probably even for the same bank at different times. But then again, what other security can always be presumed to be correctly priced on a risk-adjusted basis?

HOW MUCH DOES BANK EQUITY REALLY COST?

Perhaps the inapplicability of the M&M Propositions to banking may stand out more clearly if we shift focus to the other side of the capital structure equation, the equity component rather than the deposit liability side. And indeed, people often tell me they can easily imagine a viable bank with 95% deposits and 5% equity, but they can't imagine a viable bank with 5% deposits and 95% equity. Well, I can certainly imagine one. That seems hard only to those who think of the cost of equity capital as a single fixed number like, say, the 12% that investors have earned on average on U.S. equities over the last seventy years. And clearly, if a bank were earning only 8% on average on its loan portfolio, financing that portfolio with 12% money wouldn't make a lot of sense. But the cost of equity is *not* a fixed number; it's a *function* that depends both on the risk of the firm's earning assets *and* the degree of leverage in the firm's capital structure. The 12% figure I quoted is merely one point on that function reflecting the average business risk and average leverage position of U.S. equities. For any firm with less than average systematic risk and less than average leverage, the cost of equity would be lower; at zero leverage, much lower, perhaps as low as, say, 6%. At that rate, even an all-equity bank with an expected return on assets of only 8% would not only be viable, but would presumably sell for a 1.3 premium over book value.

But what if the market expected the bank could earn only 5% on average on its assets in the years ahead? Then it would sell for only about 80% of book value. Now comes the heartbreaker. The market value of the equity would still lie below its book value even if the bank levers up its capital structure and hence its expected earnings per share with deposit money for which it pays only 4%. The leveraging will indeed raise the expected earnings per share on the equity, but not by enough to compensate the shareholders for the risks added by the leverage. All this, I might add, is just standard M&M Proposition II stuff.

In summary, an essential message of the M&M Propositions as applied to banking is that you can't hope to lever up a sow's ear into a silk purse. You may *think* you can during the good times, but you'll give it all back and more when the bad times roll around.

Some will object at this point, that while an all-equity bank might well exist in principle, no such banks exist in practice, which suggests that the M&M Propositions really don't apply to banking. But, of course, taken literally, they wouldn't apply anywhere else either. Much of the research focus in finance in the last thirty years has been precisely on those departures from the strict M&M assumptions that will give a push or a tilt toward more or less leverage in a firm's desired, long-run target capital structure. No very simple or coherent set of tilting principles have emerged. Nor, for that matter, has any clear pattern of capital structures been observed across firms. Even banks display some substantial (and not always easily explainable) differences in their choice of operating and financial risk profiles.

But this is neither the time nor the occasion to review all or even the most important extensions and qualifications of the M&M Propositions that have accumulated in the academic literature. Let me conclude instead by homing in on what the M&M Propositions *can* contribute to the vexing policy issue of bank capital requirements.

BANK CAPITAL REQUIREMENTS IN LIGHT OF THE M&M PROPOSITIONS

In taking up issues of bank capital requirements and the M&M Propositions, I am actually returning to a subject treated in a paper on the regulation of bank holding companies that Fischer Black, Richard Posner and I wrote back in 1978. We start there with the conditional proposition that if the government is indeed insuring bank deposits either explicitly or implicitly via the too-big-to-fail doctrine, then it effectively stands as a creditor vis-à-vis the bank's owners. And its regulations, to be socially efficient, should resemble the measures adopted by freely contracting private lenders in similar circumstances. At least in a broad-brush way, they really do. Both, for example, maintain surveillance against changes in the debtor's business activities that might jeopardize the safety of the loan. Both impose equity capital requirements and both monitor any dividend diversions to the shareholders that might pull the capital ratio below the agreed-upon levels. So close is the mimicry, in fact, that I can't help smiling at complaints from bankers about their capital requirements, knowing that they have always imposed exactly the same discipline on people in debt to them.

The regulatory and the market creditor policies may indeed be similar in outline, but they clearly differ also in significant details. One is the way they define the capital that goes into their capital requirements. Surely no private lending institution that came up with anything as arbitrary as the definitions under the Basel accords could hope to survive long as a major player in a competitive lending market. But we called attention in our 1978 paper to a far more important difference: "in private markets, the capital requirements imposed by the lender involve a *quid pro quo:* the benefits of additional capital put up when the loan is being negotiated are passed on to the borrower in the form of a reduced administrative cost component in the interest rate. This is not the case with government regulation of banks."

Or at least it wasn't the case back in 1978. In the years since then, and especially in the recent bank reform legislation, steps have been taken to attach rewards and punishments particularly, but not only, in the insurance premiums charged for increases and decreases in a bank's capital. It was certainly a move in a sensible direction and I applaud the ingenuity of some of the original proposals. But by the time Congress got through with them, it's not clear how much closer to the efficiency boundary we really have come.

Nor is that in any way surprising or remarkable. Standard government blunderbuss, one-size-fits-all regulations cannot and should not be expected to match the kind of delicate balancing of interests achievable through private contracting. Hence bank capital requirements will continue to be a source of friction and of inefficiency particularly when it comes to forcing banks to pony up more equity capital. As bankers often say when finally turning down a long-standing but troublesome customer: it's time for a new creditor to take a fresh look at this problem.

Fischer Black, Richard Posner, and I hinted obliquely at what that new approach might be, but we weren't ready for radical steps at that time. Remember that our paper was written before the first threatened S&L and bank collapse of the early 1980s, the Continental Bank bailout of the middle 1980s, and the even bigger bank and S&L bailouts of the late 1980s and early 1990s. It was still possible to believe in the 1970s that a simple, enhanced capital-requirements approach could adequately protect depositors at relatively low cost, thanks to the M&M Propositions, or at least at a much lower cost than bankers seemed to believe, and certainly at a lower cost than some of the alternatives then being proposed. Capital requirements, we recognized, were no panacea. They could not prevent embezzlement, of course, a frequent cause of past bank failures in the United States. Nor would it be easy to keep the banks from offsetting the added depositor protection by increasing the risk of their assets still further. But given the then existing structure of bank surveillance and examination—which, like most outside observers in that more trusting age, we believed were, if anything, too conservative—we concluded that enhanced capital requirements would be the cheapest solution within the existing regulatory framework.

But why must we stay within that framework? It certainly hasn't been a conspicuous success, to put it mildly. Why not just scrap the whole costly system of deposit insurance, capital requirements plus risk surveillance in favor of a variant on Irving Fisher's 100% money proposal, under which insured deposits—and there need be no limitation on the size of the accounts—must be invested only in short term Treasury bills or close equivalents? *That* will surely guarantee the safety of the payment system and head off any future taxpayer bailouts. And it won't deprive small- and medium-sized businesses of needed bank financing. It will just force banks to raise the funds to support their loan portfolios by issuing nonguaranteed securities of any of a variety of kinds at rates and prices that will surely reflect the bank's risk posture more accurately than any feasible scheme of insurance premiums.

But there are many other advantages to the Fisher scheme as well. It will end, once and for all, any threat of a monetary implosion like that of 1930–1933. That's why Fisher proposed it in the first place. With the ending of that threat, the monetary authorities can finally begin to take a more positive view of financial innovation and experimentation. It's hard, understandably, for people who feel they have the responsibility for the country's (and indeed the world's) whole payment system on their shoulders to look kindly on the explosive growth of off-balance sheet derivatives transactions, even though, on balance, derivatives may be reducing the level of risks in the economy.

And, of course, there is at least one additional benefit from the Fisher solution: it should put a merciful end, finally, to all further concerns over whether the M&M Propositions really do apply to banking.

An address given at the Conference on Risk Management of Financial Institutions and the Role of Capital, sponsored by The Wharton Financial Institutions Center, Philadelphia, PA, March 9–11, 1994. Thanks are owed to my colleagues Geoffrey Miller and Anil Kashyap for helpful comments on an earlier draft.

REFERENCES

Black, Fischer, Merton H. Miller and Richard A. Posner, "An Approach to the Regulation of Bank Holding Companies," *Journal of Business*, 51, No. 3, July 1978, pp. 379–412.

22

How Much University Research Is Enough?

If my title has you bracing for the standard academic hymn to research you can forget that. This will be a lecture in economics. But a short one. I need no reminder, after all, that my words will be the least of the memories you carry from this happy occasion. I can barely remember the words of my own commencement speaker in 1943, who happened to be Winston Churchill. Something about the Nahrzis, as he called them. He was against them.

In those days, two topics were taboo for commencement speakers at universities in the genteel tradition: sex and money. Now, only one remains, and I propose to break it today by talking about the money side of research. Are we spending too much on it? Or too little? Both views are argued with some passion these days.

A report, issued recently with great fanfare by the National Science Foundation, urges more taxpayer-financed spending for commercial, product-development research. At the same time, *The Chicago Tribune*, in a weeklong series of articles, calls on the University of Illinois, and by extension all major universities, to cut back spending on faculty research. But in my view neither the NSF nor The *Chicago Tribune*'s reporter makes a convincing economic diagnosis of the illnesses they seek to cure.

Let me begin with the NSF's recent call for subsidies to industrial research.

The NSF panel surely knows that research in new product development is a profit-motivated activity. If, therefore, private-sector, profit-motivated firms are currently not doing more such research, one of two propositions must be true. Either the firms believe the expected future payoffs, discounted back to present value, are too small to recover the current cash outlays required. Or the activity really *is* profitable, but the firms are too dumb to realize it. And that, essentially, is the NSF's position.

The NSF report argues, among other things, that Japanese economic growth has surpassed our own because U.S. business managers and shareholders, especially institutional shareholders, are too narrowly focused on immediate, short-term profits. Patient Japanese firms, by contrast, are said to worry less about the current bottom line than about long-term market penetration. They outspend us on long-term commercial product development. And it shows.

This legendary farsightedness of Japanese firms and myopia of U.S. firms has by now become the conventional wisdom. That view was already approaching cliché status when I last addressed this summer convocation nine years ago. I argued then, however, and on many occasions thereafter, that differences in managerial style did not explain our seeming economic decline relative to theirs.

Note that I say seeming decline. Economic theory predicts that in a world with no permanent technological secrets, all market-driven economies will converge to the same standard of living eventually, though it may take decades, and perhaps even centuries for those starting furthest back. But since we in the United States start at the front of the pack, the rest of the converging world must always be gaining on us. (Yes, despite current campaign rhetoric we *do* have the highest standard of living or close to it when it's computed properly with purchasing-power adjusted exchange rates. Just check out the cost of a McDonald's *Grosser Mac* or *Viertel Pfunder* on your next trip to Germany).

Admittedly, the Japanese have been closing the gap on us even more rapidly since 1945 than during their equally remarkable spurt after the Meiji Restoration of the 1870s. That should not be surprising. Countries recovering from losing and destructive wars, like Germany and Japan, can be expected to have high per capita savings rates and hence rapid growth rates, while their capital stock is being rebuilt. By the same token, countries like ours, with no wartime destruction to make good, will consume more, save less and hence grow more slowly. Our inherently slower growth as a winner was masked for a while by our catching up with the investment backlog left over from the depressed 1930s. But by the middle 1960s we were back to the slower, long-run growth path appropriate to our high levels of accumulated wealth per capita.

Japanese economic policies not only reinforced the natural processes of postwar recovery in their country but almost surely overdid it. The stock market inflation fueled by the easy-money posture of the Bank of Japan during the 1980s made capital look dirt cheap to many Japanese firms. It's easy to be lavishly far-sighted if you think equity capital is costing you only one percent. Many U.S. firms with high price/earnings ratios made the same mistake in the 1960s.

But those days of wine and roses are over now in Japan. The Bank of Japan has taken the punch bowl from the party, as William McChesney Martin liked to put it. The Japanese stock and real-estate markets have collapsed and with them, the capital cushions that made Japanese commercial banks such eager lenders to business borrowers, especially those in their own *keiretsu*. Many Japanese firms are suffering losses for the first time in their recent history. Bankruptcies are rising and industries are plagued with overcapacity. Budgets are everywhere being pruned back. The Japanese financial press, in fact, now worries about Japan falling behind the more farsighted Koreans.

The NSF's concerns over too little commercial research in the United States may thus be misplaced, but are at least understandable. What, however, are we to make of the worries over too *much* research by U.S. universities? The research output of a university is not, after all, like the smoke by-product of a factory that makes air harder to breathe or clothes harder to wash. No one believes university research is actually harmful, though many believe it's not worth very much. And, indeed, some of it isn't. But the same is true, alas, of much art, literature, or music. Some research, however, *is* worth a great deal, though such is the cruelty of our fate that we often won't know which is which until many years have passed.

So great, in fact, is the worth of the best basic research that all modern governments subsidize its production. Unlike narrowly focused commercial research, the full benefits of basic research are spread too widely in time and space for the researchers to recover the costs of development in product prices or in royalties. How do you establish property rights in the inverse square law of gravity? A market economy left solely to its own devices, will thus produce too little of it. That's what the NSF should really be worrying about.

Some critics of university research may accept subsidies to basic research, at least in principle. Their quarrel rather is with *how* it gets subsidized, and, in particular, with that part they see as being diverted from the universities' teaching programs. To the critics, as payers of tuition, the cost of faculty research seems a matter of simple arithmetic. If a university has a hundred faculty members each teaching and researching half time, then surely the same teaching could be done with fifty full-time faculty. But at half the tuition.

It's not quite that simple, however, for a number of reasons, among them, some important self-regulating market forces that are being overlooked. No university charging its customers double the costs of producing its teaching services could hope to survive for long unless it had an unbreakable monopoly. Otherwise competitors would unbundle the product and offer a research-free teaching product at half the price.

In the very competitive U.S. higher-education market some institutions of higher learning have done just that, though perhaps not quite at half the price. Many colleges in the United States today focus entirely on teaching, and so do most graduate schools of business. So be it. A hundred academic flowers are blooming. That's one beauty of our approach to higher education, after all, in contrast to the European one-size-fits-all approach.

That specialized teaching institutions can survive is thus in no way remarkable. The more challenging question, is, how, in our highly competitive industry, have the handful of still fully bundled, private research universities, like ours, managed to thrive despite sacrificing the efficiency gains that specialization to a single task normally brings.

The answer can be only that combining teaching and research raises the *quality* of the teaching by enough to offset the higher costs of producing it. I have never understood why some critics of academic research find that idea so far-fetched. The time and thought dedicated to creating new music surely enhanced Haydn's performances as an orchestra conductor, Vivaldi's as a convent music master, and our own Easley Blackwood's as a teacher of harmony. Why should it be different in any other field of serious intellectual activity?

But achieving these quality gains in teaching is not automatic merely because the faculty also does research, even good research. It still takes two to tango. The students are equally important to the process. Too many of them and they become mere faceless ciphers on the campus. That's what *The Chicago Tribune* was really complaining about, I suspect. And above all, the students must *want* the stimulus of interacting with a faculty whose motto is not just that an unexamined life is not worth living, but that an unexamined subject is not worth teaching.

Those of you graduating today have successfully survived this sometimes grueling interaction with the faculty. On their behalf I congratulate you and wish you the very best in your subsequent careers. Keep in touch.

Convocation speech, University of Chicago, August 28, 1992.

Endnotes

Chapter 1

1. The secretary of the treasury was then George P. Shultz, a former colleague and long-time friend of Milton Friedman. The Chairman of the Federal Reserve Board was Arthur Burns, another old friend. With Milton Friedman's blessing, both gave a cordial audience to Leo Melamed of the CME and at least a *nihil obstat* to his proposal for an International Monetary Exchange (Melamed 1988).

2. Under the SEC's original dispensation, only calls could be traded, because puts were regarded as potentially destabilizing. Word of the put-call parity theorem had apparently not yet reached the SEC staff.

3. The first currency swap appears to have been arranged by Continental Illinois Bank's London merchant bank in 1976. The precise dates and places remain problematic because the originators sought secrecy in a vain attempt to maintain their competitive advantage. (See Hu 1988, especially note 73, page 363.)

4. See Brennan and Schwartz (1989). Particularly interesting in their demonstration, however, is how small the destabilization potential really is, provided the rest of the investing public understands what is going on.

5. Evolution also involves "extinctions." Some of the recent innovations will inevitably fail in the competitive struggle. Others may be killed by heavy-handed regulation.

Chapter 2

1. Under the terms of the agreement, Bankers Trust agreed to pay P&G a fixed interest rate of 5.3% for five years and P&G agreed to pay Bankers Trust a floating interest rate equal to the commercial paper rate minus seventy-five basis points during the first six months of the deal. So far, just an ordinary, plain vanilla fixed-for-

floating swap. After the first six months, however, if P&G did not opt out at that point, P&G's floating rate obligation for the remainder of the five-year contract would be the commercial paper rate minus seventy-five basis points, as before, but now plus an additional "spread" equal to the difference between 17.4 times the five-year Treasury rate and the price of a thirty-year Treasury bond. If this difference turned out to be a negative number, as was the case when the contract was first initiated in November 1993, the spread would be arbitrarily set to zero. By early 1994, however, the rise in the five-year rate and the fall in the thirty-year bond price had created a positive value for the spread of several hundred basis points. (For the details of the P&G/Bankers Trust swap, see Gamze and McCann 1995.)

2. In point of fact, of course, Bankers Trust's market value actually dropped substantially during 1995. Bankers Trust's voluntary settlement in the Gibson Greetings case was taken by the public as tantamount to pleading guilty to fraud. The damage to Bankers Trust's reputation inflicted by that admission was magnified many fold by the regulators. Not only did the Federal Reserve reprimand and fine Bankers Trust, but the SEC and the CFTC, neither of them actually primary regulators for a bank like Bankers Trust, but both anxious to impress their own Congressional overseers and the public with their zeal as market watchdogs, found pretexts to pile on with additional fines and penalties. Some wags have dubbed that unsolicited intervention by the SEC and the CFTC as "regulatory ambulance chasing."

3. Is society's wealth also destroyed by bond market crashes like those in early 1994 that precipitated so many of the derivatives disasters? For the corporate bond market, the answer is clearly no. The losses to the creditors will always be matched exactly by the gains to the issuers. For government debt, however, the answer depends on whether you believe the public is rational enough to see the government bonds they own as just the present value of the taxes to be paid by themselves and their descendants to service that debt. If so (i.e., if so-called Ricardian equivalence holds), then the government debt too is just a wash; if not, then at least part of the debt may constitute net social wealth. The issue is still very much an open one among economists, but a recent and every exhaustive study by Meguire (1995) suggests the truth lies closer to the Ricardian view than to the net wealth view.

4. Orange County actually seems to have lost about as much on its reverse repos and its leveraged holdings of long-term bonds as on its inverse floaters and other derivatives. Distinctions of that kind, however, are by now of only pedantic interest. Rightly or wrongly, Orange County will forever go down in history as a derivatives disaster. (For a detailed account of the Orange County portfolio, see Jorion 1995.)

5. That may seem a far from trivial loss, though surely not to Deutsche Bank, one of the world's largest banks and MG's principal creditor as well as stockholder. Also, it was a loss that would have been more than recouped in 1994 and 1995 when oil prices bounced back. Even that is not the end of the MG story, however. In early 1994, prices began to recover. The new managers of MGRM, after liquidating most of the futures hedge, suddenly realized they were now unhedged and went on to cancel a big chunk of the still outstanding forward-delivery contracts the previous management had negotiated. But because spot prices at that point were still well below the contracted delivery prices, MGRM was "in the money" on those contracts. Canceling them, without requiring compensation, thus transferred wealth from MGRM back to its customers. To that extent, at least, some of MGRM's eventual losses were not really derivatives disasters at all, but self-inflicted wounds. (For a fuller account

of the MG episode see Culp and Miller 1995 a, b and c; see also chapter 13 in this volume.)

6. I'm often asked how the losers could possibly have thought the deals were making them better off if they really knew how bad the worst outcomes could be. In most of the disasters, the key players apparently did know but, after some initial losses, chose in effect to "double their bets"—in P&G's case by not buying back the put when the spread first became positive (see Note 2 above); and in the Barings case by plunging in Nikkei futures after having lost by selling index options on the Japanese market. The decision makers surely understood they'd be dead if their doubled bets went sour, but no deader after all, than they would have been anyway once their bosses learned about the first loss. In the MG case, on the other hand, the reverse spin could have occurred. The top management of the German parent company may have closed down the marketing program of its U.S. subsidiary rather than put more money into it because they believed, mistakenly, that the U.S. managers were doubling up rather than hedging. (See Culp and Miller 1995b). As a further irony, the losses in all the derivatives disasters considered here would have turned into substantial gains if only the positions could have been maintained for a few months longer. By May 1995 the Nikkei 225 had increased by 30% above its post-Kobe lows in February, interest rates had fallen dramatically, and oil prices had climbed back to mid-1993 levels. The decision makers just ran out of money too soon in classic "gambler's ruin" fashion (though in the MG case, "hedger's ruin" might be the more appropriate term). In the Orange County case, we show in Miller and Ross (1996) that if the county had not filed for bankruptcy in December 1994 and had not converted the portfolio into low return, liquid funds, all the county's book losses would have been more than recovered during the following year.

7. P&G's original fraud suit against Bankers Trust was expanded on October 4, 1995, by a federal judge to allow P&G to add civil racketeering, or RICO (Racketeer Influenced and Corrupt Organizations (Act)), charges to its case. A court's acceptance of a RICO charge, which opens the possibility of triple-damage award, can often coerce even the most determined defendant to seek a settlement, rather than to continue to fight. That the market interpreted the ruling as a victory for P&G is indicated by the stock price reaction: Bankers Trust stock fell $0.75 to $69.25 and P&G's rose $1 to $78.25. The P&G suit was eventually settled with P&G recovering much, but by no means all, of its claim against Bankers Trust. (See also note 17 below.)

8. Nor is the money spent on lawyers universally regarded as a deadweight cost. Steven Magee and Frances T. Magee (1996, forthcoming) offer perhaps the most articulate exposition of the "lawyers-as-waste" position, but others would emphasize the economic efficiency, given its long survivorship, of private litigation as a method for settling disputes over contract terms. The Magees stress, and rightly, the social damage from legal opportunism and from what economists call rent-seeking activity by lawyers, much of it exploiting opportunities to profit from government regulation. Still, some kinds of remedies are clearly necessary for those parties to a contract who believe a fraud has been committed against them. Otherwise, the costs of doing business—any business—could quickly become excessive. The operative question thus boils down to which approaches to redress for fraud are socially most efficient: private litigation, regulatory intervention, or the Mafia? Given that the parties to the litigation in the case of P&G and many other recent derivatives suits are all large, public corporations, private litigation would seem, to me at least, to have important advantages over the other alternatives.

9. Under the curious system of corporate big-business governance in Germany, the banks who are both the leading creditors and the dominant stockholders serve as a "supervisory board," ceding the day-to-day authority for running the company to a management board. The supervisory banks retain power to change the management, but normally only in the event of a crisis. A lead bank anxious to replace management may thus have little choice but to orchestrate a "crisis." (Further discussion of the claimed "near bankruptcy" in the MG episode is provided in chapter 13.)

10. Academic finance specialists would also stress that quite apart from the actual frequency of bankruptcies, the mere prospect of possible future bankruptcy may create social costs by inducing firms into costly strategies to avoid bankruptcy—strategies, moreover, that by leading to cuts in output, may spread the contagion to other firms. Because derivatives, properly used, can offer a low-cost way of reducing some of the risks of encountering bankruptcy, additional, safety-motivated government regulation of derivatives that reduces their use may actually turn out to be counterproductive. But surely that will hardly be news.

11. That is why treating the P&G, MG, Orange County, and Barings episodes as derivatives disasters can be misleading. Those disasters all trace not to normal business bets gone sour, but to failures by top management, for one reason or another, to make reasoned judgments about the strategies their underlings were following. Had top management only understood the real facts, the eventual disastrous outcomes might have been avoided altogether, or at least much reduced in severity. Blaming derivatives is thus much like blaming the car for drunk driving. Some believe, of course, that derivatives have made it easier for "rogue traders" to run up losses faster than ever before, but that is far from clear. As shown by Deutsche Bank's Schneider real estate debacle of a few years back, and more recently by the Daiwa Bank scandal and the Sumitomo copper case, rogue traders can still run up losses just as big or bigger in all the old-fashioned ways.

12. On the other hand, as noted in the previous note, even an institution as big as Daiwa Bank can suffer from lax internal controls. For over eleven years, neither the bank's internal auditors nor its external auditors seem to have taken the elementary step of comparing the bank's figures for its holdings of U.S. Government bonds with those of the custodian bank (Bankers Trust, ironically enough). The outside auditors eventually did spot the failure of Daiwa's U.S. branch to separate its bond trading functions from the settlement functions (shades of Barings), but any steps taken to correct that organizational flaw did not immediately expose the fraud. They simply forced the trader to work much harder to cover his tracks (even volunteering to sacrifice his mandatory vacation, something his superiors seem actually to have regarded as praiseworthy, rather than suspicious). Press accounts suggest that the internal control failures at Daiwa may have arisen from some uncertainty over whether the Japanese or the American accountants were responsible for auditing the New York branch where the trouble occurred.

13. On September 13, 1995, the California Legislature approved a plan permitting Orange County to use the proceeds from new "certificates of participation" to pay off (eventually) most of the county's noteholders. The interest payments on the new certificates are to be backed by funds diverted from transportation and other county service accounts. Even if the market accepts the new certificates (which are rumored to carry a rating of no more than Caa), several hundred millions of dollars

in claims against Orange County will still remain to be funded. The uncompensated creditors, especially the municipality depositors in the Orange County pool of funds, are being urged to make themselves whole by suing Merrill Lynch. The bankruptcy court authorized some $50 million for lawyers fees for these suits.

14. In fact, the derivatives industry could not have developed at all without legislation declaring such contracts not to be mere unenforceable "wagers." More recently, however, doubts about the legal enforceability of contracts have been arising from the actions of the regulatory authorities themselves, those presumed guardians of the marketplace. A particularly egregious example is the July 27, 1995, enforcement ruling against MG Refining and Marketing Corporation, MGRM, by the CFTC in which some of MGRM's delivery contracts with customers were ruled "illegal off-exchange futures" and hence voidable. Because the contracts in question were similar in essential respects to the "take-or-pay" agreements common throughout the oil and gas industry, a pall of uncertainty now hangs over the market. Losing counterparties on these and similar derivatives deals—and remember that every derivatives contract has a loser—now may have a "free" option: pay up and eat the loss; or default, claiming that their contracts too were illegal. A long season of contentious lawsuits is in prospect until Congress finally reins in the CFTC and clarifies the excessively vague Commodity Exchange Act from which the Commission derives authority over "off-exchange futures." (Author's note: Faced with a barrage of unfavorable critical comment from the swap dealers, however, the CFTC has recently denied any intention on its part to take an aggressive view of its MGRM enforcement action.)

15. In the months following the Barings affair, the volume of trading on the world's futures exchanges has indeed fallen relative to the previous year, but how much, if any, of that fall traces to bad publicity for futures is far from clear. The volatility in exchange rates and interest rates has also fallen substantially. Nor has the fall-off in volume been uniform. Foreign currency futures seem to be down, for example, but stock index futures are up, as are corn and soybean futures. Short-term interest rate futures are down heavily, but long-term products are down only slightly. Simex itself, which presumably should have suffered most from the Barings episode, actually had a higher volume to date (June 1995) than in 1994. (See also chapter 11 in this volume for a somewhat updated perspective.)

16. Although the U.S. Congress is unlikely to enact new suitability restrictions for derivatives, many state governments either have already passed or are considering rules limiting, and in some cases even banning, the use of derivatives by their own local and municipal governments and boards. While economists usually insist that a more constrained solution is never better than a less constrained one, keep in mind that the government employees responsible for major investment decisions are often chosen more for their political skills than their financial expertise. Limiting the investment strategies they can follow may thus be cheaper than monitoring them intensively.

17. The tape recordings of Bankers Trust's traders released in the P&G case, as well as the similar tapes from the Gibson Greetings case, make one wonder how the corporate treasurers on the other side of the deals failed to see what seemed so obvious to the traders (even after discounting for the notorious bragadoccio of traders generally), namely that the treasurers were selling their puts far too cheaply. While hubris on the part of the treasurers over their prowess in forecasting interest rates was undoubtedly part of their problem, they may also have been misled by defects in their professional vocabulary. Corporate treasurers, even with MBA degrees, tend to think

in terms of yield differentials rather than present values. Unfortunately for them, the much harder to compute present values are what really counts, something the traders knew full well. The salty trader recordings have received much attention, as would be expected, but the press has yet to pick up the irony in P&G using the losses suffered by other firms in their Bankers Trust deals as evidence of a pattern of "racketeering" on Bankers Trust's part. The irony being, of course, that someone must be a loser (*ex post*) in every derivatives deal. If none of Bankers Trust's counterparties had ever suffered a loss, Bankers Trust would have been the loser on every deal. Its deal book would have been hopelessly unbalanced and it would surely have had to go out of business.

Chapter 5

1. In response to public clamor, MOF has recently set up an SEC-style investigating unit, but unlike the U.S. SEC, it is not an independent agency. And until it actually brings a case and wins, it will have to be considered just a paper tiger.

2. The futures exchanges were also able to maintain fixed commissions, but more by direct collusion than by force of law. They too were forced to abandon fixed commissions in 1975 under pressure from the Justice Department's Antitrust Division.

Chapter 7

1. The "disasters" and the supposed damage they have caused are the subject of chapter 2 in this volume.

Chapter 11

1. The episode *could* have been a more serious blow to Simex and possibly to futures exchanges generally, if the Dutch bank, ING, had not stepped up to the plate and bought what was left of Barings. Without that $2 billion cash injection, untangling who owed what to whom would have been a costly and time-consuming ordeal for all concerned. In the event, however, the incident has served actually to dramatize how strong the exchange customer protection systems really are when competently administered.

2. Although interest-rate contracts are likely to bear the main brunt of the long-term decline in the level and volatility of the inflation rate, contracts for physical commodities will also be affected. Empirical studies show that, in general, the higher the level of aggregate inflation, the greater the average volatility of the individual commodity components of the index. For equities, of course, volatility is closely related to the level and changes in the level of stock prices. Volatility goes up when stock prices fall.

3. Short-term bursts of interest rate and exchange rate volatility are also likely from time to time as the dwindling number of foreign countries with serious inflation problems (or, in Japan's case, deflation problems) come back into line. In Japan's case, some substantial rise is likely eventually in short-term interest rates (and some rise in the value of the yen relative to the dollar) as Japan pulls out of its long slump. But nothing like the currency turmoil of 1992 or late 1994 seems in sight. In fact, if the Europeans do succeed in instituting a common currency, many in the foreign exchange trading community will have to seek alternative employment.

4. Relations between the sectors can have elements of complementarity as well as competitiveness, of course. Just as the trucking sector sends loaded trailers piggyback on railroad flat cars, the swap dealers use Eurodollar and T-bond futures to balance out their net interest rate exposures. But the exchanges and the swaps dealers are still basically competitive sectors.

5. One telltale sign of this productivity surge is the loud moaning that low profit margins are forcing many smaller firms to go out of business or to sell out to larger firms. The smaller firms, of course, are more likely to be the marginal, highest-cost firms and their exit serves to raise productivity in the industry as a whole. This exploitation of the economies of scale by the process of exit is often cruel, but it's effective.

6. See Miller (1991), especially chapter 3. See also chapter 18 in this volume.

7. Many of the congestion costs of accessing and using the trading floors efficiently stem from the reluctance of the exchanges to create "property rights" for the trading positions within the pit. Hence the best positions do not automatically gravitate to the most active traders who would presumably value them most highly. There are too many "one-lot traders" crowding in to get a piece of the action. Fortunately for the exchanges, informal systems of property rights have sprung up to alleviate the worst inefficiencies. But here, as elsewhere with similar congestion problems, conscious resort to price mechanisms would clearly lead to better and lower-cost solutions.

8. Another cost of using the exchanges is "market impact" and here some observers claim to detect a recent relative deterioration in the trading pits—a loss of liquidity that they trace to the declining role of floor traders, who are mostly individuals, relative to off-floor traders who are increasingly financial institutions or commodity pools with much better access to information and with vastly greater capital resources. As a long-time trader recently lamented to me: "In the old days, the heavy hitters were on the floor and the pikers were off the floor. Now it's the other way around." No loss of liquidity, however, is yet detectable in pits as active as those for the S&P 500, the Eurodollar or the Treasury long-term and medium-term bonds. The impression of deterioration may perhaps have arisen in some quarters because spreads in some competing OTC transactions (particularly in foreign exchange trading) are not only often narrower than those of the exchanges, but sometimes even smaller than the minimum tick size for the exchange contract. To the extent that large tick sizes are leading to competitive disadvantage, the exchanges clearly have incentives to reduce them. The CME already allows for "half-ticks" on some Eurodollar contract months and "quarter ticks" are currently under discussion.

9. See, for example, Grossman and Miller who estimate that the costs of the CFTC's audit trail proposals in 1985 exceeded the benefits by at least one and possibly two orders of magnitude.

10. Particularly galling to the exchanges has been the refusal of the CFTC to allow CTAs (Commodity Trading Advisers) and managed futures firms to report a single average price for the trades they have entered on behalf of their many customer accounts during the day. Unlike the case with trades on the options exchanges, each futures trade and the (substantial) paper trail it generates must be parcelled out separately. After strong pressure from the exchanges, the CFTC has recently authorized the use of "all-or-nothing" (AON) large order trades in the currency pits. The initial response has been encouraging.

On the other hand, it must also be conceded that the regulatory structure has conveyed important competitive benefits to the futures industry as regulatory structures so typically do to those they are regulating. (See Miller 1993 and Stigler 1971.) The benefits, however, are not in projecting the kind of Good Housekeeping Seal of Approval mantle that the Securities and Exchange Commission offers firms in the securities industry. The CFTC's justly earned Keystone Kop image largely precludes that. But the 1974 Congressional Act that gave jurisdiction over futures to a federal agency, the CFTC, effectively preempted regulation of futures by the states—regulation that was often extremely hostile and restrictive. Absent federal jurisdiction, for example, the "cash settlement" so vital for contracts like the S&P 500 contract or the Eurodollar contract would have been impossible under many state laws.

The CFTC Act, moreover (or, more properly the Commodity Exchange Act of 1936), by requiring that all "futures" contracts be traded on an "exchange" regulated by the CFTC, has undoubtedly kept the OTC industry from duplicating popular contracts and such key tactical features of exchange-traded contracts as standardization, fungibility, collateralization and daily marking to market lest they be ruled subject to CFTC jurisdiction. The inherent ambiguity over what exactly constitutes a "futures" has certainly inhibited competitive innovations by the OTC sector. But the exchanges pay a price for this by being forced to submit their own contract innovations to CFTC approval—a process that can take as much as eighteen months or more. Thanks to the recent change in the political control of the Congress, the exchanges have finally succeeded in persuading the Agriculture Committee overseers of CFTC to consider reducing the CFTC's power to hold up contract approval. The CFTC has sought to weaken the impact of the proposed new Lugar-Leahy legislation by "voluntarily" agreeing to move faster (as fast as 10 days in trivial cases!), but not surprisingly, the commission continues to insist that retaining its power to approve new contracts is somehow necessary to protect the "public." How the CFTC thinks it can continue to justify the public benefits for "certificates of convenience and necessity" even after the Interstate Commerce Commission has been deregulated out of existence remains a mystery.

11. The futures exchanges have also lagged behind both the options exchanges and the stock exchanges in offering automatic execution systems for small retail orders. Programs comparable to the RAES (Retail Automatic Execution System) program of the Chicago Board Options Exchange (CBOE), in which randomly selected floor traders are allocated small lot trades at the current market price, are seriously being considered by the futures exchanges to discourage the OTC dealers from trolling more intensively for the retail customer trade, once the primary preserve of the exchanges. Automatic systems like RAES on CBOE or like SOES (Small Order Execution System) on NASDAQ may well help attract more retail trade, but can create so many other problems at the same time as to leave the net profit balance somewhat uncertain.

12. The same argument applies, of course, to new contracts even at the established exchanges. Because the opportunity costs for traders are so high, substantial financial inducements typically must be offered to get members to man the pits for new contracts and even those inducements are likely to prove unsuccessful unless volume picks up quickly. Some exchanges are therefore currently considering the alternative of introducing new products first for screen trading and shifting to floor trading only when volume and liquidity in the contract has become sufficient to support a pit.

13. The first sighting of what may turn out to be the proverbial cloud no bigger than a man's hand appeared in the spring of 1996 at a small manufacturing firm in Pennsylvania. The company chairman invited any stockholders seeking to expand or contract their share ownership in the company to signify their wishes via the Internet. Although SEC investigators quickly came on the scene, the SEC has so far taken no punitive steps against the company.

In the months since that first unconventional Internet sighting, novel applications of Internet technology have been appearing at what seems the rate of one a week. Some of these may perhaps just be "bucket shops," as the exchanges would call them, designed to exploit holes in the regulatory blanket, but others seem to represent real innovations in transaction technology.

14. The Chicago Mercantile Exchange, for example, has recently formed a subsidiary, called the CME Depository Trust, offering swap dealers collateral management service utilizing many features from the CME's regular clearinghouse programs (except that the CME Depository Trust's guarantees against counterparty default are limited strictly to the collateral deposited). The CME, however, currently does extend its clearinghouse guarantees, and on a fairly substantial scale, to a certain class of off-exchange transactions known as EFPs (Exchange for Physicals). EFPs had long been a common, though minor, type of transaction in agricultural futures, used mainly for facilitating closeout via delivery at contract expiration. But in recent years EFPs have become important in financial futures, particularly currency futures, not for facilitating delivery, but for adjusting portfolios after regular trading hours and for allowing dealers to "cross" some customer orders in house. Because the EFPs bypass the trading floors, some members of the exchange favored banning such transactions, but the CME chose instead to impose a fee on EFPs and is now enjoying nontrivial additional revenue from these "clearing charges."

Chapter 12

1. The calculations to follow are adapted from the finite growth model presented in Miller and Modigliani (1961). I have taken the value of rho (the risk-adjusted cost of capital) as 10% (what else?) and the value of k (the investment-to-earnings ratio) as 1.0. A firm with a market-to-book ratio of 1.0 corresponds to a "no growth-premium firm" with average internal rate of return (rho-star) just equal to the cost of capital.

2. For an account of how MOF systematically uses its regulatory powers to sustain the Japanese brokerage industry cartel and to support the level of stock prices, see chapter 3 in this volume.

3. See Merton Miller and Myron Scholes, "Executive Compensation, Taxes and Incentives," in *Financial Economics: Essays in Honor of Paul Cootner,* William Sharpe and Catheryn Cootner (Eds.), Prentice-Hall, Englewood Cliffs, NJ, 1982.

Chapter 15

1. In the original M&M paper, that underlying real earning stream was taken as a given, independent of the financing decisions. Subsequent research has identified

many possible interactions between the real and the financial sides of the firm, but their effects on risk are not always in the same direction and for present purposes, they can be regarded as of only second-order importance.

2. Note, incidentally, that this story would have exactly the same conclusion if the two defecting common stockholders had opted for preferred stocks rather than junior bonds. Even though accountants classify preferred stocks as equity, preferreds are functionally equivalent to junior debt. Preferred stocks, in fact, were effectively the junk bonds of finance (often with the same bad press) prior to the 1930s when the steep rise in corporate tax rates made them less attractive than tax-deductible, interest-bearing securities of equivalent priority.

3. The deadweight costs of bankruptcy, and of financial distress more generally, may be small in the aggregate, but they do exist. A case can be made, therefore, on standard welfare-economics grounds for eliminating the current tax subsidy to debt implicit in our current unintegrated corporate income tax. Achieving complete neutrality between debt and equity, however, would require elimination of the corporate tax—a step not likely to be undertaken in the foreseeable future.

4. Actually, according to recent press reports, Trump's creditors have allowed him to keep control, at least temporarily. Should he fail to meet stipulated cash-flow targets, however, the creditors can take over his remaining interests in a so-called "prepackaged" bankruptcy, a far quicker and less costly bankruptcy proceeding in which the economic terms have been negotiated prior to filing. Further use of this ingenious and efficient method for transferring control can confidently be expected.

5. True externalities arise, as in the case of air pollution, only when actions by one firm increase the costs of others. A possible analog to pollution for corporate debt might be the shifting to the government and hence to the taxpayers, of the pension costs of failed firms. Once again, however, the aggregate impact is of only second-order significance.

6. The process of swapping equity for debt (essentially the reverse of the parable in "Does increased corporate leverage add to society's risk?" above) would have gone even further by now but for an unfortunate feature of U.S. tax law. Swapping equity for debt selling at less than face value creates taxable income from "cancellation of indebtedness." An exception is made for firms in bankruptcy, making that option more attractive than it otherwise might be for firms whose debts are at a sizeable discount.

7. Examples of such restrictions are the guidelines, recently promulgated jointly by the Federal Deposit Insurance Corporation, the Comptroller of the Currency, and the Federal Reserve Board governing so-called Highly Leveraged Transactions (HLTs). These guidelines have effectively shut off lending for corporate restructuring, whether friendly or hostile. But the rules are so vaguely drawn and so uncertain in their application as to inhibit other kinds of loans as well. Bank loans these days often carry provisions calling for automatic interest-rate increases of 100 basis points or more if the loans are later classified by the bank examiners as HLTs.

Chapter 19

1. In principle, the same rules should apply to real estate. Banks, including the housing finance banks that are among the worst offenders in the current banking cri-

sis, should not be able to hold real estate directly and should be forced to divest themselves quickly of any they take over as collateral. That would not only make the real estate markets more liquid, but knowing they would have to recognize their losses more quickly would be a useful discipline in real estate lending by banks.

2. Actually short-term interest rates have now been driven so far below long-term rates on government bonds that almost any bank is likely to show some profits. But restoring capital via this route will not be quick.

3. The suggestion will also horrify those who believe that the close ties between firms and banks under the Japanese/German approach offers major benefits in the form of better corporate governance and especially in permitting firms to "take the long view" in undertaking highly capital-intensive projects. This is not the appropriate place to argue the point (though I must admit to my long-standing skepticism about the presumed benefits of Japanese/German style bank ties), but the issue may be becoming moot. As in the United States, the really big firms have steadily been reducing their reliance on bank loans for financing.

Index